PRIME SUSPECTS IN A GRISLY TRIPLE HOMICIDE, ATIF RAFAY AND SEBASTIAN BURNS CLAIMED THEY HAD NOTHING TO HIDE.

SO WHY DID THEY RUN?

Detective Bob Thompson was livid.

"I do believe that they fled to Canada. They never told me they were leaving. They knew I was the primary investigator. They had my pager number. They had my cell phone and desk number," Thompson said with contempt.

Thompson believed the only reason the boys left without informing him was because police were closing in on them.

"After their interview in the park, I think that they sat and said, 'You know what? They're on to us. Let's get out of here.'"

Atif and Sebastian left behind more than an angry detective. They also left behind a mosque filled with mourners. Later that day, Sultana, Tariq, and Basma Rafay were buried after a funeral service. The inscription on their gravestones, written in Arabic, read: "In the name of God, the merciful, the compassionate. To God we belong, and to God we return."

The only surviving member of the Rafay family wasn' ... ilogue. Atif Rafay ha ... Canada, a world aw ... aw and the Bellevue

D1053756

PERFECTLY EXECUTED

PETER VAN SANT
AND JENNA JACKSON

Pocket Star Books
New York   London   Toronto   Sydney

Pocket Star Books
A Division of Simon & Schuster, Inc.
1230 Avenue of the Americas
New York, NY 10020

Copyright © 2007 by CBS Broadcasting Inc.
All rights reserved.
48 Hours Mystery and related marks are
trademarks of CBS Broadcasting Inc.

All rights reserved, including the right to reproduce this book
or portions thereof in any form whatsoever. For information
address Pocket Books Subsidiary Rights Department,
1230 Avenue of the Americas, New York, NY 10020

First Pocket Star Books paperback edition September 2007

POCKET STAR and colophon are registered trademarks
of Simon & Schuster, Inc.

For information about special discounts for bulk
purchases, please contact Simon & Schuster Special Sales
at 1-800-456-6798 or business@simonandschuster.com

Cover design by Anna Dorfman;
Photograph of Atif Rafay © Anthony P. Bolante/Pool

Manufactured in the United States of America

10 9 8 7 6 5 4 3 2

ISBN-13: 978-1-4165-4531-6
ISBN-10:   1-4165-4531-X

From Peter . . . for my wife, Sarma,
and my children, Erik, Jeff, Stefan,
Kristina, Liana, and Lukas.

And from Jenna . . . for my boys:
Jackson, Parker, and Rees.

The nerve center at *48 Hours* is in a corner office area on the sixth floor at the CBS Broadcast Center in New York. This is the beehive where story editor Kathleen O'Connell oversees a research staff that combs America's newspapers—and works with attorney sources nationwide—to discover compelling murder cases for the broadcast.

O'Connell is a larger-than-life character, a personality a screenwriter might concoct: petite, shapely, pretty—and tough as nails. She runs her office like a general, combing through reports from the front lines.

In 2001, O'Connell came across a story that she instantly knew was a winner. She quickly pitched the idea to *48 Hours* executive producer Susan Zirinsky, who green-lighted the project. O'Connell's next call was to one of her most dogged field producers, Jenna Jackson, who had built a reputation for getting "the gets."

The story was very strong: brilliant, young best friends accused of plotting the murder of one of the friend's family. The suspects had been in custody for years, maintaining a wall of silence put up just days after the murders had occurred. That's where Jenna Jackson went to work. It took several years, numerous face-to-face meetings, and an exchange of letters over many months before the lead suspect in the case, Sebastian Burns, agreed to speak with *48 Hours*. Once Sebastian was on board, Jackson encouraged him to get his family, friends, defense team, and codefendant, Atif Rafay, to speak as well.

Correspondent Peter Van Sant made numerous trips to Seattle and Vancouver, British Columbia, to help convince prosecutors, the Royal Canadian Mounted Police, and friends of the defendants to participate in the program. Van Sant became obsessed with the case, knowing he would be the first reporter ever to interview Burns and Rafay. Van Sant also had one extra motivation—the murders had occurred in the small, quiet town where he grew up: Bellevue, Washington.

Another key player in this case was associate producer Gayane Keshishyan, who met with Atif Rafay over the course of many months and helped persuade him to participate. Keshishyan's dedication to the story helped to keep lines of communication open among all the important parties. She also played a major role in convincing the Royal Canadian

Mounted Police to grant us an interview, a first for its undercover operatives.

Special thanks also goes to producers Nancy Kramer, Susan Zirinsky, Al Briganti, and senior producer Katie Boyle for their talent and guidance. And to Carlin DeGuerin, Eric Marripodi, and Domenico Montanaro.

The authors also wish to thank editors Mike Vele, Basil Pappas, and Gary Winter for their remarkable creativity.

And we could not have learned of or been able to tell this story without the significant help of numerous people in Bellevue and Seattle—including, but not limited to, detective Bob Thompson; prosecutors James Konat and Roger Davidheiser; defense attorneys Jeff Robinson, Song Richardson, Amanda Lee, and Theresa Olson; Sebastian Burns, his friends and family, and Atif Rafay.

On a more personal note, beginning with Peter Van Sant:

I want to thank my wife, Sarma, for surrendering a portion of the house to a giant mess of transcripts, documents, and background articles, and for her advice. I'd also like to thank those who inspire me the most, my children: Erik, Jeff, Stefan, Kristina, Liana, and Lukas. And of course, the two people who made me possible, my parents, Joy and Richard.

Finally, I wish to thank my coauthor, Jenna Jackson, for her remarkable work and gifted storytelling.

And from Jenna Jackson: I'd like to thank Dan for his constant example, Chip for never allowing me to settle—and my friends and family for their encouragement and patience throughout this project. And Peter Van Sant for his incredible writing, attention to detail, and persistence in making this book happen.

CONTENTS

PART III
THE TRIAL

A Perfect Murder

It was a house of horrors.

The first police officer who nervously entered the Rafay family home just after 2 A.M. on July 12, 1994, wasn't prepared for what he was about to see. Never in the 130-year history of the wealthy suburb of Bellevue, Washington, had a crime of such shocking brutality been committed.

Just minutes before, a desperate-sounding teenager named Sebastian Burns had called 911. He had just returned from a night out on the town with his best friend, Atif Rafay. The two brilliant nineteen-year-olds had been staying at the Rafay house while on summer vacation from college.

When the first patrol car arrived in the hilly Somerset neighborhood, Sebastian and Atif darted out of the darkness and pounded on the trunk of his car to get the officer's attention. They pointed at the Rafay house and shouted for the officer to enter the home. Something terrible waited inside.

The officer himself had never seen a dead body, but that was about to change.

Once inside, his flashlight beam discovered Sultana Rafay, Atif's mother, lying facedown on the family room carpet. The back of her head had been crushed. A pool of blood surrounded her face, like an ink bottle that had been spilled.

Upstairs, in the master bedroom, was a macabre scene: Tariq Rafay, Atif's father, was lying in the middle of the bed, with his hands clasped just above his stomach. It was a pose a body might be placed in inside a casket. The officer turned on the bedroom light. Tariq's head appeared to have exploded. Blood and material covered every wall, even the ceiling.

Downstairs, Atif's younger sister, Basma, was lying unconscious. Her face and head were battered. She would die a few hours later.

At first, investigators thought it must have been a murder-suicide. Tariq's head was so obliterated that it was at first assumed he must have shot himself with a shotgun. But no weapon was found. The police quickly realized this was murder—and one of the worst in Washington State history.

Suspicion quickly fell on the two boys who'd discovered the gruesome scene—Atif, the lone surviving member of the Rafay family, and his best friend, Sebastian. Within hours, police had checked their clothing, hands, arms, and hair for traces of blood.

None was found—not a single drop.

But more important, the boys had an alibi that

checked out: They had left the house shortly after 8 P.M., gone to a local restaurant for a light meal, and then taken in the 9:50 showing of *The Lion King*. Employees at the restaurant and movie theater remembered seeing them.

That was significant, because neighbors on either side of the Rafay home told police that they had heard pounding and moaning sounds coming from the house sometime between 9:45 and 10:15 P.M., a time when the boys were seen at the movies.

Sebastian and Atif said that after watching *The Lion King*, they had driven across Lake Washington into downtown Seattle, where they got some ice cream and French fries at an all-night diner. A waitress there also remembered the boys. The two then drove back to Bellevue, discovered the carnage, and called 911.

Detective Bob Thompson was assigned to lead the murder investigation. He was a veteran of the police department but had never led a homicide inquiry. Thompson conducted two long interviews with Sebastian and Atif. There was no forensic evidence that linked them to the murders, but Thompson had suspicions. He thought the two acted oddly. And in the days after the murders were discovered, no one saw Atif shed a single tear.

Those suspicions solidified into resolve one morning a couple of days after the murders: Detective Thompson dropped by the motel where the boys were staying, but the two were gone. They had taken a Greyhound bus to Vancouver, British Columbia, where Sebastian's parents lived.

Within hours of discovering that the boys had crossed into Canada, Bellevue police contacted the RCMP: the Royal Canadian Mounted Police. Like Sebastian, the Rafays were Canadian citizens. Detective Thompson described the details of the murders and speculated that the boys may have been involved. And if so, they may have conspired to kill the Rafay family while in Canada. The motive, Thompson believed, was money: Atif stood to inherit nearly half a million dollars.

The Mounties sent a representative to Bellevue to look at the case file. Detective Thompson, meanwhile, spent time in Vancouver, trying to learn what he could about the two boys.

Both the Bellevue police and the RCMP concluded that Sebastian and Atif were the most likely suspects in the murders. But lacking direct evidence, there was little they could do.

Within months, the RCMP decided on a plan to ensnare the boys. They launched "Project Estate," the most elaborate undercover operation in British Columbia history. It played out over three months, involving a cast of unsavory make-believe mobsters, guns, theft, money laundering, beautiful women, fast cars, and greed. The number one target of this Hollywood-like production was Sebastian Burns, the genius who dominated Atif, and whom police came to believe was the mastermind behind the murder plot.

What unfolded was a modern Leopold and Loeb story of two teenagers who police said thought they were among the smartest people in the world; young men who thought that the rules of society didn't apply to the intellectually superior; young men who thought they could outsmart anyone and craft the perfect murder.

It was a case filled with bizarre twists and turns, and with details that included sex, videotape, a manhunt that reached to Japan, a screenplay, and, ultimately, betrayal. It was a notorious murder case that took ten long years to bring to trial.

And it ended as it began: with mystery and controversy.

PART I

THE CRIME

911 call—July 13, 1994—2:01 A.M.

"There's—I need—an—an ambulance."

"What's the problem there?"

"The—there's just some kind of break-in—I—"

"OK, well, just calm down. What's the problem?"

"The—the—I don't—my friend, his mom and dad are—they're—they're—I—we—think they're dead."

"Why do you think they're dead?"

"There's blood. They're not breathing. There's blood all over his face. They're like—I don't know. Please just come! I don't know—if you—COME FAST!"

1

A Quiet Cul-de-Sac

Sultana Rafay couldn't have been happier than at this moment. It was the early evening of July 12, 1994, and Sultana had just gently laid out her Muslim prayer rug in the family room of her new home in Bellevue, Washington, an affluent suburb right outside Seattle. She had so many gifts for which to thank God: Her husband, Tariq, a gifted structural engineer and bridge builder, had recently started a new, $59,000-a-year job as a project manager with Alpha Engineering. Her nineteen-year-old son, Atif, a brilliant student and in many ways her best friend, had just finished his freshman year at Cornell University and was home for the summer. She loved spending time with Atif, discussing classic literature and philosophy. She wished that Atif would join her in prayer, but understood that, for now, her son didn't share the family's love of Islam. In fact, Atif had told his parents that he didn't believe in Islam. The three had held spirited discussions at times about religion, but

Sultana thought Atif was just going through a phase. With time, she believed, that would change. Sultana and Tariq were devout Sunni Muslims and had long been active in religious and cultural events.

Also at home was the Rafays' twenty-year-old daughter, Basma, who since birth had needed special attention. Sultana was happy that Basma seemed to be adjusting well to her new neighborhood.

The Rafays' new home was in the Somerset section of Bellevue, a postcard-perfect community of contemporary houses built among tall Douglas fir and western red cedar trees that, on this cloudless summer evening, cut jagged silhouettes against the deepening blue sky. The Rafay home sat at the top of a cul-de-sac, with large living room windows that looked out at the houses below. Sultana felt as if she was on top of the world.

Even though it was after 9 P.M., the soft summer daylight was only slowly yielding to darkness. Nearly everyone in this peaceful, hilly neighborhood had settled in for the night. It was so quiet; neighbors said you could hear the slightest sound, from a door closing inside a home to someone walking across a driveway.

Sultana was a devoted mother. Her smooth face was dominated by her big brown eyes and radiant smile. She looked younger than her fifty-six years. Sultana had met her husband while earning a master's degree in nutrition at Colorado State University in Fort Collins. They had quickly fallen in love. Tariq had written poetry for her, a loving tradition he continued throughout their marriage. Once her children were born, Sultana had decided to become a stay-at-home mom. She prided herself on her dedication to her children and on running a well-organized household. It bothered her that there were still moving boxes around her that had not yet been unpacked. Scattered on the window ledge in front of her were half a dozen books and some business files. Perhaps tomorrow she would finish tidying up the family room.

Upstairs in the master bedroom, Tariq had put on his long-sleeved blue pajamas and turned in for the night. He was in his usual sleeping position—lying flat on his back in their queen-sized bed. With his head comfortably positioned between two pillows, Tariq was sound asleep. It was a warm evening, so he had left the covers at the foot of the bed. Like Sultana, Tariq was fifty-six. He was a slender man of medium height whose face bore the constant serious look of scientific intensity. He had a large, bulblike nose and dark eyes that were underlined with brownish folds, the permanent markings left from a childhood of poverty in his native Pakistan and years of hard work in Canada and the United States. Tariq was known as a solemn man, but at home he had a dry sense of humor. Where others might not get the joke, Sultana would often break an awkward moment with a giggle. She was her husband's best audience. But on the night of July 12, 1994, Tariq wasn't in a mood for jokes. After a week of long workdays that often stretched into the evenings, Tariq was using his Saturday night to catch up on his rest.

Down the hall, Basma was in her room, getting ready for bed. She had laid out the clothes she planned to wear the next day on the clean carpet between her bed and closet. Atif wasn't home. He had left the house earlier in the evening with his best friend from high school, Sebastian Burns, who was also on summer vacation, from Capilano College in North Vancouver, British Columbia. Both boys had graduated from West Vancouver High School in June of 1993. Sebastian had been staying at the Rafays' for several days, visiting Atif. The boys left the house around 8:30 P.M., planning to eat, take in a showing of *The Lion King* at a local cineplex, and then go hang out in downtown Seattle.

Back in the Rafay family room, Sultana, dressed in a traditional Pakistani *abaya* and flip-flop sandals, finished smoothing out the wrinkles of her prayer rug. She took off her reading glasses and placed them on the carpet, just above her right shoulder. Sultana paused for a moment, taking several deep breaths to focus her concentration. She then slowly kneeled down and began to pray.

As she softly mouthed her words of thanks to God, Sultana never knew who suddenly ended her life with a crushing blow to the back of her head with an aluminum baseball bat. She rolled to one side, with blood from her fractured skull flowing onto her prayer rug and the family room carpet. The killer then made sure. He smashed her skull in exactly the same spot again.

Whoever delivered these merciless strikes stood by Sultana's lifeless body and had an unexpected moment of compassion or shame. The murderer placed a silk scarf across Sultana's bloody face and head.

The killer quickly moved on to the next target. He seemed to know exactly where to go. Blood drops left a red trail from Sultana's body to the stairs. He made his way upstairs, then down the lighted hallway to the master bedroom. He crept in undetected. Tariq was still asleep in his cotton summer pajamas, still faceup on the left side of the bed, with his right arm lying gently across his chest. His left hand was touching Sultana's pillow. Taking aim, the killer raised his bloody bat high and delivered a perfect deathblow to Tariq's forehead. Forensic experts later determined that this first strike must have killed Tariq, because they believe he never moved. There were no defensive wounds on his arms or hands.

But whoever did this wasn't satisfied with his efficient kill. He raised the bat again and again, pulverizing Tariq's head. Blood spatter and brain matter flew in all directions and would later be found on every wall of the room, and even the ceiling. It was as though a balloon full of blood had exploded.

After his murderous frenzy with Tariq, the killer stepped back into the hallway. Small drops of blood showed that he now quickly made his way down the hall toward the last surviving member of the Rafay family, Basma. The killer must have been running— the blood drops had a forward smear, a pattern that resembled paint being thrown from an artist's brush. Basma was awake. God only knows what she had heard and what it must have been like to wait behind her bedroom door for the monster to enter.

Breathing heavily, frozen with fear, she must have watched the doorknob turn.

2

Sounds in the Night

Sometime between 9:45 and 10:15 P.M.—he wasn't quite sure of the time—neighbor Marc Sidell, a private pilot, took some aviation charts out to his car for a flight he had planned for the next day. The car was parked in the driveway. But Sidell had something more important on his mind that night—his cat Abby. She had been missing for nearly twenty-four hours. After he put the charts in the backseat, Sidell took a few steps down his driveway and cupped his hands to his mouth.

"Abby! Abby!" he called. He listened for his cat's familiar meow, but there was no response. Instead, he heard something else—a pounding sound. It appeared to be coming from the home of his new next-door neighbors, the Rafays. In the twilight, Sidell stopped calling the cat and tried to figure out what he was hearing.

"They were hollow banging sounds, like hanging a picture with something hollow," Sidell said. "Usually, you hang pictures at eye level. But this sounded like they were hitting down below. I thought that was sort of unusual."

Sidell, a gregarious, rotund man in his mid-fifties, knew that the Rafays had just recently moved in, and he gave some thought to knocking on their front door to see if they needed any help putting things on the wall. He had seen Sultana and Basma only once, days before, when they were outside gardening. He had said hello but didn't stop to have a conversation.

The sky was still managing to hold the last glow of that glorious summer night. Sidell looked away from the Rafay house and again called out to his cat. After a few more minutes of unanswered calls, Sidell went back inside.

The temperature was quickly falling. Even on warm summer days, breezes off Puget Sound acted as a wonderful air conditioner. The smell of warmed fir and cedar trees added to the soothing nature of this summer night. Sidell and his wife, Judith, had the windows wide open, taking it all in. The outside air was also welcomed because the Sidells had recently painted their home, and the smell of the oil-based paint still lingered in the house.

The pounding next door went on and on, lasting about twenty minutes. As Sidell listened, he thought the Rafays must have been having some trouble with their picture hanging. Maybe he should have gone over, he thought. Instead, he couldn't help but listen.

"It sounded hollow, like the hammer missed and

it went into the drywall. And you could hear the drywall give," Sidell said.

Of course, Sidell didn't realize that he was actually hearing the Rafay family being bludgeoned to death. The killer was now in Basma's room, which was the closest bedroom to Marc Sidell's house, just fifteen feet away.

"There was some moaning sound in there," Sidell said with a chill.

Those odd moans were Basma's cries for help. They were the only sounds she could make. Basma was severely autistic. She hadn't spoken a word since childhood. She couldn't speak now. She couldn't call 911. But she could fight. Her bedroom became a battleground. The killer—his back blocking the door, the room's only escape route—raised the bat over and over again, landing glancing blows as Basma darted from place to place in her room. She suffered numerous wounds to her hands and arms as she tried to block the baseball bat. Some of her teeth were knocked out of her mouth and were scattered across the room. So powerful were the blows, tiny shards of aluminum would later be found on her body.

The sounds reaching the Sidell house next door then changed, from moaning to something else.

"A female, low type of mooing—low grumbling type of noise," Sidell said. He had no idea what was taking place, just a stone's throw away.

Basma's terror must have been unimaginable. The killer was covered in blood from his mutilation of

Basma's parents. His bat was dripping with blood and debris. Fresh from his destruction of Rafay, the killer must have been wild.

After Basma was knocked unconscious to the carpet, the killer headed to the downstairs bathroom. Investigators would later say the killer, covered head to toe in blood, did something remarkable for someone who could not have known whether Atif would shortly return home: He took a shower. He rinsed off the bat. The sound traveled.

"I heard some water running," Sidell said. "You know how you can hear water go through the plumbing of a house."

When pressed on how he could have heard all of this sound coming from the Rafays' home, Sidell became adamant.

"Look, there are very thin walls. This is a very quiet cul-de-sac, as you can hear. There's not really any traffic. Occasionally a plane flies by, but not too often. And basically, there's nothing to kill the sound. And the sounds coming from the Rafays' were pretty loud."

Sometime after 10 P.M., the last light of the summer sunset had finally faded. The neighborhood was again quiet. The pounding and muffled moans from next door had stopped. Marc Sidell occasionally stuck his head outside the door, calling his cat. He finally went back upstairs, and was standing near an open window when he heard one last sound before getting into bed.

"I heard some running coming out of the driveway," Sidell said with certainty. "One set of feet went over the grass, then another set of feet—young, quick feet. The other one went on the driveway and they ran around—running away from the Rafay house."

Inside that house, two people were dead. And a third, Basma, was dying from numerous bat strikes across her body and head.

The Rafay family murders were the worst single criminal act in Bellevue history. They would touch off one of the most extraordinary murder investigations ever in Washington State and in British Columbia, Canada, where the Rafays had recently lived. The initial investigation would pit a homicide detective leading the first murder case of his career against the two young men who, early on the morning of July 13, 1994, walked into the Rafay home, discovered the carnage, and called 911.

3

Best of Friends

Atif Rafay said he was lucky to be alive. At about 8:30 on the night his family was bludgeoned to death, Atif had left his home with his best friend, Sebastian Burns. The two teenagers had planned a long evening together. They drove to The Keg, a local restaurant, for some fries and a milk shake. They then caught a showing of *The Lion King* at the Factoria Cinemas. From there, they traveled about eight miles into downtown Seattle, where they ended up at Steve's Broiler, a diner-style all-night restaurant.

"They came in around eleven-twenty or so," Christine Kuykendall, a waitress, remembered. "They were just cutting up, having a good time. They were talking about going to a nightclub, wanting to know where the good spots were."

Atif and Sebastian settled into a booth and ordered a chocolate sundae.

The boys made a distinctive pair. Physically, they were opposites. Sebastian was tall, about six-two, thin, yet athletic, in a distance runner sort of way. His face was smooth and handsome, with piercing blue eyes. His smile was playfully mischievous. His hair was dark brown, thick and wavy, and stylishly cut. He was the kind of young man who was noticed the moment he entered a room, which was typically with a self-assured confidence. He looked like an actor, and at West Vancouver High School he had been, taking the lead role in a school play.

"He's a special kind of person, a very interesting, thoughtful person," said Sarah Isaacs, Sebastian's high school sweetheart. "And when I met Sebastian in grade twelve, everything became wonderful. He's insightful, wonderful to talk to. He's a lot of fun. We had a lot of fun together."

It was the start of a five-year romance. Sarah said Sebastian was her first love. In high school, they made a striking couple. Sarah was as beautiful as Sebastian was handsome. Her face was dominated by her large, soft eyes and loving smile. Her hair was long and thickly curled. Her speech was firm, with a British Columbia accent that gently stressed the vowels. Her walk was fluid, a product of her years of training as a modern dancer. She was strikingly intelligent and articulate, projecting beauty, brains, and warmth—an all-Canadian girl.

"I was Miss Congeniality," she grinned. "People liked Sebastian. He was well-liked by girls in high school. He went to parties. He was athletic. He was charismatic. He always had interesting things to say. He was what I would describe, in those days, as a deep thinker."

Sarah thumbed through pictures of her and Sebastian.

"I was in love with him," Sarah said wistfully. "It was a very exciting time. He was my first love." She looked away and sighed. "I thought I was going to marry him someday. He was everything I wanted."

She added, "He's very sentimental, a very emotional person."

Sebastian grew up in posh West Vancouver, British Columbia, which has been called the most expensive municipality in Canada. In 2006, the average price of a home in the Burnses' beautiful bedroom community, just across the Lions Gate Bridge from downtown Vancouver, exceeded $1.2 million. Nestled above the picturesque North Shore, West Vancouver was home to Canada's first shopping mall. Nearby was one of Vancouver's most popular tourist attractions, Grouse Mountain, which rose 4,100 feet high. Along a sloping, winding road, set amid towering Douglas fir trees, was the home of Dave and Carol Burns. They raised Sebastian, and his strikingly beautiful big sister, Tiffany, in a home filled with music and literature.

"My brother's a wonderful person," Tiffany said with family pride. Tiffany worked as a news anchor in Cleveland. She stood about five-ten with shoulder-length blonde hair and piercing blue eyes. The camera loved her. "He's very smart," Tiffany continued. "He's definitely what you would call an intellectual. We were the ultimate nuclear family. We always got along well."

Sebastian was never into organized sports. He never played hockey, baseball, or softball. His parents said he had terrible hand-eye coordination. He preferred solo sports, like snowboarding, Rollerblading, and mountain biking.

"He's a sweetie pie," said his mother, Carol Burns, a soft-spoken woman of obvious sophistication. Carol grew up in Toronto and moved to Vancouver when she was about twenty-five years old. That's where she met Dave, an engineer, who had come to Canada from his native England to do some graduate work. Carol raised two children while also having a successful career in finance.

"Sebastian was a loving son, very thoughtful. He always had a very good, zany sense of humor. And he enjoyed tickling people and bringing them out."

"And he never had a fight of any kind, to my knowledge," Dave Burns added.

Dave was raised in a working-class neighborhood in Liverpool, England. But his accent is more BBC than Beatle.

"He would never get involved in a fight," Dave said, quite properly. "He would always go into defense mode. He wasn't an aggressive kid."

"He never wanted the physical stuff," Carol said with a chuckle. "But he could outargue anybody."

Most of all, Sebastian's parents said, their son loved music. Both Tiffany and Sebastian played classical cello. They had a tradition every Christmas where brother and sister woke up their parents by playing carols on their cellos.

In his teenage years, Sebastian joined the Royal Canadian Air Cadets, whose motto is "To Learn, To Serve, To Advance." Air Cadet training, which ran throughout the school year, included instruction on how to fly an airplane, how to navigate, and how to use an aircraft radio. Sebastian learned other special skills as well, including how to survive if his plane went down. The Air Cadet program also involved community service and academic achievement. Sebastian spent five years in the program. He did so well that he received the Duke of Edinburgh Gold Medal. It was pinned on his uniform by none other than Prince Edward.

Sebastian's father recalled that receiving the medal from a member of British royalty was a proud moment for the entire family.

"You might say that he has been acknowledged as being a top-caliber citizen in the making," Burns said in his cultured accent.

As Sebastian's father spoke, he often paused before answering a question. It was a trait passed down to both his children. Tiffany laughed when asked about Sebastian's unique way of carrying on a conversation.

"My brother is very complex. If you ask him if he

wants milk with his coffee, he's got to think about it. 'Hmmm, what kind of coffee do I really want?'"

Tiffany then leaned in to make a point.

"Sebastian is not the type of person that can give a straight answer to a question. That is simply the way he is."

In conversation, Sebastian had a peculiar speaking pattern. When asked a question, he tended to do his father's "pause and contemplate," while oddly puckering his lips. To someone who didn't know him, it might appear he was pausing to make something up, when, in fact, it was just the way he talked. His accent had "a mid-Atlantic" quality to it, like the almost British accent many American actors used in the 1930s and '40s.

"His manner is strange," Sarah said. "You probably know that. He's stiff. He's square."

"I said all kinds of arrogant jokes," Sebastian himself said after a quick pucker, referring to his high school days. "I'm sure I was a jerk lots of times."

Tiffany said her brains and confidence earned her a reputation for arrogance in high school. She believed her brother, always self-assured, often struck people the same way.

"The whole Burns family, apparently, is arrogant," Tiffany said with a sardonic sigh.

"He was always told that he was smart," Sarah Isaacs added. "And so he was a little arrogant. But not dangerously arrogant."

Sebastian acknowledged in an interview with *48*

Hours correspondent Peter Van Sant that he could be condescending toward his fellow students. He once described himself as one of the smartest people on earth.

"I was an arrogant teenager who had a habit of shooting his mouth off," Sebastian said, like a professor summing up a lecture topic.

"I think that everyone who knew Sebastian thought that he was going on to do something interesting with his life," Sarah said proudly. "I think he was voted 'Most Likely to Go into Politics.' You know, people expected him to be a leader."

Atif Rafay was the physical opposite of Sebastian. He was short, about five-two. He looked like his mother, with gentle, almost feminine features, including doe-like eyes and a pleasant smile. He met Sebastian in the tenth grade, but they didn't become buddies until their senior year, which in Canada is called grade "twelve." Theirs was a friendship based on mutual intellectual respect. Both were voracious readers. In each other, they found someone of sophistication, someone they could talk to.

"I didn't hang around with most of the kids, because, first of all, I was sort of an outsider in the sense that I had come from Pakistan," Atif said with a flat exactness in his pronunciation, as if he were reading from someone else's diary.

"High school was a very sudden and drastic change," he said. "I wouldn't say it was culture shock, particularly. I think the absence of culture would be . . . the shock, I suppose. I certainly was not typical. I just didn't have the same sort of interest in sports. I guess I sort of wouldn't have fit into the mold of most students at West Van High."

Atif participated in the British Columbia Youth Parliament, where he was an outstanding debater. In an interview with *48 Hours,* Atif said he felt he could outthink just about anyone.

"I had been raised to have high expectations of myself," Atif said matter-of-factly. "Did I look down on the other students? Intellectually, if you're talking about the majority of students in my graduating class, sure. I had a reasonably high opinion of my own abilities."

Atif was best known at school as a quiet, brilliant student, with a gift for creative writing. But while he could debate with the brightest young minds in western Canada, he was socially withdrawn. Sarah credited Sebastian for bringing Atif out of his shell.

"When they first met, Atif had big goggle glasses and was a little nerdy-looking," she said with a smile. "Sebastian would never have been cruel to someone because they were a nerd, overweight, or unattractive. He just doesn't have that side to him."

Atif eventually got contact lenses and upgraded his wardrobe.

"Sebastian wanted to help him basically to get girls. And so he helped him look cool. And he became friends with Atif and showed Atif how to dress.

They'd go out. He'd introduce Atif to girls. He sort of helped Atif be a stud, like he was," Sarah said with a giggle.

Atif may have been shy, but academically he was a big man on campus. He spoke with correspondent Peter Van Sant about his intelligence—and how he viewed himself in high school.

"Do you consider yourself intellectually gifted?" Van Sant asked the young man.

"Yeah, I think that's fair to say. I had a reasonably high opinion of my own ability," Atif said frankly.

"Were you a little arrogant back then?"

"Oh, absolutely. I'm sure I was, sure. A sense of superiority."

"Condescending?"

"Probably."

"Judgmental?" Van Sant pushed him.

"Judgmental? Absolutely, sure," Atif answered without hesitation.

"Atif's one of the most immediately likeable people I've ever met in my life," Sebastian said with great fondness. When the two teens met, he connected immediately with Atif's academic seriousness. "And he's very charming, pleasant to spent time with."

Sebastian brought Atif into his circle of friends, which included Sarah Isaacs and Jimmy Miyoshi, another academically gifted student. They shared common interests—including philosophy, art, Shakespeare, books—and they had a special fondness for movies and screenwriting. In grade twelve, Atif earned first prize in a University of British Columbia essay competition. His winning paper was on tolerance.

Atif laughed as he looked back on his friendship with Sebastian.

"We probably did cut . . . sort of an odd couple. I mean, you know, short Pakistani guy, tall white guy."

Because of their differences, many of their classmates at West Vancouver High School thought that Sebastian led Atif around by the nose. But Sarah Isaacs said that notion was nonsense.

"Atif is a confident, assertive person. He's not a follower," Sarah said, somewhat annoyed by the idea. "Sebastian was taller. He was white. He was popular. And so people looking at the relationship would have assumed that he was the leader. And that really was not the case. They were equals."

Atif spoke of Sebastian with warm affection.

"Sebastian is bright, charming—a sincere guy. And he was sincerely curious, intellectually curious. He was very funny. I mean, certainly, he was one of my best friends."

Atif paused, tilted his head slightly, and concluded his thought with flawless articulation, "And I don't know what more to say."

4

The Discovery

Back at Steve's Broiler in downtown Seattle, it was about 1:30 A.M. when Sebastian and Atif ran out of things to say, finished their ice cream, and settled their bill.

"It totaled up to about two-seventy," waitress Christine Kuykendall said. She remembered the boys because they did something unexpected for two teenagers. "They paid for it with a ten-dollar bill and left five dollars for me. That was unusual. I wouldn't have expected more than a dollar or so."

The boys walked over to a nearby bar, the Weathered Wall, but the bouncer told them it was closed. They stopped back by Steve's Broiler, where they used the restroom facilities, then got into the Rafay family's Honda Accord and headed back to Bellevue. Their route took them about six blocks to Interstate 5, which they took south to the I-90 exit. That led them across the Mercer Island Floating Bridge, heading toward the wealthy Eastside suburbs. It was just before 2 A.M. when they pulled into the Rafays' drive-way. The night was still. They got out and entered through the garage door, which led directly into the downstairs family room, where the lights were still on. Sebastian was the first into the house.

"We saw Atif's mom lying on the floor. I saw her lying there, and there was a lot of blood around her head," Sebastian said, his voice lowering to a whisper. Sebastian paused and cleared his throat. "I saw her lying there and there was a lot of blood around her head."

Peter Van Sant encouraged him to continue. "Did you turn her over?"

"No."

"Why not?"

"Atif and I were shocked out of our minds. Almost to the point of hysteria. And we recoiled—or I recoiled."

"How do you not turn her over to check if she's breathing?" Van Sant asked.

Sebastian seemed almost ashamed as he tried to answer. "I don't know. I don't know. I don't remember everything that we did. I cannot describe to you how shocking it was, just how completely confounding it was. And there was nothing sensical about my reaction at all."

Atif stood and looked at his mother. He found her as the killer left her, and he did nothing.

"I don't think that I really want to go into this,"

Atif said sadly. "Because it's the single worst experience of my life. And because I've really spent almost every single day since then trying to avoid thinking about it. I was closer to my mom than anyone ever has been or ever will be close to. To the extent that I am loyal or generous or a warmhearted person, I am so because of my mother."

Sebastian didn't remember clearly what they did next. But they must have run upstairs to the master bedroom, where Tariq was dead, in a near decapitated state. Sebastian recalled quickly looking inside the room.

"We saw that he was in his bed. And we could see there was blood around him. It was clear that he had been attacked."

Atif would not speak about seeing his dead father. His relationship with his dad had always been quite formal. Looking back, Atif described his father in analytical, rather than emotional, terms: "He was a brilliant person. Probably a far better mathematician than I will ever be. He had elegant and beautiful handwriting. He also had a really deep and genuine reverence for knowledge and learning."

Atif then paused, reflected, and resumed his thoughts—without any sign of emotion. "I was never able to satisfactorily explain to myself, I guess, how he could have simply disappeared out of my life in this way. I can't even fathom it. There is nothing that I can imagine about my parents that could have justified anyone to do what was done to them." Atif looked away and then back. "I—I—I'm really at a loss to fathom that."

The boys said they made no effort to see if Tariq was still alive; his condition seemed obvious to them. But there was still one family member left to check on—Basma.

"She was in the adjacent room, and I could hear her breathing and moaning," Atif said, lowering his volume.

"Did you go in?" Van Sant asked him.

"I did not."

"Why not?"

Atif tried to explain himself. "It wasn't a reasoned decision. It was simply a question of acting out of habit and instinct and fear and confusion. I was horrified and completely beside myself."

Atif said that instead of opening the door to Basma's room, he retreated to the living room, where he walked around in circles, pulling out chunks of his hair.

But Van Sant pushed him on how he could leave his sister there, moaning for help. "You could hear her moaning. How do you not go in and give first aid?"

"Well, for one, I don't really know first aid. And I didn't even think of that. I acted in a cowardly and shameful way," Atif answered, slightly agitated.

"Atif, you're a bright guy. If someone's bleeding, you know how to stop the bleeding, right?"

"You're right."

The more Atif thought about his actions that

night, the more he theorized about why he didn't act to help his autistic sister.

"It would be fair to say that I had no real relationship to her. Because if anything was happening with her, I essentially left it to my parents to look after her. In that moment of crisis, it never occurred to me to go in there," Atif said.

Sebastian didn't enter Basma's room either. Instead, the two boys ran back downstairs—and Sebastian, not Atif, called 911. His voice on the tape was excited, but not necessarily panicked.

"There's—I need—an—an ambulance!" Sebastian told the 911 operator.

"OK. What's the address?" she asked.

"4610 144th," Sebastian said without hesitation.

"Is that a house or an apartment?"

"It's—it's a house. It's a house."

"What's the problem there?" the operator asked.

"The—there's just some kind of break-in—I . . ."

"OK, well, just calm down. What's the problem?"

Sebastian's pace quickened. His tone became higher. He was obviously shaken.

"The—the—I don't—the—the two—my friend, his mom and dad are—they're—they're—I—we—think they're dead."

"OK. And what—are they at that address there?" the operator asked him.

"Yes, please!! I don't know if it's safe here. I just—I . . ." Sebastian sighed heavily. "We'll be outside."

"Why—why do you think that they're dead?" the operator asked.

Sebastian's breathing picked up. He was clearly stressed.

"There's blood. They're not breathing. There's— blood all over his face. They're like—I don't know—if you come fast—I . . ."

Sebastian didn't mention Basma, who was still alive, unconscious, in her bedroom.

"OK. Just calm down. Where are they at in the house?" she asked him.

Sebastian started to describe where the bodies were in the house, but interrupted himself.

"I don't think it's safe here. I want—we'll—we'll be outside."

"OK. Go ahead and go outside."

Sebastian was now pleading. "Please! Please! OK."

"They're on their way," the operator reassured him.

"We'll be outside."

Terrified, Sebastian hung up the phone. He and Atif ran out of the house and went to the curb to wait for help.

Sebastian lit up a cigarette.

5

Help Arrives

Bellevue police and paramedic units were dispatched. With their emergency lights flashing but sirens turned off, they raced to the Rafay house. The first officers arrived in the Somerset neighborhood within six minutes.

Marc Sidell was startled awake by voices drifting into his bedroom window from the front yard. He said it was 1:33 A.M., explaining that he'd glanced over at his digital clock on the bedside table. Sidell shot out of bed and went to the window. He quickly kneeled down, too embarrassed to stand, because he was naked.

"There was somebody outside the window making a lot of noise," Sidell said.

Judith Sidell also came over to the window to see what all the fuss was about. Judith remembered the time being closer to 2 A.M., which matched police reports.

"I looked outside, and I saw two teenagers talking," Judith said. "They were right by the curb of the cul-de-sac in between the Rafay house and our house. I had no idea who they were."

With his head poking over the windowsill, Marc Sidell watched the young men for several minutes. It was deathly quiet outside, except for those two boys. Sidell remembered that one of the boys was much taller than the other.

"I could see them conversing to each other. They didn't look like they were real excited about anything," Sidell said. "I didn't know what was going on, why didn't they just go to bed or whatever."

Walking in the direction of those two boys was Lt. Greg Neese, a rookie, who felt a combination of nervousness and excitement. Like many police officers in this peaceful community, he had never been to a murder scene before—never seen a dead body. He said he thought, "Just don't get lost."

Officer Gary Hromada was converging from the opposite direction of Lieutenant Neese, about one minute ahead of him. Getting to 144th Place South East was no easy task. It was deep inside a neighborhood maze of streets, places, and circles. At about 2:06 A.M., Officer Hromada turned onto 144th. He slowed down his Ford Crown Victoria cruiser as he approached the end of the cul-de-sac. He had been advised that two young men would be waiting outside, but Hromada didn't see anyone in the darkness. He turned on his searchlight to check house addresses, and was startled.

"I'm driving around, and I hear loud pounding on the back of my police car, as if you took your hand and hit the car as hard as you could on the trunk and back window," Hromada said. "I also heard people yelling, and I stopped my car."

"He initially had driven past, right past the house," Atif later said, in defense of the boys' over-the-top reaction. "We had to chase him down."

Officer Hromada quickly got out of his car. Sebastian and Atif were both standing just off his back bumper, screaming at him. They seemed to be on the verge of tears. Sebastian appeared to be shaking.

From his window perch, Marc Sidell said he heard Officer Hromada ask Atif a question.

"He said, 'Where are your parents?'" Sidell said.

"Another thing struck me," Sidell said. "They [the boys] weren't excited. They were sort of like, 'Oh well. We got caught.'"

"Yeah," Judith Sidell quickly added. "That's why I thought they robbed the house."

But from Officer Hromada's experience on the street, he felt he was dealing with two hysterical teenagers.

"I told them to back off," Hromada said, "but they kept yelling. They were yelling something about the house. But I didn't know if they were suspects, witnesses, or victims."

Despite Officer Hromada's instructions, the boys, obviously distraught, started describing what was inside the Rafay home.

"They were saying things like, 'There's blood everywhere. There's bodies everywhere. It's terrible inside. And there's [pointing toward the Rafay house] the house!'"

Hromada said the boys kept screaming. But one thing struck him: There were no tears. He listened to the boys for a few more seconds and then sternly ordered them to sit down on the curb. Sebastian and Atif fell silent.

"It was like a light switch," Hromada said. "When the light switch was on, they were very incoherent, they're yelling and screaming. When the light switch went off, they were quiet, emotionless, and acidic."

Hromada said the whole scene seemed odd to him.

"They became very calm. They didn't move," Hromada said, as he thought back to that night. "It surprised me that they didn't ask me any questions."

"He thought we were—I don't know what—that we were somehow crazy, criminal or something," Atif said. "He then yelled at us, and so, yes, we quieted down pretty quick, because he seemed pretty aggressive about it."

Atif's face then took on a look of disgust.

"As to whether it was like a 'light switch,' I think that's just a ridiculous, fantastic invention."

Officer Hromada said he spent about ten minutes with the boys. In all that time, neither Atif nor Sebastian asked about the status of any of the victims or inquired about when the ambulance was going to arrive.

Shortly after Officer Hromada's dramatic scene with Sebastian and Atif, Lt. Greg Neese pulled up in his patrol car. He grabbed a camera, putting the strap around his neck. Neese then pulled his service revolver from his holster. His pulse racing, Lieutenant Neese entered the Rafay home. Right behind him were two paramedics, who had just arrived. They could hear Basma.

"It was what I describe as a death rattle," one of the paramedics said. "It's a big gasping noise, just gasping for air basically."

Lt. Neese holstered his gun and raised his camera. He took two pictures of the paramedics trying to save Basma.

"They attempted to resuscitate her," Neese said. "They put her on a gurney and took her out of the house."

Another officer, John Bosseler, was heading into the house as Basma was being brought out. He looked at her.

"She was bleeding profusely. They carried her down the steps. She came within two feet of me," Bosseler said. "I noticed a lot of blood around her head. Some blood was dripping onto the ground."

Basma never regained consciousness. If she had, her autism would have prevented her from telling investigators what had happened. Basma, twenty, died six hours later at Overlook Hospital in Bellevue. The Rafay family was now down to one member—

Atif. Officer Hromada was keeping an eye on the teenager, who was sitting on the curb alongside Sebastian.

"They were sitting so close together, their hips were touching," Hromada said. "They were occasionally murmuring to one another. I could not hear what they were saying."

Inside the Rafay house, the rookie left Basma's room to continue his search. He made his way upstairs. It was dark. As he approached the master bedroom, another officer turned on a light in the hallway.

"I don't know who turned that on," Neese said, "but it threw a little light in there [the bedroom]. But I couldn't really see all the way back to the far wall."

He stepped into the room, and his eyes adjusted to the low light coming from the hallway. Neese raised his camera in the direction of Tariq and took several pictures of the first dead person he had ever seen.

Twenty miles away, Homicide Detective Bob Thompson, a sixteen-year veteran of the Bellevue Police Department, was awakened by the blaring ring of his bedside phone. On the line was a lieutenant standing outside a home. The worst multiple murder in Bellevue history had just been discovered. And in a night of firsts, Thompson was assigned, for the first time in his career, to lead the homicide investigation.

"I had just come into the homicide unit, so for me,

personally, I think it was a lot of pressure. And there was a lot going on in my mind, making sure things were done and trying to go through a checklist. In some respects, it was kind of exciting," Thompson said with a sad smile. "And in some respects, it was . . . kind of nerve-racking."

Bob Thompson is a man straight out of a Norman Rockwell painting. Married, the father of three daughters, Thompson stands about six-one and weighs 180 pounds. He has perfect posture, square shoulders, and the chest of a mountain climber. Thompson, an avid gym rat and outdoorsman, once scaled Mount Rainier in Washington State, they stood atop its 14,410-foot summit. Thompson's face is angular, his jaw squared, his eyes blue, all topped by detective-cut brown hair, neatly combed with a part on the side. He is always dressed in a sports coat, tie, and slacks. Thompson's accent is pure Northwest, with that slightly Minnie-soh-tan sound. His voice is friendly, with a gee-whiz kind of attitude. He was known for investigating like he climbed—methodically, one step at a time.

Thompson quickly dressed, got into his unmarked black Buick Regal, and roared off through empty streets toward the Rafay house.

The sun had still not risen on the morning of July 13, 1994, but the Somerset neighborhood was full of light—created by more than a dozen police and paramedic vehicles that were now parked around the cul-de-sac in front of the Rafay family home. The sole survivor of the Rafay family, Atif, and his best friend, Sebastian Burns, had been in and out of squad cars and observed by a number of police officers and para-medics. Their every word and facial expression was being interpreted. Although there was no suggestion by anyone that the boys were somehow involved in the murders, they represented the only direct link to the family. Police refer to such people as "persons of interest." It does not mean that someone is a suspect, but in any murder investigation, detectives begin with the immediate surviving family members and then work their way out to friends, neighbors, and business associates. Police reports varied wildly in the descriptions of the boys.

One officer wrote, "Sebastian was extremely emotional and could hardly speak because of it."

Another officer said the boys "were just sitting there with kind of a glazed look. No real emotion that I could tell. Neither of them were crying or, you know, upset. Their emotions . . . didn't seem like they fit with what they had just discovered."

Some officers were struck that Atif didn't ask about his sister or request to go to be with her at the hospital.

"He seemed, you know, real calm," one officer said of Atif. "He wasn't crying."

But another policeman at the scene saw something completely different.

"Throughout my contact with Atif Rafay, he was

very subdued and acted stunned and shocked. He was cooperative and answered all questions."

Still another officer summed up Atif's behavior as "nothing suspicious."

Atif said he was overwhelmed by what had happened to his family, but being stoic, he said, was a family trait.

"I was trying to distract myself as much as possible and not remember what had occurred," Atif said with determination. "Doing my best to avoid the images of horror that crowded in on my head. People have different mechanisms of coping. And mine was to avoid and divert myself from even thinking about it."

Atif also blamed some of his reaction on the police, who he claimed seemed uncaring about his loss.

"It certainly didn't feel like they were being the least bit sensitive or even humane."

Sebastian said some of his emotion that night was for his best friend and the sorrow Atif was experiencing. Sebastian said he wasn't very close to Atif's parents, but he respected them. He had just spent five days visiting Atif and living at the Rafay home.

"I thought they were very nice. Sultana was very quiet, but very attentive," Sebastian said. "She was always very kind to me when I came over. Tariq was very witty, but very dry. I didn't really see much of his personality."

Sitting in a squad car, Sebastian was the closest thing to family Atif had left. He had relatives in Ontario, Canada, but didn't know them much beyond their names. The two nineteen-year-old boys told several officers their story of being out on the town and coming home to discover the bodies. They felt like victims.

Soon, they'd feel like suspects.

6

So Many Questions

Detective Bob Thompson knew these murders would get a lot of attention, so he was doing everything by the book. He requested a search warrant of the Rafay home while driving to the scene. It was standard operating procedure in a homicide case to get a warrant before a detective entered a home. It was just after 4 A.M. when he arrived at the scene.

"As I pulled up, there was a crime scene van already there. The whole area had been cordoned off with crime scene tape," Thompson said. "As I drove in, there were a number of police cars. Atif and Sebastian were each in a separate patrol car."

Thompson didn't speak to the boys. At 4:55 A.M., his search warrant was issued. Thompson met up with another detective, Jeff Gomes, who would work alongside Thompson throughout the investigation. Gomes was a nineteen-year veteran of the Bellevue PD and was known for his shrewd interrogating techniques. A third officer, carrying a video camera, joined them to document their exploration of the house. The three men entered with the camera rolling.

"We walked downstairs, where we found Sultana," Thompson said. "She was facedown in a pool of blood. It appeared she had some trauma to the back of her head."

Looking at Sultana, Thompson tried to imagine the last moments of her life.

"You start absorbing what you actually are seeing," Thompson said. "That's when I thought she may have been attacked by someone she knew. Because she didn't appear to have any defensive wounds. Also, it's a large room down there. It would be very difficult for someone to sneak up on her."

The three men moved on, walking into the bedroom where Sebastian stayed. The area was a mess.

"It appeared to have been ransacked," Thompson said. "Boxes were tipped over; drawers were opened."

Such a scene was typical of a robbery, as thieves tended to throw things about, looking for valuables. But something about this mess caught Thompson's eye.

"Nothing appeared to have been gone through. The boxes are literally dumped over. But nobody really rummaged through them."

Thompson filed away the thought, and the men continued their inspection.

"Then, we went upstairs, where we discovered Tariq Rafay in his bed."

The video shook from side to side as the cameraman walked into the room. He panned about and found Tariq on the bed.

"He was faceup," Thompson said calmly, with the detachment necessary for a detective to do his job. "He was in his pajamas. And literally, the entire wall behind his head was just a rainbow of blood, flesh, hair, and—to be blunt—brain matter. I'll tell you what it looked like: It looked like a shotgun blast to the head. But I quickly noticed there wasn't a gun in the room."

Other officers who had been in the room initially thought that a murder-suicide had taken place. Thompson moved in to get a closer look at Tariq.

"His face, literally, was caved in. It looked like someone had hit him forty or fifty times. It told me that somebody had something against Tariq. Or that somebody just went off the deep end." Thompson paused, took a breath, and continued. "And once they started killing, they either enjoyed it or they couldn't stop themselves."

Thompson made a mental note to himself. "Who were Tariq's enemies?"

The cameraman was still working the room. He tilted up to the ceiling, then down, panning side to side, making sure each wall was recorded on video.

"There was blood all over the room—on the ceiling, on the floor, on the walls," Thompson said with disgust. "It was basically an overkill. He was probably dead on the first blow."

Thompson examined the rest of Tariq's body and came to a quick conclusion.

"His legs were crossed and he never—he never felt anything. He never knew what hit him."

The final stop was Basma's room.

"Instantly walking into Basma's room, you could tell there had been a struggle. Sultana appeared to have been killed instantly. Tariq had been killed instantly. Basma, it was obvious right from the beginning that she had struggled and fought. She had been chased around that room."

Thompson, who had daughters of his own, appeared to have been most affected by Basma's murder.

"There were indentations in the wall where someone was swinging at her and it appeared that they had missed. There was blood in different locations on the bed, on the wall, and on the floor. There were teeth on the floor and bed."

When the tour of the house ended, Detectives Thompson and Gomes huddled and talked over what they had just seen. Thompson knew that once the community awoke and heard news reports, all hell would break loose.

"You know, things start running through your mind," Thompson said nervously. "Like there's some kind of a serial killer running through the neighborhood. I knew there would be pressure to solve this crime."

But the more Thompson and Gomes discussed the evidence, the more they became suspicious of the two young men who had called 911.

"Obviously, the area of suspicion would be: Who would Sultana be comfortable with, and who would be in that room? And the only two people that she would appear to know in that situation were Sebastian and Atif."

Outside the Rafay home, the two boys had done everything asked of them by the various patrol officers and crime scene investigators. They had been photographed, examined for gunpowder residue, checked head to feet for blood, and fingerprinted.

"I allowed them to run a Lumalight [which illuminates blood] over me," Atif said. "I gave them as many statements and interviews as they requested. I gave them complete access to my computer files."

Atif handed over his eyeglasses for examination. Both boys also gave police their clothes for laboratory testing and even agreed to go down to Bellevue police headquarters for questioning. That's where Detective Thompson first met them.

"I think I did every single thing they asked," Atif said with some annoyance. "I can't imagine what more I could possibly have done. I simply did whatever I could to assist them in any way I could." Atif's tone became more serious. "Even when it was becoming clear to me that my information was not for investigating the case, but in making a case against me."

7

Ask Us Anything

Atif and Sebastian both said they felt investigators turning against them during their interviews at police headquarters. It wasn't anything specific that was said to them, just the tone. The questioning felt more like an interrogation. It was now 6:50 A.M., on the morning of July 13. Neither boy had slept or been offered any food. They had not chosen to contact attorneys—both teens later said they were trying to cooperate with police. Since they both believed they had done nothing wrong, they didn't think that they needed to contact attorneys. Sebastian hadn't spoken to his parents, who were 150 miles away in West Vancouver, B.C. They were still in yesterday's clothes. They were each interviewed separately. Atif was first.

"Tell me what you did during the daytime. What happened?" Detective Thompson asked Atif.

"We woke up really late, as usual," Atif began.

Detective Gomes walked in, interrupting the interview. "Excuse me. I just came into the room. I'm Detective Gomes. And it is six fifty-one. OK. Go ahead."

"We woke up really late—twelve, I guess—I had a small breakfast," Atif continued.

"What did you have for breakfast?"

"Sebastian made me some French toast," Atif said.

The questioning went on in excruciating detail. Atif said they went to Safeway, Barnes & Noble, and a music store called Silver Platters.

"I had dinner with my family," Atif said. "Sort of a small one, though, like, like a salmon or whatever."

"Everyone there for dinner?" Thompson asked.

"Everyone was there, right. And around eight-thirty, we left to go to The Keg."

The Keg was a restaurant chain, offering everything from burgers to steaks. The restaurant was in the same shopping center as a multiplex movie theater, where the boys planned on taking in a show.

Detective Gomes asked something that was bothering him.

"Why did you go eat again?"

"Basically because we're hungry," Atif shrugged.

Atif said that at about 9:30 P.M., they bought tickets at the Factoria Cinema for the 9:50 showing of *The Lion King*.

"Did you see it?" Gomes asked.

"Yeah," Atif said. "It was a really bad movie."

Later that day, police began checking out Atif's story. The time of the movie, and whether or not the boys were there, would soon become a critically important part of the investigation. Neighbors on either side of the Rafay home told police that they heard pounding coming from inside the house. Police later concluded they were earwitnesses to the murders. The neighbors would soon tell police the time they believed they heard the pounding. Their recollections could implicate or exonerate Atif and Sebastian, depending on whether the boys' alibis checked out. For now, detectives were trying to establish a time line based on the boys' memories of that night.

"What time did the movie get out?" Detective Gomes asked Atif.

"It must have been, I can't remember exactly, but it must have been eleven-twenty or something like that," Atif said.

"After that?"

"After that, we drove down to central Seattle because we figured we'd hang out and go to a café and we'd go to a club at Fourth and Virginia."

That café was actually Steve's Broiler, a twenty-four-hour diner-style restaurant. It was located just a few blocks from the Space Needle and is a fixture for Seattle night owls.

"And then we ate there," Atif told the detectives. "I had a little dessert sundae and Coke, and I think Sebastian had hash browns and something else. Then we basically asked around if there was a club nearby or anything, and about one-twenty or something, about one-thirty, they told us there was a place called the Weathered Wall."

The Weathered Wall was a grunge-rock dance

club, located about two blocks from the restaurant where the boys had just left their five-dollar tip. They tried to enter the club but were turned away; it was closing time. Atif said they stopped again at Steve's to use the restroom, then went back to his car. He let Sebastian drive. The two drove about one mile through downtown city streets to Interstate 5. They went south just a few miles, exiting at I-90 East. That took them to the Mercer Island Floating Bridge, which spans Lake Washington. There were two floating bridges that take motorists to what is called the Eastside, which includes the wealthy suburbs of Mercer Island, Newport, Kirkland, and Bellevue. Once on the Eastside, it was about a ten-minute drive to the Rafay home in Somerset.

As they approached the house, Atif said he opened the garage door with a remote. He then unlocked the door leading to the hallway and walked into the house.

"And then I saw my mom," he told detectives. "And I sort of walked up to her and I knelt over her, but I just ran."

"Did you touch her?" Detective Gomes asked.

"I knelt near. I don't know if I touched her."

Gomes remembered seeing a scarf placed over Sultana's head. He looked straight at Atif.

"Did you put anything over her?" Gomes asked.

"No, I don't think," Atif said.

"So you run and you're starting to lose control at this point?"

"Well, yeah. I can't really remember anything. No, I remember like, you know, seeing they disarranged Sebastian's room."

Sebastian had been staying in a guest room at the Rafay house. That was the bedroom where Detective Thompson noticed that boxes had been turned over but not scattered about.

"Sebastian entered his room and noticed that everything was upturned, so I went, I went to follow him into his room," Atif said.

"So Sebastian's room is downstairs?" Detective Thompson clarified.

"Uh-huh. And then we went right up the stairs and went to my dad's room."

"Did you call out or anything?" Thompson asked.

"Yeah," Atif said. "I was saying, 'Dad?'"

Sebastian had followed Atif up the stairs. But he passed Atif and entered the master bedroom first. Atif followed quickly behind.

"I could hear my sister at this point," Atif told detectives. "I could hear her. And so I went into my dad's room and I saw the blood on the wall, and then I freaked, I was freaking out. I don't know what I did."

"Did you touch him?" Gomes asked.

"I didn't touch him. I could hear my sister. I just didn't want to, didn't want to hear that, so I left. I just ran. I went into my room, basically told Sebastian."

"Did you go into your sister's room when you heard her?" Thompson asked the teen.

Atif shook his head, as if trying to erase the memory. "No. No."

Later in the interview, Atif said he then went into his own room and "just looked around." Gomes asked a question that immediately raised suspicions. Atif had been short on detail about his parents. But suddenly, he remembered something that seemed trivial.

"Did you notice anything missing from the house?" Gomes asked.

"Not at that point, but now that I'm thinking of it," Atif said, "I don't remember seeing my Discman or my receiver in my room."

"Your what?" Gomes looked at the teen, thinking he must have heard him wrong.

"My Discman or receiver," Atif repeated.

Hearing Atif's answer was like having a light switch turned on for Detective Thompson.

"He had just seen his dad obliterated and murdered. And he notices that his Discman is missing from another room?" Thompson is dripping with sarcasm at this moment. "That is odd."

Thompson continued questioning Atif on this statement. "You indicated that maybe your CD player was taken from your room."

"Uh-huh." Atif looked at the detective.

"Anything else in the house taken?"

"I haven't checked. I don't know."

"Did you indicate a VCR?" Detective Thompson asked.

"Yes, yes," the teen said.

"From where?"

"From the cabinet—on the TV stand."

"In the family room?"

"Yeah."

Thompson looked hard at Atif. "You recognized that because . . . why?"

"Because the door was open," Atif said.

"The door to the cabinet was open?"

"Yeah."

Thompson moved the story forward.

"And then where did you go?" Thompson asked.

"Then I went to the living room area, and Sebastian called 911," Atif said.

Detectives Thompson and Gomes now turned their attention to Sebastian. In his interview with the detectives at 7:30 A.M., Sebastian told basically the same story. Except when he described making the 911 call. Sebastian said he told the 911 operator the Rafays' house address after reading it off a magazine. Atif remembered it differently.

When the detectives interviewed Atif, he told them, "I was trying to give him the address of the place, and he's just telling them to get over here."

During the talks with both boys, Detective Thompson said he was picking up something from Sebastian and Atif that just didn't make sense: an attitude.

"Just trying to talk to them, they just seemed aloof. They just seemed like, 'Hey, we've already talked to the patrol officers. What do we have to talk to you for?'" Thompson recounted, imitating the boys in a whiny voice.

Thompson said he shot back that it was because Atif's family was dead.

"They acted suspicious," Thompson said. "When talking to Atif, I said, 'Hey, you need to get hold of your family. You have some funeral arrangements.' He didn't want to do any of those things."

Detectives said Atif told them that he didn't have any family in the area and that he didn't want to contact anyone at this time.

But Atif told *48 Hours* a very different story.

"Your family is murdered and you don't contact any relatives. Why?" Peter Van Sant asked Atif.

"The very first female officer told us that she thought that the Royal Canadian Mounted Police and the Bellevue police would certainly help us, help me do that. And, in fact, would do it *for* me," Atif said emphatically. "And I then mentioned that subsequently to Thompson and Gomes, and they both promised me that they would do so. But quite frankly, I was in no condition to call anyone and make those announcements. I couldn't even think of what to do with myself."

Based on his experience with other cases, Thompson said that family members usually drive him crazy in the opposite way, asking what they can do to help or demanding constant updates on the investigation.

"They didn't do any of that," Thompson said.

"Their attitude was 'Why do you keep bothering me?'"

Thompson had now spent several hours observing the two boys.

"It appeared to me that Sebastian was very dominant over Atif," Thompson said. "And he seemed to be the person who always seemed to answer for Atif. If you asked Atif a question, Sebastian would always step in."

At police headquarters, both boys gave their clothes to investigators. Sebastian had on the most memorable item of clothing, a colorful cartoon T-shirt that read "Reid Fleming: World's Toughest Milkman."

At 8:30 A.M., the boys were finally taken out for breakfast. Sebastian had still not called his parents. After breakfast, they were taken to a local dive, the Bellevue Motel, the kind of place that offered hourly rates. It stood out in the affluent community like a nasty boil. The boys had no money. All their possessions had been seized by the police. They were given a room that had no telephone. It was now about 10:30 A.M.

Within minutes, they were fast asleep.

8

We Have Alibis

While Sebastian and Atif rested, police were hard at work checking out their alibis. An investigator went to The Keg, where a waitress remembered seeing the boys around 8:30 P.M. They had been friendly, striking up a brief conversation. They had also asked the time, not wanting to be late for their movie. The waitress told them it was 9:30.

Police then moved on to the Factoria Cinemas, where the boys said they had seen the 9:50 P.M. showing of *The Lion King*.

"We were having a managers' meeting," said Jose Martinez, an assistant manager. "Someone called upstairs saying there were two police officers that wanted to talk to the head manager."

The manager headed down, with Jose right behind him. The police produced photographs of Sebastian and Atif and asked the manager if he recognized them. But Jose quickly jumped into the conversation.

"I do," Martinez said he told the two officers.

The police asked him why he remembered the boys.

"Because he [Atif] was wearing the same jacket—the same jacket he's wearing in the police picture," Martinez said.

Atif had worn a camouflage army jacket that night. It stuck in Jose's mind because he wondered why anyone would wear a heavy coat on such a warm summer night. He also remembered the boys for another reason.

"They were just acting stupid—just goofy I guess," Martinez said. "It seemed like they wanted attention drawn to themselves. They seemed to be in a good mood."

Police also spoke with several other theater employees. One remembered Sebastian because the teen made a point of asking an employee at the concession stand if he liked his milkman shirt. Another remembered Atif coming out of the theater a little after 10 P.M. to let the employees know that the movie curtain hadn't properly opened and that the film was being projected onto the drapes.

During their interviews, police asked each of the boys separately if they knew how the movie—which ran an hour and twenty-eight minutes—ended. Both described the end accurately, including the climactic battle between Simba and Scar. Atif was even asked if he could remember any of the film's credits.

"Whoopi Goldberg was one of the hyenas," Atif

said confidently, like a student having the right answer in class. "Matthew Broderick was Simba."

Jose Martinez also remembered several other things about that night. All the alarms on the exit doors had been turned off. They did that on nights when the crowds were small, he told police. Martinez also remembered that he didn't see the boys leave. He was working outside on a planter, and he thought he would have remembered those two "goofy" guys exiting.

Other police officers went to Steve's Broiler, the downtown Seattle eatery. The waitress there remembered the boys from that large tip they left. The boys' alibis appeared to be airtight. In fact, Bellevue police spokesman Lt. Jack McDonald told reporters that Atif and Sebastian were not suspects in the murder.

"It all checks out," Lieutenant McDonald told the *Seattle Times*. "People saw them at those locations."

Witnesses from later that night confirmed that the boys were wearing the same clothes they had on earlier in the evening, when they'd been at the restaurants and movie theater. Those clothes, including that wacky milkman T-shirt, don't have a speck of blood on them. Sebastian and Atif's shoes were also tested for blood.

The results were negative.

Inside the Rafay house, Bellevue's CSI team, using the best technology available in 1994, combed every inch of the house. They took hundreds of photographs, examined each room for hair, blood, and fibers. They dusted for fingerprints everywhere they could. There wasn't a single bloody fingerprint or footprint that in any way linked the two boys to the crime. Sebastian and Atif's fingerprints were found in the house, but both had been there for days prior to the murder. In the shower, twenty-two human hairs were recovered and examined. Only one hair displayed Mongoloid characteristics, consistent with the Rafays' racial group. The remaining hairs displayed Caucasian characteristics. Some of Sebastian's hairs were found in the drain, in the same spot the killer washed himself off. But this was the shower Sebastian had been using during his five-day visit to the Rafay house. The hairs were insignificant.

One crime scene investigator did find an intriguing potential piece of evidence—a single thick black hair, described as "coarse," on the fitted sheet in the master bedroom. It was obvious to the naked eye, lying there all on its own. Was this a hair left by the killer? Investigators believed if they could learn whose hair it was, the triple murder case might be solved. DNA tests were ordered to see if the hair was a match for anyone in the Rafay family or for their houseguest, Sebastian. It would take months for the results to come back from the lab.

While a colleague was telling a frightened public that the boys were not suspects, Detective Bob Thompson had his doubts. Did the boys' alibis really check out? Another Detective, Jerry Johnson, canvassed home owners who lived near the Rafays. On the evening of July 13, he interviewed Marc Sidell. It was less than twenty-four hours since Sidell had said he heard pounding coming from the Rafay house. His memory was fresh. Sidell told the detective about the "muffled cow" sounds he had heard. He was then asked when he had heard them.

"So this was about um . . . nine forty-five?" the detective asked.

"Yeah, about nine forty-five . . . nine-fifty," Sidell said.

At that exact time, several witnesses confirmed, Sebastian Burns and Atif Rafay were at the movie theater. If Sidell's memory was correct, the boys could not have committed the murders; they simply could not have been in two places at the same time.

Sidell wasn't the only neighbor who heard the pounding sounds at a time the boys were at the movies. On the other side of the Rafay house lived Julie Rackley. She estimated that her bedroom window was about twenty-five feet from the Rafay house. On the night of the murders, Rackley's bedroom window was open. She spoke to police numerous times about what happened that night. Rackley was a person of habit, with a nightly routine. She went to bed at about the same time each night. Her time line remained consistent in her various police interviews.

Rackley remembered lying in bed, reading the book *Que's Legacy*. "I think it was about nine-thirty, nine thirty-five or so. It could have been a little sooner than that," she told Detective Dale Foote.

She read "until about page sixteen," when she heard something that caused her to lift her eyes from the book.

"And that was at about nine fifty-six," Rackley said. "I just remember thinking, Gee, it's sort of late in the evening for somebody to be hammering." She thought the sound was "weird."

"Normally when a metal hammer strikes a nail, you get a resounding, you know, a very sharp sound," she said. "This was not a sharp sound. This was more muffled-sounding."

The hammering went on for some time, she told the officer.

"Bang, bang, bang, bang, bang, bang," Rackley said in a nervous way. "Just over and over. And then I was thinking, you know, When is this going to stop? Because I kind of want to sit and read and not hear this noise."

"And so can you give me a kind of window of time that this banging sound probably occurred?" Detective Foote asked.

"I'd say that it probably occurred before, definitely before ten-fifteen and probably after nine-forty. So somewhere in between that time," Rackley said.

If Rackley was also correct, Sebastian and Atif were in their seats at the movie theater, complaining about that stuck curtain.

Julie Rackley's recollection troubled Detective Bob Thompson, the man heading up the murder investigation. So he asked Rackley if she would consent to participating in a reenactment of that night, right down to reading the same pages in her book. Julie agreed. She went through her routine and read to the end of page 16 of *Que's Legacy*.

"When Julie Rackley ends the reenactment and she looks at the clock, what time is it?" Peter Van Sant asked Detective Thompson.

"It was nine fifty-six," Thompson said, knowing where this was going.

"Where are the boys at nine fifty-six?"

"At nine fifty-six, they were at the movie theater," Thompson said.

"Case closed," Van Sant said.

Thompson's blue eyes narrowed. He responded with one, emphatic word.

"No."

9

Suspicions Grow

Sebastian and Atif had been asleep for about four hours when they were awakened by police. Detectives Thompson and Gomes wanted to speak with them again. There were more questions to be asked about the boys' odd behavior.

Sebastian and Atif agreed to speak with the detectives at Bovee Park, just a few blocks from their motel. When Detective Thompson arrived to pick them up, Sebastian told him that he and Atif wanted to speak to the detectives together, side by side.

"No, we'll talk to you individually," Thompson shot back. "At that time, Sebastian put his hand across Atif's and said, 'We will go together.' Their demeanor kind of took me back."

Investigators never want to interview two witnesses at the same time. There is the concern of creating a false memory if one listens to the other describe a crime. Thompson wanted independent versions of what happened.

After a brief discussion, the boys agreed to Thompson's ground rules. Atif went first. It was a beautiful summer day, with not a cloud in the sky, as the three men sat at a picnic table in the heavily wooded park. The interview was tape-recorded.

Atif explained that he and Sebastian had taken a Greyhound bus from Vancouver, B.C., on July 7 to Seattle. They'd been up visiting Sebastian's family and some friends, including their other best friend, Jimmy Miyoshi. Once in Seattle, they took a taxi to Atif's house. Atif then matter-of-factly told the detectives that he and Sebastian slept in the same bed. That comment woke Detective Thompson up.

"OK. Do you guys have a relationship together, any kind of other relationship?" Thompson asked Atif.

"Are you talking about a sexual relationship?" Atif asked back.

"Sexual relationship," Thompson clarified.

"No."

Atif was clearly agitated by the question. Gomes tried to calm him down, "OK. It's just a question."

Police would later find traces of semen in the bed where Atif and Sebastian slept. It was Atif's.

Atif said his dad cleared out the guest room the next day, and Sebastian slept there the rest of his stay. Atif then told, for the third time, what he and Sebastian did before they discovered his family. He offered specific details about where they had been, what they ate, and who they saw. Atif said that while waiting for *The Lion King* to begin, he played a video game out in the lobby, "Mortal Kombat II." Atif described the waitresses he had seen later that night at Steve's Broiler.

"This waitress there, she had glasses on," Atif said.

Detective Gomes interrupted, asking for more detail. "What kind of glasses?"

"Just regular glasses—very bookish glasses or owlish glasses, rather. And we were asking about a club. So she brought this other waitress who is wearing a black shirt. And we asked, she had sort of a weird voice because it was long and drawn or whatever. It was like a drawl."

But when the interview eventually got to the moment when the boys entered the Rafay house, Atif's memory started to fail him.

"We go in, walk straight through to Sebastian's room because, you know, it's fairly late, probably my parents are asleep, whatever," Atif said. "And I saw my mom. And then, I saw my mom and, uh, can't remember . . ."

"What did you do?" Gomes asked.

"I may have gone up. I can't remember. I don't know. I don't know if I touched her."

"Was the light on in that room?" Gomes asked him.

"Yeah."

"Was that unusual?"

"Yeah. In fact, I remember thinking, when I was

pulling on—when Sebastian was pulling into the house—I remember thinking it was odd that the lower light was on."

Gomes made an entry in his notebook. "And then what did you do?"

"I probably ran up there," Atif said, not sure at all. "I think I went up to her?"

"Did you call? 'Hey, Mom.' Did you say anything like that?"

"I think I may have mumbled it. I don't know. I, I don't think I shouted hard. I think I mumbled it," Atif said.

"Did Sebastian say anything?" Gomes asked.

"He may have said, 'Fuck, Christ,' I don't know."

Detective Gomes pressed Atif for more details. Atif said he may have touched his mother and then run away. He said he went to find Sebastian, who had run to his room.

"Your mom was there laying dead, blood around her head. He went to his room? To do what?" Gomes asked.

"I don't know," Atif said.

Atif said he ran to Sebastian's room, where he noticed all of those overturned boxes. But Detective Gomes brought Atif back to his mother. For the first time in three police interviews, Atif added an intriguing detail.

"Maybe I touched her and then I maybe got my hand dirty," Atif said.

"Got your hand dirty?" Gomes asked.

"Like, like, I don't know."

"So you got blood on your right hand?"

"Yeah. Maybe. No."

Atif then said he may have gone to the upstairs bathroom to wash his hands, but he wasn't sure. Then he was asked about entering the master bedroom, where his father lay dead. He was asked which hand he used to open the door, and Atif said he didn't know.

"By that time, I was in quite a state," he later told Peter Van Sant, before adding sarcastically, "I had been living in the motel that they had so kindly provided. Sleeping on and off, trying to distract myself as much as possible and not remember what had occurred, trying to avoid the images of horror that crowded in on my head."

But the detectives pressed on, demanding ever more specific details. There was a purpose for the tough questioning. They were suspicious that Atif's memory was so fuzzy about what he had seen and done after discovering his parents. Why, they wondered, was Atif so unclear about his mother and father, while providing such sharp detail about his alibi and his missing possessions and Sebastian's ransacked room?

"I go to my dad's and open my dad's room," Atif continued his story.

"What do you mean—open your dad's room?" Gomes asked.

"I pushed the door open."

"Was the door closed?"

This confused Atif. "It wasn't. I don't think it was. I don't know."

Gomes continued. "Did you go walk over to your dad?"

"Um, no. No. I don't think so. No. No."

Thompson broke in, clearly getting frustrated. "Well, you'd know, wouldn't you?"

"Yeah. I . . . I . . . I don't."

Atif said the light was off in the master bedroom. He was clearly being made anxious by the questions. The nervousness was evident in his voice.

"Was he dead?" Gomes asked.

"I guess so," Atif said.

"How do you know he was dead?"

Atif stated the obvious. "Because there's blood on the wall, because my mom isn't moving, because, because he's not moving."

"OK, was the blood his?"

"Who the fuck else's would it be!" Atif shouted.

But Gomes kept his cool—this was all an age-old interrogation tactic. "Now you're calling it a bloodstain. Before you just said a stain."

"Well, it looks like a bloodstain," Atif said. "I can't tell 'cause the lights were off."

"Did you check?"

"No. No."

"What if he's still alive?" Thompson asked.

Gomes echoed his partner. "What if he is still alive?"

"I don't know first aid. I don't know any. I, I, couldn't do anything," Atif stammered.

"OK. How about turning on the light and seeing the body?" Gomes said sarcastically.

"No, I don't want to look at anything like that."

Atif told the detectives that instead of doing something, he began talking to himself.

"I think I was muttering something like, I don't know, 'This isn't happening. Fuck! This is a dream.'"

Later at police headquarters, as he remembered the conversation in the park, Detective Thompson leaned back in his chair. He shook his head when he thought about what Atif didn't do inside his own home.

"This is his mother! His very own mother. You see your mom laying on the floor, you grab her. I mean, that's the natural thing to do. And he just refused to walk up and touch her. But he seemed to know that she was dead. And the same thing with his father."

Thompson's gut told him something was very wrong with the story he was hearing. But there was no actual evidence suggesting Atif was involved. There were only his actions and his befuddled words.

"You know what?" Thompson asked rhetorically. "He is a strange kid. He is a strange kid. But all these things add up to suspicion."

The detectives grew even more suspicious as they revisited another baffling moment involving Atif: his refusal to help his dying autistic sister, Basma.

"Did you hear your sister?" Thompson asked Atif.

"I could hear her," Atif said. "She's just moaning, she wasn't, she wasn't saying anything. She hasn't said anything for fifteen years."

Thompson had already heard this story twice before, but he still couldn't believe it. He zeroed in and elicited an answer that shocked his sensibilities.

"And then you said, 'I'm not going to go to my sister,' the only one that was actually alive?" Thompson asked.

Atif nodded his head up and down.

"That's truly odd," Thompson said, looking at Atif. "Please be honest with us, because it'll come out in the end."

"I'm being honest with you, and I'm telling you," Atif said.

"Now's the time. Now's the time to tell us—tell us what happened."

Atif took a deep breath and looked Thompson in the eye.

"I can say that I never really liked my sister— once," Atif said. "I was scared of my sister. My sister was, my sister—my sister is gross."

Thompson, the dedicated family man, was rocked by what he had just heard.

"So even if she was dying, you wouldn't want to save her—as gross as she is—even if she was dying, you wouldn't want to save her?" he asked the teen.

"I couldn't save her. That was the thing."

Thompson was stunned. Atif had been nervous throughout the conversation, but never emotional. There was a coldness to his answers and his stare.

"I'm sitting here looking at this guy thinking, You know, here's his family . . . there's a possibility that he could have committed this crime."

For the first time since the police had arrived at the Rafay home and walked into that house of horror, Detective Thompson was about to suggest that Atif was more than just a lucky survivor. It was a technique he used to try and elicit a confession. The idea was to make a person think you knew much more than you were revealing. In essence, it was a bluff, like making a big wager when you have a bad hand. Thompson paused, signaling with his silence that something important was about to be said.

"Somebody who did this is very close to your family. There has to be a tie-in there someplace," he told the teen. "And you know what? I think you know who it is."

Atif's voice turned from nervousness to anger. The interview was now a confrontation.

"Ridiculous," Atif answered. "No, I would tell you. I would tell you if I knew who did it. Do you think I'd tell you if, if I even did it?"

Thompson shrugged. "No. I don't know. Depends on who you're going to give up—you know what I mean? Maybe it's a friend of yours that wants to get—maybe there's so many problems that you and your family are having. And they'll say, 'Hey, if I can just get rid of that family, then you could get out from under that religion.'"

Atif's mind must have been swirling. How did Thompson know about his harsh feelings about his parents' religious beliefs? The truth was, Thompson *didn't* know. He was just playing a hunch. Atif's heart was racing. He started stammering.

"My parents, never, never, never, never, never at all—in any way—a problem at all. They were the most supportive family in the world. They did everything for me. How could it possibly be better for me, now that I'm out from everything? Now, I have nothing."

Atif's tenor became more defensive than angry. His voice moved to a higher pitch.

"Why would I . . . why would I keep from you the name of somebody who'd do that to me—to my family??"

"I don't know," Thompson answered back. "I guess that's what we're asking."

The implication of Thompson's line of questioning was clear: Atif was becoming a suspect in the murders. *48 Hours* correspondent Peter Van Sant later pressed Atif about his decisions not to check his parents or help his critically wounded sister.

"You know that for the average person, it sounds terrible that you didn't go in there," Van Sant told him. "It sounds like you wanted her to die."

"Well, I suppose that if I had planned these

murders, I certainly would have rushed in and made heroic efforts to save her," Atif said. "Unfortunately, I had not planned these murders."

Atif just didn't seem to understand why people would think his behavior was strange.

The questioning in the park was coming to an end. It was obvious to Thompson that Atif wasn't going to confess to anything. So the detective concluded with a straightforward question.

"Would Sebastian do it?"

Atif regained his confidence when he heard the question. His answer was firm.

"I don't know if you know Sebastian Burns, but no—never in a million years."

10

Sebastian's Turn

Sebastian Burns was in a foul mood when it came his turn to sit on the picnic table. He complained that the detectives' questioning of Atif took too long. He was hungry.

"You understand we're trying to catch some people that murdered a family in Bellevue," Detective Thompson told the cranky teen.

"I understand that," Sebastian said. "I just, I don't know, when I wait for hours, I guess I become skeptical."

"Do you want us to get to the bottom of this? Or do you want to . . ."

Sebastian sighed. "Yes, of course I do."

Sebastian was asked if he and Atif were lovers. He said no. The detectives then asked about what the boys were doing in Vancouver before driving down to Bellevue. Sebastian mentioned seeing Jimmy Miyoshi.

"He just came outside, and we just talked to him

for not very long. We just wanted to say, you know—
what's up, kind of thing," Sebastian said.

"Was anything up?" Gomes asked.

"Not really."

Sebastian recounted what the boys did the night
of the murders, including going to see *The Lion King*,
a movie Sebastian described as "pretty shitty."

"How was the ending?" Gomes asked.

"The ending was like, it was, it was unsatisfying,
like basically, you know, good prevails."

As the questioning continued, Sebastian's tone
became more irritated. He was asked why he didn't
touch Atif's mom after he discovered her lying on the
floor.

"I guess I suspected that she was deceased," Sebastian said. "I'm trying to remember if there was a
scent. I'm not really sure."

"But you didn't go over to touch her to see if she
was dead or if she needed some help maybe?" Gomes
asked.

"No, I didn't."

The detectives then had Sebastian, in excruciating detail, take them through exactly what happened
after they discovered Sultana Rafay's body. They
wanted to know precisely what Sebastian did and
where he went in the house. The conversation became
heated when Sebastian said "I can't remember" one
too many times.

"We're just going to have to keep doing this and

doing this and doing this," Thompson told the teen. "Because just 'I don't remember' isn't really going to cut it."

"Regardless of whether it's going to cut it or not, then I can't remember," Sebastian retorted.

"OK."

Sebastian backed off a little. "I'm sorry. I've never fucking seen dead bodies before, OK? I've never seen anything like this. So if I can't remember, I'm sorry that I didn't take notes at the time."

Sebastian said he didn't see Atif touch his father.

In his subsequent interview with *48 Hours'* Peter Van Sant, Sebastian's answers were still frustratingly short on detail.

"Did you go to Basma's room?" Van Sant asked the teen.

"No, I didn't," Sebastian said.

"Why not?"

"I don't know."

"Could you hear Basma?"

"I don't remember."

"There's two of you," Van Sant pointed out.

"That's right."

"One goes to Basma, one goes to the phone."

Sebastian conceded this made sense logically. "Yeah."

"One stops the bleeding, one calls for help. Why didn't you do that?"

"I don't know."

The two detectives wrapped up their interview of

Sebastian by having him theorize who may have committed the murders.

"Do you think a member of the family did it?" Thompson asked.

"No, not really," Sebastian said. "I mean, I haven't met them all, but I've met some of them. I don't think so."

The boys were taken back to the Bellevue Motel. They had been through an investigative meat grinder since discovering the bodies at 2 A.M. on July 13. They had been subjected to a total of six hours of questioning—all without the advice or consent of an attorney. They believed they'd done everything in their power to help police with their investigation. But what they were starting to sense was that the more they talked, the more they were becoming the focus of this investigation. And in an interview with *48 Hours,* Thompson said the teens were right.

"Entering this park on July fourteenth, Sebastian and Atif were witnesses," Van Sant observed. "By the time they left, at the end of these statements, were they suspects?"

"Yes. Definitely," Thompson said. "By the time they left, they were suspects."

For Thompson, it was a combination of little things that told him the boys were involved, beginning with their night out on the town. Everywhere they went, they had done something to draw attention to themselves: asking the time, chatting up waitresses and leaving big tips, acting "goofy" at the movie theater, complaining about the malfunctioning movie curtain, and wearing clothing that caught the eye—Sebastian's cartoon milkman T-shirt and Atif's heavy camouflage jacket worn on a warm summer night. Thompson felt it was all part of a plan to establish an alibi.

Based on his experience, Thompson thought that even the 911 call was unusual, almost scripted.

"First of all," Thompson said, "he rattled off the address to this residence when the dispatcher said, 'Where are you?' He said, '4610 144th Place South East,' not like—I'm at my friend's house. How did he know that address that he could just rattle that off?"

Sebastian said he read the address off a magazine, but Thompson found that a bit too convenient. The dispatcher asked Sebastian what the problem was, and his answer also struck Thompson as suspicious.

"He indicated in there that there had been some sort of a break-in. What is the problem there? The problem there is that there's two dead people—and a third who's alive. That's the problem."

Raising the idea of a break-in at that moment, Thompson believed, was a planned attempt to divert police attention away from the boys and toward a mystery intruder.

Thompson said he was also struck by how Sebastian seemed to take control of the emergency call, telling the dispatcher that the boys would meet police outside on the curb.

"To me, it appears like it was scripted—practiced—like a script he was reading," Thompson said.

And why, Thompson wondered, would two frightened boys, worried that a killer could still be inside, go out to the curb and sit down—with their backs to the house?

"It just doesn't make sense," Thompson said.

Sebastian said that nothing he and Atif did that night made any sense because they were in shock and panicked by what they had seen.

"We didn't do it," Sebastian said forcefully. "Atif and I are innocent."

After their grilling in the park, Sebastian and Atif went back to their moldy room at the Bellevue Motel. The boys had not been told directly by the detectives that they were considered suspects. They were free to do whatever they wanted. So they took a four-block walk toward downtown, where they entered a Blockbuster Video store. Police later picked up hidden video from the store's surveillance cameras which showed Sebastian and Atif renting a VCR player and three movies—a Chevy Chase comedy, *The Shogun* television miniseries, and *Enter the Dragon*, a Bruce Lee kung fu film. They walked back to the motel and started watching the movies.

Sebastian had still not called his parents, although police had finally put a telephone in the boys' room. What Sebastian didn't know was that for much of the day, while he and Atif were being questioned in the park, his parents had been frantically trying to get in touch with him.

Atif had not spoken to any of his relatives. But police had managed to find a man Atif referred to as an uncle, although he wasn't a blood relative. The man contacted some relatives of the family who lived near Toronto. Some flew to Seattle to begin making funeral arrangements. No one tried to contact Atif.

Why Atif's relatives kept their distance from him was never fully explained; they declined requests to talk about the case. But in an e-mail that police discovered on the Rafay family computer, Atif once made a passing reference to his extended family.

"My relatives are to me an enigma," Atif wrote. "I would trust the most casual acquaintance more than them in many matters, let alone my friends."

11

Homecoming

The murders of Sultana, Tariq, and Basma Rafay generated front-page headlines and extensive television coverage in Bellevue, Seattle, and Vancouver, B.C. The Rafays were Canadian citizens and had moved only recently to Bellevue from their West Vancouver home.

On the morning of July 14, 1994, Sarah Isaacs was starting to get concerned about her boyfriend, Sebastian Burns. He hadn't phoned her in a few days. Sarah was at her parents' home when they asked her to come upstairs. They had something important to tell her.

"They told me there had been a terrible tragedy," Sarah said. Her heart started pounding. "I asked them what it was. And they told me that Atif's family had been murdered. And that they had read it in the paper. So I was horrified."

Sarah had no way of reaching Sebastian. She went to work in a daze. Suddenly, she wondered if Sebastian's parents knew what had happened.

"So I left work," Sarah said. "And I called Mr. Burns."

It was about 10:20 A.M. when Sebastian's father, Dave Burns, answered the phone. He instantly recognized Sarah's voice.

"Hi, Mr. Burns, have you heard the news?" Sarah asked.

"Well, what news is that, Sarah?" Dave Burns asked calmly.

Sarah couldn't believe she was the one to break the devastating news to the Burns family.

"Atif and Sebastian came home and they found— Atif's parents had been murdered."

He made Sarah repeat what she had heard.

"This occurred on Tuesday?" Burns said. "I hadn't heard any of this."

Dave Burns described himself as not being a news junkie and said he hadn't read a newspaper or watched the TV news recently. He hung up with Sarah and called the Seattle Police Department. Wrong city. Someone told him to call the Bellevue PD. Panic was setting in.

"We were as frantic as you can imagine," Sebastian's mother, Carol, said.

Burns said he then made about six phone calls to the Bellevue police. He demanded to know where his son was, if he'd been arrested, who was in charge of the case, and, most important, why he hadn't heard from anyone.

"I remember being struck by the strange answers

I was getting from police," Burns said. "And I said, 'Look, are you holding these guys for any reason?'"

Burns said the officer responded by asking why he would ask that.

"Why would I ask that? Well, I'm not hearing from them. Why wouldn't I hear from them?"

Burns said the officer responded, "I can't answer for your family dynamic."

"And that was the first time I'd ever heard that phrase, so I wasn't quite sure what this meant," Burns said.

Burns said he then told the officer that if the Bellevue police weren't holding the boys, he'd like them to come home. Burns said they were in an "ugly situation in a foreign country."

Burns said the officer seemed to take offense at the fact that he'd just referred to the U.S. as a foreign country. Burns responded, "Well, I don't quite know how to put this, but I live in one country, you live in another. So I'm in a foreign country to you, and you're in a foreign country to me," Burns said.

The conversation continued in that manner. Burns said the officer talked about how Canadian men had fought alongside Americans in Vietnam and how he considered us all one people. Getting nowhere, Dave Burns hung up and called again. He got a different officer this time, who said he was familiar with the case. He told Burns that his son was "a big eater." Burns hung up the phone again. This time he called a lawyer friend in Vancouver.

"And he said, 'Well, if it was my kids, I'd bring them home,'" Burns said, referring to the phone call.

By 10 P.M., the boys had finished watching their movies and Sebastian finally called home. He told his dad that he planned on staying in Bellevue "until the inquiry is over." But Dave Burns said no, that he would come right down and pick him up. Sebastian told his father there was no reason to come to Bellevue—and said that he and Atif would catch a bus home the next day.

On Friday morning, July 15, Carol Burns phoned Cindy Taylor Blakely, who headed up the Canadian Consulate in Seattle. She explained what had happened to Sebastian and asked for help. Blakely hung up the phone and immediately called the Bellevue Police Department. She spoke to an official and asked if the boys were under arrest. She was told no. She then asked if the boys could leave Bellevue and was told "sure." Reservations were made on a 10:30 A.M. Greyhound bus bound for Vancouver. Blakely met the boys at the bus depot before noon to make sure they got on board. She then followed the bus in her consulate vehicle. Blakely drove ninety-nine miles north, all the way to the Canadian border, just in case a border officer had any questions. By late afternoon on the fifteenth, Sebastian and Atif arrived at the Burnses' house in West Vancouver. They were relieved to be home.

Detective Bob Thompson was livid.

"I do believe that they fled to Canada. They never

told me they were leaving. They knew I was the primary investigator. They had my pager number. They had my cell phone and desk number," Thompson said with contempt.

Thompson believed the only reason the boys left without informing him was because police were closing in on them.

"After their interview in the park, I think that they sat and said, 'You know what? They're on to us. Let's get out of here.'"

Atif and Sebastian left behind more than an angry detective. They also left behind a mosque filled with mourners. Later that day, Sultana, Tariq, and Basma Rafay were buried after a funeral service. The inscription on their gravestones, written in Arabic, read: "In the name of God, the merciful, the compassionate. To God we belong, and to God we return."

The only surviving member of the Rafay family wasn't at the cemetery to read the epilogue. Atif Rafay had crossed the 49th Parallel into Canada, a world away from the jurisdiction of U.S. law and the Bellevue police.

The boys' unannounced trip home became big news on both sides of the border. Sebastian and Atif watched the story that night on the local news.

Atif later told *48 Hours* correspondent Peter Van Sant that all of this could be explained.

"Why did you leave Bellevue for Canada?" Van Sant asked him.

"Well, it was either that or stay in the motel and wait for whatever Detectives Thompson and Gomes had in store next for me, I guess," Atif said.

"Did you flee to Canada?"

Atif laughed. "It was certainly the most well-announced fleeing that I can imagine. The consulate was informed. The Bellevue police were informed. The customs people were also informed."

But the boys left so quickly that they never returned the VCR they had rented, and it was later reported stolen by Blockbuster. That report led police to check the store's security cameras, where they discovered the video of Sebastian and Atif. The VCR was never recovered.

"Why didn't you attend the funeral?" Van Sant asked Atif.

"I didn't know about it," Atif insisted. "I learned of the funeral when I returned to Vancouver and saw it on television. I was never told."

"Atif, the impression is you didn't give a damn."

"Well, that certainly isn't true. That certainly would be the opposite of the truth."

Locked on Atif's face, Van Sant voiced what Detective Thompson suspected.

"Atif, did you and Sebastian Burns meticulously plan the murder of your family?"

Atif didn't hesitate, didn't flinch.

"Absolutely not."

"Are you telling me you had absolutely nothing to do with these murders?" Van Sant asked.

"Precisely."

"Why should we believe you?"

"I think the evidence speaks for itself, with respect to that."

In fact, Atif was right. Despite days of intensive CSI work, with the Rafay house turned upside down by fingerprint, hair, and blood spatter experts, there wasn't a shred of evidence that could form the basis of a case, let alone an arrest warrant. If this was a planned murder, then it was perfectly executed.

But within days, new, dramatic leads surfaced in the investigation. Instead of implicating Sebastian and Atif, however, the leads took the inquiry in a whole new direction—into the realm of religious fanaticism and murder-for-hire.

PART II

THE SUSPECTS

12

A Professional Hit

Soon after the Rafay family murders reached the news media in Washington State and British Columbia, people started coming forward to investigators in both countries with stunning new information.

The first tantalizing tip came six days after the triple homicide was reported, from the Royal Canadian Mounted Police in Vancouver. Constable Patrice Gelinas told Bellevue investigators that on July 19 a reliable street informant told him of a potential murder-for-hire plot that sounded like it was related to the Rafay case. Constable Gelinas gave Bellevue detectives an "information packet" on what he had learned. Here was the complete transcript:

> *Source advised that he/she has learned from an un-*
> *specified source approximately a week and a half ago*
> *a contract was placed on an East Indian family resid-*
> *ing in Bellevue, Washington, by the Dosanjh Group.*
> *Source learned that a Jessy {sic} Brar was offered*

$20,000 Canadian to execute the contract. Source indicated that this East Indian family originated from Vancouver, B.C. Source stated that he/she has recently viewed a news report on television channel "KIRO 7" reporting that an East Indian family has been recently murdered in Bellevue, Washington. That is how the source linked this homicide to Jessy {sic} Brar. Source has no personal knowledge of the murder. Source will provide further information and contact Cst. GELINAS if more information becomes available. Finally, source stated that the Dosanjh Group will get involved most likely in future homicides.

The RCMP passed along the information to Bellevue police because its informant had provided solid information on two previous homicides in Vancouver. The informant wasn't paid for his information. And as far as the RCMP was concerned, the man had no motive to lie or get involved in the case.

Peter Van Sant asked Detective Thompson the obvious question. "What family fits that description?"

"Well, obviously, the Rafays fit that description."

"Did you go check this out?"

"Oh, immediately," Thompson said. "That sounded like a good lead. It sounded startling."

Thompson said he immediately traveled to Maple Ridge, B.C., about an hour's drive east of Vancouver, with two other investigators to meet with the constable who had received the tip. Thompson said he wanted to speak with the informant.

"But the RCMP has a policy that doesn't allow people to talk to the informant," Thompson said. "So then, we wanted to talk to the person that the informant heard this from [Jesse Brar]. But that person wouldn't come forward either."

The next step, Thompson said, was to try and find Brar, a man described by Thompson as "a low-life criminal."

"Jesse Brar had a criminal record in Canada," Thompson said.

Thompson then spoke with the Vancouver Police Department, and asked for its assistance. Brar's residence was eventually located. Vancouver PD decided to send a SWAT team to Brar's front door.

"And so we actually went there a couple of times and he wasn't home," Thompson explained. "And what we learned is that Jesse Brar rarely stayed at that house. He would float from house to house—wherever he could find a place to put his head. And so, it would be futile for the Bellevue police to be roaming around Vancouver trying to find Jesse Brar."

Investigators finally found Brar—Brar denied killing the Rafays and denied ever claiming that he had done so.

Thompson said investigators researched the Dosanjh Group, which sounded like a financial firm but in reality was a ruthless organized crime family that specialized in drug trafficking, especially cocaine. The group had been involved in turf wars around Vancouver and had lost two of its top lieutenants in the past year.

The Dosanjh Group was known to use fire-arms in its murders, but never baseball bats. And Thompson learned that the Dosanjh brothers had been murdered three months before the Rafays were killed.

Thompson's team dug still deeper. Officers researched to see if Tariq Rafay had any ties to this group. They found none. Tariq had no debt, except for his mortgage, and no history of any sort of relationship with any nefarious groups or individuals.

Thompson and his team of investigators never found Jesse Brar and never spoke with him.

"Is it fair to say that you didn't *properly* check out this lead in Vancouver?" Van Sant asked.

"You know, it may be fair to say that that lead was not fully checked out and that it should have been done more thoroughly," Thompson admitted. "But we—I developed the opinion that this had nothing to do with the Rafays."

Thompson said that the way the Rafays were killed told him, and other homicide investigators he spoke with, that this wasn't a professional hit.

"This was someone who used a baseball bat to kill the family. Then they took a shower in the house—felt comfortable enough to go into the shower and clean up. And then—there was no forced entry." Then Thompson added, "If it was a professional hit, why wouldn't they take out the eldest son?"

"At this point in your investigation, is it true that you're biased now toward these boys?" Van Sant asked. "And you really don't want to hear about these other potential leads?"

"Well, that's not true at all."

Carol Burns, Sebastian's mother, felt otherwise.

"They've decided that my son and his friend are the guilty parties. They've decided that," Carol said firmly. "They have no evidence, but they've decided that. And so the rest of the case is about proving circumstantially that they are the killers."

Carol took a breath after her strong denunciation.

"I'm sorry, but that's how I see it."

Carol and Dave Burns's frustration with police would soon reach new heights, as they learned of another tantalizing lead, with more specific information, that suggested an Islamic fundamentalist connection to the murders.

When Atif Rafay was interviewed in the park in Bellevue on July 14, he was asked who might want the family dead. Atif suggested the family had adversaries—fundamentalist Shiite Muslims.

"My mom used to talk about those things, but, nothing, no one would do that," Atif said.

"Your mom would talk about what?" Detective Thompson asked him.

"Well, she talks about, you know, these people were enemies of the family and whatever."

"What?" Gomes broke in.

"It's another religious group, Shiites and stuff, but . . ."

"Shiites?" Gomes clarified. "Do you know who she talked about specifically? You've got to help us here, Atif. Who do we look at?"

But Atif wasn't much help. "They wouldn't . . . I don't know that for sure. My mom, you know, personally broke off contact with those people."

Thompson never gave the notion of a possible religious assassination another thought—until about two weeks after the killings, when he received a call from a man named Douglas Mohammed, who had once been an FBI informant.

"Douglas Mohammed said that he had information that he thought he should share with this investigation," Thompson said.

Mohammed told Detective Thompson that he thought a Seattle-based Muslim cleric ordered Tariq Rafay's murder because of his interpretation of the Koran. He said one of the enforcers for this radical cleric was known to use a baseball bat in his attacks, and that the baseball bat might be in the trunk of a car. Mohammed then offered to give Bellevue police a series of names, addresses, phone numbers, and license plates of people he considered to be suspect.

"Is it true that Douglas Mohammed mentioned a baseball bat before it had been publicized in the media that a bat had been used at the Rafay house?" Van Sant asked the lead detective.

"Yes," Thompson conceded. "He did say that. But it had been publicized that the victims were bludgeoned to death."

"You could use a tire iron to bludgeon someone to death."

"He could have, yeah."

And there was more to suggest a possible hit. After Atif and Sebastian returned to Canada, Bellevue police received a call from a very reliable source, the Seattle Police Department's Intelligence Division. An officer there told investigators that they should check out a radical, extremely violent Pakistani-based terrorist group called Jamaat ul-Fuqra for a possible link to the homicides. The group was known to have an active cell in Seattle and was believed to have been responsible for fire bombings of Hindu and Hare Krishna temples in the city. Jamaat ul-Fuqra would become infamous years later for the 2002 beheading of the *Wall Street Journal* reporter Daniel Pearl in Karachi, Pakistan.

Fuqra believed in the purification of Islam through violence. Its enemies included fellow Muslims, those who didn't practice the faith in a way consistent with Fuqra's interpretation of the Koran. Tariq Rafay may have been one of those Muslims.

Though a quiet, reflective man, Atif's father, Tariq, was also a man of courage and profound religious conviction. While living in Canada, Tariq had helped found the Canadian-Pakistan Friendship Organization, a moderate religious and cultural group based in Surrey, B.C., just outside Vancouver. He served as the group's president. Another man who later headed the organization, Riasat Ali Khan, a close friend of Tariq's, was murdered outside his home in Vancouver, B.C.

That murder was never solved.

Tariq caused some controversy in the Muslim community in British Columbia when he did calculations that determined, in his opinion, that mosques in the province were not built in the proper directional alignment toward Mecca. Tariq concluded that, as a result, Muslims in B.C. were not praying in the right direction. That finding reportedly angered a lot of people.

"My family did have enemies," Atif said in his interview with *48 Hours*. "Did my parents have enemies that I think would do what was done to them? I couldn't believe that, if it weren't for the fact that— apparently that is the case."

Atif said his mother, Sultana, had complained that some groups of people didn't get along with her and Tariq. But Atif said his mother was always vague.

"Obviously, there was more going on than I was ever fully clued in to," Atif said.

"Is it your belief today that this was some kind of hit?" Van Sant asked. "That your parents and your sister were essentially assassinated?"

"Well, they were," Atif said. "And the question is, who did it? I can't imagine what else could have prompted someone to literally destroy my father in his bed while he was sleeping."

Detective Thompson never took Douglas Mohammed, or any of his accusations, seriously.

"To be honest with you," Thompson said, shaking his head, "I thought the guy was kind of what we call a two-twenty."

That was police code for crazy.

"I thought he was a little bit of a nut when he came in," Thompson said. "In fact, if you just spoke with him for a few minutes, you would think—I think most people would understand that Douglas Mohammed was not a credible person to start putting your eggs in a basket with."

But the FBI had a higher opinion of this "two-twenty." Douglas Mohammed had once provided information to the Bureau that led to the conviction of several people in a credit card scheme.

In his interview with *48 Hours,* Sebastian Burns condemned Detective Thompson's decision to ignore what he considered to be one of the most important leads in the case.

"Douglas Mohammed told the police about people who wanted to kill Atif's father," Sebastian said. "And he told them what the murder weapon was. That's information only the killer would know. If Douglas Mohammed had told the police the victims were shot, or the victims were strangled or poisoned or stabbed—then they would know that he was lying."

Then, in that unusual speaking style of his, Sebastian contemplated, puckered his lips, and concluded.

"But he knew what the method of death was—before anybody else knew."

Detective Thompson, however, said the evidence in this case pointed in only one direction—north to Canada, to the two best friends who were now trying to restart their lives in Vancouver.

13

Exhausted and Dazed

Dave and Carol Burns had met the Rafay family only once.

"They came to our house two or three weeks before the murders took place. And I met them when they were sitting in my living room," Dave said.

Tariq, Sultana, and Basma had all dropped by to meet the parents of their son's best friend.

"And that was when I realized that Atif—who I didn't know particularly well at that time—that his parents were fundamentally Islamic," Dave Burns said. "Both the ladies were wearing full-length—to the floor—gowns. The gowns were black. And both were wearing veils."

Dave Burns remembered Basma trying to speak, but "she had no words."

"It was quite unearthly watching her," Dave said with a shudder. "She's quite a big girl, too—bigger than her mother. So she would sort of scratch at her mother to get attention."

Dave Burns was struck by how kind Sultana was toward her daughter.

"Sultana would just very gently, without apologizing or explaining anything, would soothe her and keep her calm."

Carol Burns watched Sultana from a mother's perspective.

"Sultana had to put Basma's shoes on and off," Carol remembered. "I mean, she really could not even tie her own shoelaces."

Now, on Friday, July 15, 1994, Atif was back in the same living room where he had recently sat with his family. With no place to go—no relatives in Vancouver—Atif had accompanied Sebastian back to the Burnses' West Vancouver home. Sebastian's parents said the boys arrived home exhausted and dazed. The Burnses invited Atif to live with them until he could get his life in order.

Dave Burns took his son aside and asked him what had happened in Bellevue.

"He told me, relatively unemotionally—without editorializing—roughly what had happened," Burns said. "He said they had been cross-examined by the police in a variety of settings."

Carol Burns later tried to explain something that had baffled Bellevue police and reporters following the case: Why had Sebastian waited so long after the murders to speak with his parents?

"You know the whole thing with him—and in a

way it runs in our family—is if anybody has problems, they tend to want to solve them without making the rest of the family feel bad," Carol said. "If anybody's got bad news, they'll tell you after it's over. He was just, you know, trying to maintain a presence of calm."

But the calm in the Burnses' West Vancouver home was soon shattered, when Dave Burns turned on the local television news.

"Atif, take a look at this," Dave remembered saying. "Atif comes in and sees his family's funeral on the TV. Atif just lost it. He was just unbelievably upset over that."

Both boys said they didn't know anything about a funeral.

"Atif was swearing, which he usually doesn't do," Carol said. "He wanted to get hold of Thompson. He called him a bastard."

Carol said Atif was stunned that the Bellevue police were saying the boys had knowingly skipped the service.

"I mean the whole thing was bizarre," Carol said. "And for them [the Bellevue police] to put that kind of a slant on it just made us sick."

Detectives Thompson and Gomes were angry over the boys' bus ride across the border. Early the next morning, they, along with two other Bellevue detectives, drove to West Vancouver.

"We figured they must be staying at the Burnses' home, since Atif didn't really have any family left,"

Thompson said. "And we had a few questions for them." It wouldn't be long before the boys were once again face-to-face with Bellevue detectives.

One surprise meeting, however, would occur in an unlikely location and lead to an incident that would forever damage the boys' image with the public.

Two days after the boys settled into the Burns home in West Vancouver, Carol Burns noticed two men outside their home. She told her husband about what she saw.

"This was at our house!" Dave Burns said incredulously. "They were wandering around looking at—eyeballing our house. And they spoke to Carol."

The two men were Detectives Thompson and Gomes.

"One of them said that they had helped solve the Green River Murders in Washington State," Carol said. "I thought that was an odd thing to say to me." After more than twenty years and forty-eight women killed, the Green River Murders were solved in 2003 with the arrest and subsequent confession of Gary Ridgway.

Carol spoke with the men and agreed that they could come back the next day and speak with Atif and Sebastian. But when Dave Burns got home that night, he learned that several Bellevue detectives had approached Atif when he was with some friends at another house. Thompson and Gomes were not present at this run-in.

Veteran detective Tom Wray rang the doorbell at the friends' home. Wray was a man Thompson described as "old school" in his investigative style. He was blunt and liked to use profanity for effect. Atif answered the door, surrounded by his buddies. Wray asked if he could speak to Atif alone.

"And as I understand it," Burns explained, "Atif responded by saying, 'I've got nothing to hide. You can talk to me here in front of my friends.' To which the officer responded, 'Don't fuck with us, Atif, get your ass out here.'"

Atif and his friends closed the door. Afterward, Atif called over to the Burns household and told Dave Burns what had happened.

The next day, Thompson arrived at the Burns home to speak with the boys—not having been told about Detective Wray's curse-laden conversation with Atif. Dave Burns answered the door, assuming that Thompson was the foulmouthed detective.

"I certainly wasn't going to let him into the house," Burns said. They spoke briefly, then Burns ended the conversation. "I wouldn't slam the door, because the door's got a leaded glass frame in it."

But Thompson remembered the good-bye differently.

"He slammed the door so hard, the entire house shook," Thompson said.

But before the door was closed, Dave Burns gave Thompson a slip of paper with the name of an attorney.

"Talk to him," Burns told the detective.

Thompson later called the attorney, who demanded printed copies of all the previous police interviews with the boys. Thompson refused. The attorney then informed Thompson that the detective couldn't interview the boys. In fact, he told Thompson that all cooperation with the Bellevue Police Department was officially over.

But no one was leaving Sebastian and Atif alone. Television news camera crews shot video of them going in and out of the house of their close friend Jimmy Miyoshi. TV crews were also on hand outside a local mosque in nearby Richmond on August 7, where a memorial service was being held for Tariq, Sultana, and Basma Rafay.

Inside the mosque, the family was being eulogized. Atif appeared to be deep in thought when a man came in and sat down next to him.

"Hello, Atif," he calmly said.

It was a Bellevue police detective. Atif quickly glanced over at Sebastian. Behind him was another detective, who gave Sebastian a big Bellevue hello. The two boys quickly looked at each other—and panicked. They got up—in the middle of the ceremony—and speed-walked out of the mosque, directly into the lenses of waiting cameramen. Reporters started shouting questions. Sebastian and Atif broke into a run, and their faces inappropriately broke into smiles. On the tape, you could see and hear them laughing.

The images were broadcast throughout British Columbia and western Washington. Thompson saw it that night on the news.

"It was kind of disgusting watching them run out—prior to the service being over," Thompson said. "They were running out, jumping into a car, laughing and giggling. And I think, knowing what had happened to the family—knowing that they had missed the funeral—and now the son is at the memorial service in Vancouver. And he just leaves! It was rather disgusting."

At best, the boys appeared to be insensitive and immature. At worst, the video could easily have led someone to think they were coldhearted killers.

48 Hours' Peter Van Sant confronted Atif about his demeanor. "I've got to tell you, it's one of the most disturbing pieces of video in all of this. What was so funny, Atif?"

"I guess, you know, it was the media that was funny," Atif tried to explain. "It just seemed absolutely grotesque. And I suppose, I couldn't help laughing at it. It was because the car started while Sebastian wasn't fully in the car, and he kind of bumped his head on the sill of the door. And that's what inspired that particular burst of merriment."

What was merriment for Atif only served to motivate Detective Thompson even more. He and his team of investigators now sought to find out everything they could about these two odd young men. They focused on Sebastian and Atif's alma mater, West

Vancouver High School. They discovered strange writings, a fascination with a nineteenth-century German philosopher, and a starring role in a high school play that seemed to Detective Thompson to provide a possible inspiration for murder.

14

Leopold and Loeb

In early 1993, the drama club at West Vancouver High School needed to select a play that would become the signature stage event of the school year. In the past, a play from Shakespeare or a popular musical was selected. But this year's group of seniors wanted something different, something unforgettable, something—risky.

Robin Puga would direct the play. He was a good friend of Sebastian Burns's and Atif Rafay's. They hung out in and away from school. After high school, Puga, Sebastian, Atif, and their other close friend, Jimmy Miyoshi, would all rent a house together. The group was considered the intellectual elite of the class of '93. They all shared an interest in the German philosopher Friedrich Nietzsche, whom they had studied in class.

Nietzsche was best known for his "superman" theory, the belief that the morals and rules of society don't apply to the intellectually superior. Nietzsche wrote about the *wille zur macht,* the will to power, referring to a superman's use of violence and deceit to get what he wants. Nietzsche also once famously declared that "God is dead." Adolf Hitler referred to Nietzsche as "one of the founding fathers" of Nazism, even though Nietzsche lived in another time and condemned anti-Semitism.

Sebastian now said his interest in Nietzsche was minimal in high school.

"I once thought a quote about the eternal recurrence was interesting," Sebastian said matter-of-factly, as if "eternal recurrence" was a well-known topic. "And that's pretty much the sum total of my familiarity with Nietzsche back then."

Whatever Sebastian's interest level was, his good friend, director Robin Puga, found a play that would break with West Vancouver High's tradition of fluffy productions: *Rope,* by Patrick Hamilton. It is the story of two brilliant friends, devotees of Nietzsche, who plot the perfect murder. There is no real motive, but as "superior beings" they feel entitled to do whatever they want. The two men kill a former classmate—". . . done to death by strangulation and rope," according to the script. They then stuff the victim in a chest in their living room and invite friends over for a party. Alfred Hitchcock made a movie in 1948 based on the play, starring Jimmy Stewart.

The play itself was inspired by a real-life murder in 1924 by two young boys who were also followers of Friedrich Nietzsche. Best friends Nathan Leopold and Richard Loeb believed they were supermen. Like Sebastian and Atif at the time of the Rafay murders, Leopold and Loeb were nineteen. Loeb was said by police to have no conscience—and they theorized that he dominated the friendship.

The two set out to commit the perfect crime. They meticulously planned a murder, including rehearsing what they would tell police afterward. Eventually, Leopold and Loeb killed a fourteen-year-old boy. After a long investigation, police arrested the two best friends. Their trial received worldwide attention, called at the time "the trial of the century." Leopold and Loeb were found guilty and executed.

In *Rope,* the dominant friend is named Wyndham Brandon. When *Rope* debuted at the Strand Theatre in London in 1929, Brandon was played by an actor named Sebastian Shaw. Now, in West Vancouver, another Sebastian was cast in the role, Sebastian Burns.

Arianna McGregor acted on stage with Sebastian. She vividly remembered the character he portrayed.

"The character is or believes he's really intelligent, a genius-level person that is sort of above the general man and believes that people of lesser intelligence are expendable and you can kill them," McGregor said. "He did a really good job with his character. I mean, he really nailed it."

McGregor remembered Sebastian as very intelligent and very friendly.

"He was always really nice to me and never made

me feel inferior or not wanted there or anything like that," she said.

Detective Bob Thompson found out about the play when he looked through the high school's 1993 yearbook.

"I saw that Sebastian Burns was in a play called *Rope,* about two kids who commit the perfect murder," Thompson said. "So we went out and rented the movie. That's where Nietzsche first became involved in this case."

Thompson started working on a theory that the boys' interest in Nietzsche and Sebastian's role in *Rope* had somehow inspired them to attempt the perfect murder. Perhaps, he thought, Sebastian and Atif were a modern version of Leopold and Loeb.

"That's a ridiculous notion," said Sarah Isaacs, Sebastian's girlfriend at the time. "He was interested in doing the play because it was his chance to star in a high school play. And he and I made the decision together. That it's a great play. It's a great part. You'd be perfect in it. Go and do it."

Sarah believed police investigated and publicized Sebastian's role in the play because they had so little to go on in their murder investigation.

"They couldn't say he's a violent person," Sarah said, with some anger rising. "They couldn't say he's a particularly cruel person. All they could say was he was really smart."

Sebastian's sister, Tiffany, believed investigators were grasping at straws.

"Ooooh, he was in a high school play," Tiffany said with mock importance. "Must make him a bad guy. Look at the character he played. Ooooh, he's sarcastic. Ooooh, he's a teenage boy who thinks he's smarter than some people. That must make him a bad guy, right?"

Sebastian spoke with *48 Hours* about his character in the play.

"Your character on stage says, 'We've always said, you and I, that moral concepts of right and wrong don't hold for the intellectually superior. The only crime we can commit is a mistake.' There are some people who believe that those are words that the real Sebastian Burns might say," Van Sant told him.

"That's ridiculous," Sebastian said. "That was my dialogue that was exchanged between my costar and I. There was no time, ever, during any performance or any rehearsal of this play, that anybody was ever thinking anything serious about any of the supposed intellectual philosophies in this play."

"There are some who say that this play inspired you to plan the perfect murder."

"No, that's ridiculous. Absolutely not."

But Detective Thompson wasn't so sure. He began interviewing Sebastian's former teachers.

"The first teacher that we spoke to, she said she wouldn't be surprised if Sebastian Burns was involved with this case," Thompson said. "She said, 'When you're investigating Sebastian Burns, think of David Koresh.' And back in 1994, you know, of course,

David Koresh was running the cult in Waco, Texas."

Thompson elaborated on what he learned in his interview with *48 Hours.*

"Based on your investigation, and what the RCMP officers have told you, were these two boys fascinated with Friedrich Nietzsche?" Van Sant asked.

"Yes," Thompson replied. "And actually, that information came up very early in the investigation. High school teachers and other students felt like he was interested in it."

Thompson was also intrigued by an e-mail his investigators discovered on the Rafay family computer. It had been written by Atif, just before the high school play opened.

"Rope: The pursuit of murder as an act of Morality is next week," Atif wrote. "That's going to be excellent. The perfect role for Seb."

Police were also intrigued by another fact, which was either a coincidence or a glimpse into the future. The play began with the murder itself. The audience saw the killer, but not the victim. In the high school version, Sebastian was backlit, his silhouette projected on a wall. But instead of choking his victim to death, Sebastian killed with a bat—a baseball bat.

It was Sebastian's idea. He thought it would be more dramatic.

"Well, that's just a huge coincidence, and it's nothing more than that," Dave Burns said. "I think Sebastian was actually mortified when he realized that he was a suspect in the baseball bat killings of the Rafays, because he said, 'Cripes, what's going to happen when they find out about the play?'"

In obvious distress, Dave Burns continued.

"I saw the play that has damned him, because, unfortunately it was about a murder that was similar to that which took place in Bellevue."

Burns paused, contemplated, and pursed his lips.

"And here's a case in which Sebastian was on stage, using a bat to—to beat some guy—to death."

Sebastian received rave reviews for his performance. He was commanding on stage.

It was indeed the perfect role for Seb.

15

Parting Words

Flip through the pages of any high school yearbook in North America and you would find the same thing—photographic highlights of the school year, a montage of students, scenes of the various athletic teams. The yearbook for the class of '93 had one ironic photo: a picture of Sebastian Burns in a Superman costume.

In their senior portraits, Sebastian and Atif were wearing special robes, dominated by a large red stripe with white edges that form a large V-neck. It was a sign of achievement, a reward for academic excellence.

Sebastian was beaming in his photo, looking friendly and confident, almost angelic. Atif's picture was much more serious, a no-nonsense visage that suggested moving on with certainty toward future achievement.

Seniors were often given a few lines of original thought, where they could express a hope, quote a favorite writer, or perhaps reflect upon this crossroad in their lives.

When Detective Thompson read the quotes from the two boys that stood alongside their pictures, he was taken aback. What, if anything, did they mean?

Sebastian wrote: "Sebastian seized every weeping opportunity with a clenched fist, without regard for potential victims, exploited them in any way that would yield laughter."

In another printing of the West Vancouver High School's yearbook, done several weeks later, Sebastian's quote had been different, although equally unusual.

Sebastian wrote: "Striding across his realm like a titan, Sebastian's furious contempt for the petty scriptures of the plebeians about him could not be contained by the all too small hallways."

"Plebeian" was the name given to an ordinary citizen of ancient Rome. It also suggests someone who is crude, especially someone from a lower social class.

"People have looked at this entry and said, 'There's a sinister side to Sebastian Burns,'" Van Sant told the teen.

"I had no sinister intentions or thoughts at all," Sebastian said, laughing. "I thought I was making fun of myself and making fun of yearbook entries."

Atif's yearbook quote was equally unusual.

"Atif descended through the clouds. Casting aside the hollow illusions of his peers, he gazed bemusedly at the petty struggles of those around him and began to laugh."

"God, that sounds awful," Atif conceded.

"Did you write that?" Van Sant asked.

"No, I didn't write that," Atif said. "I think that actually Sebastian had some hand in the composition. I think it's kind of funny. I certainly wouldn't have objected to it at the time."

"What does that say about you that you like those words?"

"Well, I guess it certainly indicates the sense of superiority that you've—that you've asked me about. I think it certainly indicates all the estrangement, I guess, from the majority of the people at West Van High."

Detective Thompson saw the entries as another brick in the wall of suspicion. While in Canada, he briefly met with RCMP officials to discuss his investigation. Thompson returned home to Bellevue more convinced than ever that the boys were more than just suspects—they were killers. But he lacked the evidence to back up his beliefs. Any hope for a break in the case would have to come from Canada. And the only way to get new information would be if he could convince the RCMP that there were murderers in their midst.

The life story of Sebastian Burns and Atif Rafay had been played out in Vancouver's newspapers and television stations. It seemed nearly everyone had heard of the boys, the murders in Bellevue, their intellect and arrogance, and the play *Rope*.

But Michael Langford had no idea who the four young men were who moved into the house next door in Vancouver. He first met one of them several days later, when he knocked at their door, asking them to turn down their loud rock and roll music. It was after midnight and his house was vibrating from the boys' powerful speakers.

A couple of days later, Langford's wife finally got a look at their new neighbors.

"Do you know who that is living in that house?" Langford said his wife asked him anxiously. Langford said he didn't know. But his wife sure did. "It's those two guys that supposedly killed their family down in Seattle," she told him.

Langford said his wife was very nervous about their new neighbors. He tried to shrug it off. "They haven't been convicted of anything," he told her.

But it wasn't long, Langford said, before Sebastian and Atif started harassing his family.

"We used to have a barbecue just sitting out here by the back door," Langford said, pointing to some dead grass. "We'd eat out here on the deck. But as soon as I'd open that door to come out and start barbecuing the food, that window"—Langford pointed up to a second-floor window of the house next door— "that window would open up and a speaker would magically appear right there. And they would start cranking the music up. This was even in the middle of the afternoon."

Langford said the boys seemed to enjoy being antagonistic. His life became a series of walks over to the house next door to ask them to quiet down.

"Atif was very outwardly polite about it. He would say, 'Oh, OK, we'll do that. We're sorry.' But the other fellow—Burns—was very aggressive and definitely had an attitude."

Langford ran a hand through his hair, obviously reliving the moment.

"He was very aggressive and he would tell me, 'Oh, what's your problem? Oh, you just don't like the fact of who we are.' That was his big statement, 'who we are.'"

Langford said Sebastian acted as if he was proud of what he was accused of doing.

"He was very boastful of the fact that he was known to people," Langford said. "You know, like, 'I'm the guy that they think murdered these people in Seattle.'"

The blaring music continued day after day, night after night. Langford said the music was vile, full of four-letter words and vulgar lyrics. He was forced to call the police several times to complain. He said he found the whole situation bizarre and, at times, scary.

"There was a knock on our front door. And I answered the door and there were three boys sitting—actually sitting on my front steps," Langford said with a shudder. "They said they were here to settle things with me."

By this time, Langford had been speaking to the landlord about having the boys evicted. Langford said Sebastian did most of the talking.

"He said, 'You know, we can settle this really

nicely in a nice way or we can do this—another way.'"

Langford's adrenaline started pumping. He asked Sebastian if this was some kind of threat.

"He said, 'Well, you can take it any way you want,'" Langford recalled. Sebastian then repeated himself. "We can settle this nicely or we can settle it in a different way."

Langford took that as a threat and closed his door. He and his wife talked over their predicament. It struck them as odd that the boys seemed to be going out of their way to be noticed.

The harassment escalated when the boys started shining a bright spotlight into his bedroom window. They began building large bonfires out in their front yard, just feet away from the Langfords' home. They also sat on their roof and smoked marijuana at night, the unmistakable smell drifting into the Langfords' windows.

"They just didn't care," Langford said, shaking his head. "I think they just thought they were untouchable."

"This sounds like the neighbors from Hell," Van Sant said.

"Yeah. Oh, they definitely were," Langford said. "They would throw things down at people walking by. They'd suddenly pull back their curtain and look out at us and then close the curtain right away. It was just done to give us the effect that they were watching us."

Langford said that over the weeks, his wife grew

terrified of the boys. Eventually, they sought and obtained a restraining order stating that the boys could have no contact with them. But then harassing phone calls started coming in. Langford said they would answer the phone, then hear a click on the other end. He was so afraid of the boys that he didn't have the calls traced.

Then one night, Langford said the boys broke the restraining order. At about 2 A.M., someone started banging with his fists on the Langfords' window, screaming, "Fucking bitch!"

"My wife was just in a panic," Langford said. "Holy Christ, it went on for three nights in a row."

Langford called the police. The boys were arrested. But they quickly returned to the house next door. So did the loud music. Langford said this went on month after month.

"We went off to England after they'd been there for ten months. We went on a holiday. And the hardest part was leaving this house alone," Langford explained. "So we had someone move in to stay while we were gone. And I was phoning every second day just making sure the house hadn't been burned down."

The harassment didn't stop until there was a new break in the murder investigation, a break that came not from Bellevue police, but from the RCMP.

16

Convinced Canadians

Sebastian and Atif felt they were finally safe within the borders of Canada. There was no forensic evidence that linked them to the murders. The Bellevue police detectives had suspicions that the boys were killers but lacked anything but hunches and a weak circumstantial case—not enough evidence for an arrest.

"At the time they left for Canada, the best we had was a circumstantial case. And had they not left for Canada, based on what we had then, I don't think we would have been able to make a case," said Detective Bob Thompson, leading the investigation back in Bellevue.

Months went by, and Thompson's investigation had hit a wall. He kept reviewing the CSI and officer reports from the murder scene. He started to wonder if somehow he'd gone in the wrong direction. Thompson then decided to have several different investigators look at the evidence, to make sure he wasn't focusing too much on the two teenagers. "And everybody came to the same conclusion," he said. "Your suspects are in Canada. And their names are Atif Rafay and Sebastian Burns."

On January 11, 1995, almost six months to the day after the murders, Detectives Thompson and Gomes—and their lieutenant—traveled to Canada to meet with three RCMP officers. The detectives went over their case file on the Rafay murders, telling their Canadian counterparts the details of their circumstantial case against Sebastian and Atif. They wanted to file formal charges against the two teens, but said they needed more evidence.

Once the Canadian officers read the investigational summary report supplied by the two Bellevue detectives, a Sergeant Rinn sent a memo back to RCMP headquarters in Vancouver that concluded: "There is no question—the deceased's son/brother Atif Ahmed Rafay and his close friend, Glen Sebastian Burns, are responsible for the homicides."

The Bellevue detectives asked the RCMP for specific help. They needed a sample of Sebastian's DNA—to see if it would match DNA they'd recovered from the crime scene. They were especially hoping to match that single coarse body hair discovered on Tariq Rafay's bed. If it was Sebastian's hair, the Bellevue Police believed, they had found their killer.

The RCMP agreed to help. They assigned several detectives to tail Sebastian for a few days. They finally got what they were hoping for when Sebastian came out of a restaurant in Vancouver. He stopped, blew his nose, and discarded the tissue in a public trash can. A constable scooped it up and sent the tissue—containing Sebastian's DNA—off to a lab. It would take weeks, but investigators hoped to learn whether hair found mixed with blood in the downstairs shower drain at the Rafay house matched Sebastian's. While not a conclusive piece of evidence, Bellevue police hoped it would add some substance to their circumstantial case.

Several weeks later, the RCMP sent three detectives to Bellevue. They spent one week going through all the investigative files.

Among the documents the Canadians reviewed were transcripts of e-mails taken from the hard drive of the Rafay family's home computer. In several e-mails, there were thoughts expressed that now seemed ominous. Bellevue police couldn't tie each e-mail to a specific boy, but they knew the correspondence had been either authored or received by Atif Rafay.

What the Canadians read was startling. The quotes sounded like words a Friedrich Nietzsche "superman" might say.

"Oh, yay. I'm more and more certain that being a criminal is the way to go for me. For one, I think I'd be good at it. I have an honest face. I'm not dumb. I'd be a conscientious criminal who believes in what he does. I killed someone, it would never plague my conscience. I'd be a great criminal, I think. Or assassin or something. We shall know nothing until we know whether we have the right to kill our fellow men."

In another exchange, Atif was asked by an unidentified writer if his parents would kill him if he dated a non-Muslim. "Actually no. Did I happen to mention the somewhat (completely) sexist laws of Muslim religions? My status as a guy means I could pretty much do what I want. And in any case, it becomes immaterial what they think relatively soon."

A final e-mail was signed by Atif himself. He referred to an "aphorism," a succinct statement expressing an opinion or general truth.

"Here is an aphorism I wrote myself. I really like it. 'We often condemn criminals as being not fit for society, when it is precisely the noblest among men for whom no society is fit.' Ever your friend, Atif."

The RCMP officers became as certain as their Bellevue counterparts that they had the right guys.

"And after a week of going through it, they said, 'These guys are guilty,'" Thompson said. "And they came to the conclusion that Sebastian and Atif had planned the murders in Canada, so they opened their own investigation."

The RCMP took the information in those e-mails to a judge in British Columbia. Detectives asked for a warrant to place bugs in Sebastian and Atif's house, telephone, cell phones, and car.

"The application for wiretaps was made by the RCMP," Thompson said. "And they had my entire file to look at. So I didn't personally supply information, other than say, 'Here's my file.'"

But the Canadian judge who would make the decision on whether to allow wiretaps was missing one crucial piece of evidence—evidence which might have proven critical to his final decision. Nowhere in the case file were the statements of Julie Rackley and Marc Sidell, the two neighbors who told police they had heard the murders happening at a time when the boys were seen, by several witnesses, at the movie theater.

"Does it bother you that this warrant application omitted the neighbors' statements?" Van Sant asked Detective Thompson.

"No, doesn't bother me. But—you know—these applications are all handled by Canadians, for their case. I don't have a comment on what they're doing with their case."

The judge approved the warrant applications. Undercover officers immediately launched a major surveillance operation. One afternoon, they watched Sebastian, Atif, and their roommates, Jimmy Miyoshi and Robin Puga, leave their house. Once the boys were out of sight, the RCMP officers quickly entered. Technicians placed listening devices in the home, including all the phone lines. The officers then went back outside and did something that is legal in Canada but would be illegal in the United States—they stole the boys' car so they could plant hidden microphones in the passenger compartment.

But the Mounties weren't finished yet. They also tapped the phone lines of all of the boys' known friends and of Sebastian's parents, Dave and Carol Burns.

On February 24, 1995, everything was finally in place. Nearly everywhere Sebastian and Atif went, the RCMP was secretly watching and listening. They were listening for more than casual conversation.

The RCMP hoped to hear evidence of a conspiracy to commit murder.

17

The Great Despisers

Sebastian and Atif had always been movie buffs. They were at the movies on the night the Rafay family was beaten to death. They rented movies while staying at the Bellevue Motel.

"I've loved films since I was very young," Atif said. "My initial interest was more in the aesthetics of film, this is to say, film theory and literary criticism."

But now, back in Vancouver, the boys decided to go from being movie-watchers to moviemakers. They were determined to turn their experiences in Bellevue into a screenplay. They titled their movie *The Great Despisers*.

"Where did you get the name?" Peter Van Sant asked Sebastian.

"It's part of a quote from the notorious Friedrich Nietzsche," Sebastian said.

"You named this after a writing from Friedrich Nietzsche, a man that you just told me you really weren't into. Were you into him or not?"

"Well, that one quote was something that Atif was familiar with in high school. He used it in an essay that he got a prize for in high school."

The title page of their screenplay read: "Sebastian Burns and Atif Rafay present, a Dionysus film, *The Great Despisers.*"

Dionysus was the Greek God of wine. Nietzsche was fascinated by Dionysus, whom he considered to be a liberator, "freeing one from one's self by madness, ecstasy, or wine."

In the later stages of his life, Nietzsche would sign his letters, "Dionysus." Only someone who had truly studied Nietzsche would know this obscure detail. Sebastian and Atif knew.

The title page of the screenplay was also dominated by the boys' names. They were listed five times: "presented by," "directed by," "edited by," "produced by," and "screenplay by." They were clearly the stars of the project.

"What is your screenplay about?" Van Sant asked.

"It was inspired a lot by the fact that we were being wrongfully accused, and that our lives had been ruined," Sebastian said. "It's a story about two people who were wrongfully accused, and wrongfully convicted—and we went so far as to have them be wrongfully executed."

"Did you in some way believe that this was going to happen to you?"

"Yeah, certainly. We were warned very early on

by lots of adults that we knew that—if push came to shove, that the Bellevue police would make some kind of case against us, and maybe they might even fabricate evidence against us."

Both boys had gone over and over the details of their screenplay, and they felt it was brilliant. They became determined to turn their dazzling writing into a major motion picture. All they needed was financing. It was something that they talked about for hour after hour—not realizing their conversations were being overheard, and that their dream would soon be used against them.

Over the next several months, the RCMP recorded thousands of hours of innocuous conversations. Most of the time, Sebastian and Atif were discussing normal teenage topics—fast cars, girls, sex—and, of course, their screenplay. The officers even overheard Sebastian and his girlfriend, Sarah, having sex at one point. But one thing they didn't hear—not a word—was any mention of the Bellevue murders.

The RCMP learned that the boys were all talk—no action. Sebastian and Atif were unemployed, living off Sebastian's savings bonds. After weeks of surveillance, the Mounties were growing weary of their suspects. One RCMP report noted that the two teens were "very intelligent, arrogant, self-indulgent personalities and posed a real problem in trying to approach."

The report stated that the two boys—along with

their roommates and high school friends, Jimmy Miyoshi and Robin Puga—spent their days sleeping until 4 or 5 P.M., "sitting around and debating different philosophies, watch some movie videos, work on their computer and go to bed around 4 to 5 am."

But the officers did discover an important dynamic in the lives of the four friends. There was one dominant and three recessive personalities.

"The social structure within the house was very evident in their conversations," the report stated. "Sebastian Burns dominated over all of them, with Atif Rafay a close second. The other two were simply subservient personalities."

Yet after listening to and following the teens for nearly two months and learning nothing about the murders, the RCMP officers did not decide to call off the investigation, thinking maybe they had the wrong guys. Instead, they theorized that the teens were just cagey, and decided to take the investigation to a whole new level, launching one of the most elaborate, intrusive, manipulative, and ultimately controversial undercover operations ever in North America.

And Sebastian Burns was in the crosshairs.

The most expensive and comprehensive crime scene investigation in Bellevue history hadn't yielded a single piece of forensic evidence that linked the boys to the murders. Thousands of hours of surveillance and electronic eavesdropping had not picked up a single incriminating word. Nearly eight months had passed since the murders, and Bellevue police had nothing to show for it except two oddly behaving boys who they suspected—but couldn't prove—were the killers.

But the Bellevue cops had an important ally in their investigation—the Royal Canadian Mounted Police, Canada's equivalent of the FBI. The Mounties were also convinced that the boys were guilty, and as legend had it, they always got their man.

They launched an operation that was worthy of its own screenplay. It was called "Project Estate." Its mission, as stated by the lead undercover officer under oath, was clear. "The direction from my superior was to meet the targets and attempt to get a confession from them regarding the murder they did in the States as well as determine when and how it was planned," he said.

The undercover officers were not told to find out what happened, to determine the truth. They would never directly ask the boys if they killed the Rafays. Project Estate began with the premise that the truth was already established, that Sebastian Burns and Atif Rafay did commit the murders. The only goal was to get a confession.

Enter Haslett and Shinkaruk. So as not to jeopardize their true identities, the authors were asked not to use the undercover officers' first names. These men were two of Canada's best and most experienced undercover officers. Their typical scenario was to pose as members of a powerful organized crime family. Over time, they would lure in unsuspecting citizens and make them a part of the family. Haslett described his men as "the best of the best." Their techniques were so persuasive and psychologically powerful, the two men made a remarkable claim.

"Anybody is approachable and anybody can be brought into our scenarios if the approach is done right," Haslett said.

The undercover officers walked the line between cop and criminal so well, it sometimes seemed to disappear, even to people who knew what the two men did for a living. Both men were quiet, watchful—when they spoke, their Canadian accents were strong, like those of hockey players raised in working-class families. Shinkaruk was in his mid-thirties. An ex–hockey player himself, Shinkaruk had the build and toughness to go along with it. His dark brown hair was cut in a near mullet, brushing his collar. It framed a face with small, dark eyes and a nose that looked like it had been broken in one too many street fights.

Haslett was a much smaller man—but somehow even more intimidating. He had light, close-cropped hair, except in the back, where it curled up a little above his collar. He was probably in his early fifties, but it was hard to tell. If you saw him on the street, you might cross to the other side. He played the criminal role very convincingly—and had perfected a cold, frightening stare. He wore a gold ring on his right pinky finger. When you got to know Haslett a little, which took a very long time, he relaxed and could be protective and charming.

These two men had been playing the roles of underworld criminals for years—and had it down to a science. Haslett helped to create the "Mr. Big" scenario years before—and the two men had used it successfully many times.

"I honestly don't think there's an undercover team like this anywhere in the world, and I say that very seriously," Haslett said. These two men were brilliant at creating a detailed, alternate world that lured their target in and groomed him to give a confession. By the time the Mr. Big operators met their target, it had already been decided that he was the prime suspect in whatever crime they were investigating. They just went in for the kill: a confession.

18

Too Good

The RCMP undercover specialists were so good at getting confessions that in 1996, they got a false one. It happened in the Canadian town of Rossburn, Manitoba, where a fourteen-year-old girl had been killed at the county fairgrounds. An eighteen-year-old who ran in her circle, Clayton Mentuck, was arrested for her murder. Once Mentuck was released on bail, he was lured into a Mr. Big scenario. The undercover operators were not the same two men assigned to work on the Rafay case—but the formula was the same.

Over several weeks, Mentuck was led to believe the operators worked for a far-reaching criminal organization. When asked about the murder, Mentuck denied it a dozen times—but Mr. Big made it clear that he knew Mentuck was being dishonest. He came up with a plan that would wipe out the possibility of any murder charges in the future against Mentuck. But to put this plan into motion, Mr. Big needed to know all of the details of the murder. Although Mentuck denied the charges several more times, he finally gave a confession—giving details of the murder, but saying he didn't remember some others because he was drunk at the time and must have blacked out.

A judge eventually decided that the evidence against Mentuck was not enough for a conviction—and that the level of inducement used by the undercover officers to get Mentuck's confession diminished the reliability of the statements the boy made. He found Mentuck not guilty. The decision was a jolt to the undercover unit, but it pressed ahead with its controversial techniques on a much more complicated case involving brains, ambition, and murder . . . an operation that would have been illegal if conducted in the United States.

U.S. federal courts have struck down overly invasive undercover operations that use intimidation or perceived coercion to elicit confessions. Under Canadian law, however, authorities are allowed to go much further down that road—even as far as stealing targets' private property to implant bugging devices, something that is illegal in the United States.

The RCMP launches operations such as the Mr. Big scenarios only when other attempts at gaining evidence have failed—they are time-consuming, expensive investigations. But after listening to and watching Sebastian and Atif for two months without any results, the RCMP decided it was time for Mr.

Big. Investigators first chose to target and befriend Sebastian, who the RCMP had concluded was the leader of the two teens.

The formula would be the same as in past operations. First, the undercover officers would try to meet Sebastian in a random manner, drawing him into what seemed like an innocent friendship. Once he was more comfortable, they would reveal themselves to be organized criminals. Over a period of months, they would work on luring him into a make-believe world of crime.

They launched Project Estate. The officers recorded, using audio and/or video, most of the scenarios that played out with Sebastian, always listening for clues from the teen as to how they should react and what weaknesses they could exploit. They would then use these clues to plan each future scenario.

"We don't just run off and do something with Sebastian Burns without making sure everything is covered," Haslett said. "That everything he sees is going to look extremely believable and realistic. And we're conscious of that all the time."

Going into the undercover operation, Haslett and Shinkaruk didn't know much about Sebastian and Atif. They had been given a short summary of what happened in Bellevue—but had not yet seen the investigative case file. Haslett didn't know if the two teens were guilty or innocent. He knew only that the Bellevue police considered them the sole suspects in a triple murder.

Sebastian Burns was a unique target to the two undercover officers. While only nineteen, he was much smarter than most of the street thugs with whom they dealt. But the officers were confident in their techniques and experience.

Despite his commanding intellect, Haslett and Shinkaruk had learned enough about Sebastian's dream of becoming a filmmaker to be convinced he'd be approachable. They knew he'd be caught up in their web. It all began with an innocent encounter.

19

Perchance We Meet

Sebastian Burns was bored. He had spent an hour just
driving around town. He finally pulled into his driveway, went into the house, and threw his car keys on
the kitchen counter. Sebastian noticed that the message light was blinking on the main telephone. He
pushed the play button.

"This is Crimpers Hair Salon calling for Sebastian
to confirm his appointment with Gregory tomorrow."

Sebastian Burns erased the message with a small
sense of anticipation. The haircut appointment would
at least give him something to do. It had been a terrible nine months since the murders of the Rafay family. He'd been hounded by reporters and characterized
in media reports as a murder suspect. His face had
been on television and in the local newspapers. People
occasionally turned and looked at him as he walked
down city streets. He felt like an outcast, if not an
outlaw.

His girlfriend Sarah said the teens' notoriety from

Bellevue had definitely spread to Vancouver—and they were known as murder suspects.

"Everywhere we went, people recognized them," Sarah said with some pain. "At parties, kids were talking about this big murder case, and, 'Oh, these two boys did it.' I remember a time when Sebastian, Atif, and a bunch of their friends were at a bus stop and someone drove by and rolled down the window and yelled, 'Murderers!' And that was typical."

Those kinds of incidents forced Sebastian and Atif to hole up in their house, only rarely going out.

"You have to remember that I had been totally ostracized from the community," Sebastian said with some self-pity. "I had not met any people in nine months' time. I was unable to go to college. I was unable to get a job. And to top it all off, I'd been on crutches with an injured knee. And I was stuck in our house. It was kind of like a jail."

So the next morning, Sebastian made what he considered to be a jailbreak, driving into downtown Vancouver to Crimpers Salon. It was April 11, 1995, a day that would change the course of Sebastian's life forever. He didn't know it, but Sebastian was about to become the target of a remarkable sting run by an elite undercover unit within the Royal Canadian Mounted Police. Sebastian never saw it coming.

After Sebastian got his fancy cut, he left Crimpers and headed toward the parking lot. As he neared his car, a stranger approached him. The man asked if he knew anything about breaking into a car. When

Sebastian looked confused, the man laughed and pointed to a black Pontiac Trans Am. He said he'd locked his keys in his car and asked Sebastian for help. He introduced himself as Shinkaruk and asked Sebastian to give him a ride to his hotel to get a spare key. Sebastian readily agreed—he had no other plans for the day. Shinkaruk seemed like a pleasant fellow. He was wearing a yellow dress shirt, buttoned all the way up, tucked into blue jeans.

Sebastian noticed he was wearing snakeskin cowboy boots. Shinkaruk told the teen to head to the upscale Bayshore Hotel, one of Vancouver's finest, nestled on Coal Harbor. Guests could gaze out at soaring Grouse Mountain and watch seaplanes land and taxi up to their boarding piers. Sebastian was instantly impressed. This guy must have money, he thought. The two men seemed to hit it off right away. As they were driving to the hotel, Sebastian told his new friend about the movie he and Atif had written and were hoping to make called *The Great Despisers*.

"He seemed like some kind of entrepreneur," Sebastian later said. "He reminded me of a fellow that I'd seen who looked like an ex–National Hockey League player who had opened up a trendy late-night café. And he was very friendly. And very generous."

Once at the hotel, Shinkaruk invited Sebastian to the bar and bought him a beer. He told Sebastian that he thought his boss, whom he described as a wealthy businessman, might be interested in fronting the boys some cash for their movie. Sebastian was thrilled at the prospect. The boys had been working on their script, but they had no money to finance its production. Suddenly, Sebastian was sitting in a posh bar next to a businessman with connections who was finding his every word to be fascinating. Finally, he was with an adult who could see his intellect and talent.

"I was basically just some kid who had given him a ride. And he made a special point of buying me a drink and spending some time with me," Sebastian said. "And just treated me like, you know, a friend of his. And that impressed me. I was also sort of intrigued, I guess, or excited about the way that he seemed so ready to be interested in me."

In a matter of minutes, Sebastian felt like nine months of bad luck might be coming to an end. He looked around the luxurious hotel and couldn't believe his good fortune. He reflected how he could never afford to stay at a place like this. Then, after they'd polished off a couple of drinks, Sebastian nearly fell off his bar stool when Shinkaruk made him a startling offer: He suggested they go meet his boss to talk about possible funding for Sebastian's movie. Sebastian could barely contain his excitement.

Adding to this dream moment, Shinkaruk proposed that they meet the boss, whom he called Mr. Big, at an exotic location—a strip club called the Skyline Pub in Richmond, about a fifteen-mile drive from the hotel.

Mr. Big, as his underlings referred to him, was a

shadowy figure whose real name was Haslett. As they entered the strip club, Sebastian's eyes quickly moved to the center stage, where two naked women were pole dancing. He barely heard the disco music that fueled their movement. Shinkaruk touched his elbow, breaking Sebastian's stare. He directed him to a corner table, where Mr. Big was sitting.

Haslett was a smaller man than Shinkaruk and at least ten years older. But he had the same tough guy, menacing look. He came across as a man in complete control, and obviously someone you wouldn't want to mess with. His outward mannerisms seemed fairly laid-back—but with a threatening undercurrent, like a calm pit bull. He was wearing jeans, a jean jacket, and cowboy boots.

Despite his intelligence, Sebastian was naïve. He imagined this was how important people acted. Sebastian shifted uncomfortably in his chair as he tried to adjust to this intimidating man. He only occasionally glanced back at the strippers on stage.

Once they dispensed with pleasantries and small talk, Haslett shared with Sebastian that he was involved in less than aboveboard business—but that he might be interested in branching into something legitimate, like financing a film. The conversation was briefly interrupted by a scantily dressed waitress who took drink orders. Sebastian asked for a beer. The men leaned in to talk over the pounding music.

Sebastian told Haslett and Shinkaruk more about his screenplay, *The Great Despisers.* He confidently said that his movie would "be a cultural critique of today's society." The alcohol and conversation went on for about an hour. Haslett seemed less threatening with each drink. Sebastian grew more confident. Amid some laughter and comments about the strippers, Sebastian told his new friends that he would need about $200,000 for the movie. They talked some more on various topics, including philosophy, which Sebastian brought up. Haslett didn't seem so interested in that discourse. But he told Sebastian that he was interested in the movie project. The men shook hands, and Sebastian headed home to tell Atif about his remarkable day and their potential investors.

As Sebastian was driving home, he felt that he'd especially connected with Shinkaruk—the younger of the businessmen. Because he'd essentially been cut off from the outside world of late, Sebastian was excited at the prospect of this new friendship.

"I was happy to have met him. I was nineteen. He seemed to be about thirty," Sebastian said. "This was probably the first adult friend that I'd ever had."

Peter Van Sant later asked Sebastian why he got involved with these two men—when it was clear, even from the beginning, that their business wasn't completely aboveboard.

"This was the first social experience I'd had since I'd turned nineteen," Sebastian said. "I was vulnerable."

Sebastian headed home having left one thing behind at the club: a first impression that was similar to the one Detective Bob Thompson had had nine months earlier.

"You know, he's sort of a different character," Shinkaruk said to Haslett. "He speaks differently."

Over the next three months, their observations and suspicions would only grow, as their every meeting, their every telephone conversation was recorded. But there still was never a moment in which the boys ever said they did the murders, ever discussed whether or not they got away with it, ever revealed any information that only the killers of the Rafay family would know.

Project Estate was a work in progress. Like a movie script, it had dramatic scenes yet to unfold as the undercover agents continued their mission to get the boys to confess to a crime they had publicly stated—time and time again—that they didn't commit.

20

Crossing the Line

On April 13, two days after the initial meeting at Crimpers Hair Salon, Shinkaruk called Sebastian and arranged another meeting. He picked Sebastian up but didn't tell him where they were going. They drove up through the mountains for a couple of hours to Whistler, an isolated resort town. During the drive, they discussed Sebastian's philosophies. "Burns indicated to me that he thought he and his friends were among the smartest people in the world. He said he had no use for people who weren't smarter than him," Shinkaruk wrote in his RCMP notebook after their trip. "He laughed at religion and said it was just a concept dreamed up to keep the masses content and ignorant."

They also chatted about movies like *The Godfather* and *Scarface*. Sebastian told Shinkaruk he respected Al Pacino's character in *Scarface* because he was realistic and honest. Sebastian also talked about how he liked Woody Allen as a director.

The drive seemed to go on and on, climbing the beautiful winding highway lined with evergreen trees. Occasionally, Sebastian glanced left, where he could see some of the Gulf Islands, which looked like forested footstools in the sea.

Sebastian thought they must be headed to meet other potential movie investors. But when they arrived in Whistler, they drove to Dusty's Pub—an old BBQ and beer joint described by locals as featuring "free-flowing brews, spontaneous singing, crazy antics, dogs sauntering right in, smoking." Mr. Big was the only one waiting at the bar for them.

Shinkaruk left the two men alone. It quickly became clear there were no other investors. Haslett laid out the real plan for the evening—this was a test to see if the two criminals could trust Sebastian. Sebastian was asked to drive a stolen car back down the mountain to Vancouver for Haslett's criminal organization. They told Sebastian that the car was being stolen from a former associate who'd crossed them.

Haslett made it clear to Sebastian that crossing them could be dangerous—and that stealing a car was only the beginning. The men were already upping the level of potential violence in their contact with Sebastian—Shinkaruk later said they did this so that they would be on the same level as the teen, who they increasingly suspected had bludgeoned to death three people.

Shinkaruk came back—he told Sebastian that he

had gone to try to buy gloves, so Sebastian wouldn't have to worry about leaving fingerprints in the car. When he couldn't find any, he'd bought air freshener instead. He told Sebastian that after driving the car, he should spray the freshener anywhere he touched to obliterate fingerprints, and that the scent would also throw off any sniffing dogs.

Haslett explained to Sebastian his rationale behind stealing his former employee's car—it was just a first step to the retribution that could follow.

"I'll fuck with you, and I'll fuck with your family. I am going to fucking do your wife and shit like that," he said. "You don't fucking get back at that guy. If, fuck, things that are clear to him and he's going to sit there and go, 'Holy fuck, I am still out here and they can fucking—they can fuck up everything I care about. I better fucking come through.' That is how you deal business."

When Sebastian heard the plan, he froze. His face lost all color, and he suddenly left the table and went to the bathroom. He was gone for several long minutes—the two undercover officers looked at each other, thinking they'd pushed too hard and had lost him for good. But Sebastian came back to the table a few minutes later—and when he did, he agreed to drive the car.

The men took him to the car; a car seat and several baby toys were scattered around in it. Shinkaruk used a Slim Jim to get into the vehicle, so Sebastian would believe it was stolen.

Sebastian realized at that moment that he was crossing a line into a world of crime—but he was unemployed, ostracized, a murder suspect desperate for approval anywhere he could find it. He hadn't sought this out—these men found him, convinced him to enter this world. But now this air cadet, actor, brilliant student who grew up in an affluent part of West Vancouver—a teenager who had never before been involved in this type of world—took the step that would change his life forever. He got in that car and began the drive down the mountain.

When he looked back at that moment, Sebastian would realize it was the worst mistake of his life—the beginning of the end. He later said that he had no choice but to drive the car—he was two hours away from civilization, with no car, at the mercy of two intimidating criminals.

21

Show Me the Money

Sebastian drove the car to the Bayshore Hotel, where he and Shinkaruk had gone the first time they met. After they dropped the car off, the men met up with Haslett at a pub-style restaurant, the Fogg 'n' Suds on Robson, in downtown Vancouver. Shinkaruk went to the bar to get three beers—and he could tell, when he got back to the table, that Sebastian was in a bad mood. He was friendly to Shinkaruk but directed his anger toward Haslett, the crime boss. Sebastian was upset that he'd gotten paid only $200 for driving the car back—he told Haslett that he could earn that selling shoplifted videos, recirculating ski tags, or dealing ecstasy at a rave party. He made it clear that he and his friends were only interested in making "big money"—more like $2,000 than $200.

Sebastian also told Haslett that if he was going to do anything else for them, he would need more details in advance—and he would need to be involved in the planning. He was unhappy with the car scenario because too many things could have gone wrong—he could have been seen in the car or pulled over in a routine stop by the police.

Sebastian said that when he and his friends committed a criminal act, they thought everything through thoroughly before doing it so that there were no mistakes. He trusted his friends with his life because they had done things together that he knew they would never discuss. When Shinkaruk asked him what he meant, Sebastian smiled and said, "Never mind." Shinkaruk said that Sebastian also volunteered that he was capable of being a hit man.

But Sebastian later told Peter Van Sant that he never volunteered to kill, and that when he was talking about crimes he and his friends had committed, he meant shoplifting—not the murders. And that he only said what he did so that Haslett wouldn't think he was a threat to their organization. His anger was an act—a cover for his fear.

"When Haslett saw how upset I was afterwards, and he saw that I wasn't going to talk to him . . . finally he said to me, 'I have to ask what's wrong. Because I gotta make sure you're not going to drop a dime on me.' Which means that he was worried that I was going to tell on him to the police," Sebastian said.

Sebastian's mood turned more serious as he recalled how he was becoming ever more ensnared by the crime family.

"Now, my decision up to that point had been that I was just going to play it cool—and extricate myself from this situation. And when he said that, I had to say something to make sure that he wasn't going to worry that I was going to tell on them to the police. Because I thought I'd be in danger if he thought that."

But Shinkaruk said that after Haslett left that night, Sebastian continued to talk freely and happily about the criminal world he had entered. He volunteered that he'd be interested in selling cocaine, but wasn't sure how to go about it. He said he was interested in making $40,000 to 50,000. Shinkaruk laughed and told him it would be a while before he was entrusted with enough cocaine to make that kind of money. Tired of the conversation, Shinkaruk told Sebastian he had to leave, saying Haslett had paged him. He dropped Sebastian off at a convenience store, but not before Sebastian asked if Haslett could get him a stolen car to drive. Shinkaruk said he'd check on it and drove away. Because it took place in cars and various public places, this scenario was one of the few that wasn't recorded.

Sebastian claimed that was the night he realized how dangerous these men really were—and decided to try to extricate himself from any future contact with them.

But within a couple of weeks, his actions seemed to undermine his claim. It was Sebastian who was trying to keep in contact with the two men, not the other way around.

Unbeknownst to Sebastian, Haslett and Shinkaruk got busy with other RCMP jobs during the next couple of weeks—so Shinkaruk placed a call to Sebastian on April 29, just to keep in touch with him, hoping to set up a future meeting once their schedules cleared. He left Sebastian a message on the teens' home answering machine.

Sebastian called Shinkaruk back at the number he left for the Edmonton Inn. He asked for room 939 and left a message on the hotel voice mail. Sebastian later said that he wasn't sure he was going to hear from Shinkaruk or "his pal" again. When Sebastian didn't get a return call from Shinkaruk, he continued to call back, leaving exasperated messages, saying he wasn't sure if Shinkaruk was receiving his messages but imploring him to call back. During one call, he spoke to the hotel operator and asked if Shinkaruk was still at the hotel; when the operator said yes, he hung up and didn't leave a message.

The next day, April 30, Sebastian again called Shinkaruk at the Edmonton Inn. When the voice mail answered, he sighed heavily, saying he was leaving message number three. Shinkaruk called Sebastian back; he got the machine and left a message, apologizing for not calling sooner.

On May 1 at around 1:30 A.M., Sebastian again called the hotel looking for Shinkaruk. A sleepy-sounding Shinkaruk answered the phone. He told Sebastian he'd be back in town in a few days and asked if he could call then. Sebastian said "Yeah," and the conversation ended. Shinkaruk hung up the phone, turned out the light on his bedside table, and rolled back over on his side. He knew it was only a matter of time now before they had what they wanted from Sebastian.

22

Raising the Stakes

Sebastian didn't realize that when he went home at night after meeting up with Haslett and Shinkaruk, the RCMP was right there with him. Not physically in the room, but electronically listening in. Each night, they heard Sebastian's review of the day—plots that intrigued him, suggestions that did not. RCMP officers took notes and recorded every conversation. From the information they gathered, the undercover officers could lay out a loose script for the next day—proposals they knew would keep Sebastian interested and moving ever closer to their confession trap.

On May 5, 1995, less than a week after his series of phone calls with Shinkaruk, Sebastian received a call just before 9 P.M. It was Shinkaruk. He asked Sebastian if he was free tomorrow. Sebastian said he could be but asked if Shinkaruk could switch it to tonight because he had a date planned. Shinkaruk said no, that wasn't good for him. Eager to participate,

Sebastian said fine, he'd free himself up to meet at around five tomorrow afternoon.

On the evening of May 6, Shinkaruk picked Sebastian up in a brand-new Corvette—with a beautiful woman, also an undercover agent, riding along. Sebastian eagerly got into the backseat. The sexy woman sat on his lap and draped her arms loosely around his neck. Sebastian was part aroused, part embarrassed. But either way, he was loving it. They talked about fancy cars as Shinkaruk drove to the Four Seasons Hotel in downtown Vancouver, where they would meet Haslett in a guest room. The Four Seasons was another cosmopolitan hotel, situated in a high-rise. It was the epitome of eye-popping luxury. Again, Sebastian was impressed by how much money this criminal organization obviously had to spend.

Although Sebastian wouldn't know it until much later, the room where he was meeting Haslett was wired with hidden microphones. Down the hall in another hotel room, a team of RCMP officers was listening to his every word.

The purpose of this meeting, according to the RCMP officers, was to pump up the organization to the level they felt that Sebastian was expecting—and to build further credibility with him. Shinkaruk and Haslett would further develop their characters, and their cover story, drawing Sebastian deeper into their make-believe world. They would make sure, in no uncertain terms, that Sebastian understood that Shinkaruk, at least, was a hardened criminal—"an outlaw type of person" who was capable of killing. Based on their experience, the officers believed that by causally discussing violence, they'd make Sebastian feel more comfortable talking about the murders in Bellevue.

When Sebastian and Shinkaruk walked into the guest room, another man was already there—another undercover agent who Sebastian was meeting for the first time. The woman who rode over with the men left the room to give the men some privacy. His name was Doren. He was a large, good-looking man dressed in motorcycle gear. He had a duffel bag with him. Shinkaruk told Doren it was OK to talk in front of Sebastian, and that Haslett would be arriving soon.

The two men joked around about Doren's $35,000 motorcycle and all of Shinkaruk's fancy cars. After a while, when Haslett still hadn't shown up, Doren said he had to leave to make some deliveries, but asked Shinkaruk to give Haslett "the package" he brought. He took out two handguns. He pointed to one gun and told Shinkaruk that if Haslett decided to use it, "Tell him to throw it in the salt right away, 'cause she's pretty hot . . . I don't mean 'hot' stolen, I mean still warm." They laughed, talked a little more, and Doren left the room.

"A warm gun. When you heard it, when you saw it, what were you thinking?" Van Sant later asked Sebastian.

"That means they murder people. And that means they might murder me, and I was on thin ice."

Sebastian watched this scene unfold, thinking he was in way over his head.

"Why didn't you just look at him and say, 'I am out of here. Don't call. I'm done. I'm gone'?" Van Sant asked.

"Because I felt like they were testing me, to see if I was going to tell on them," Sebastian said. "And I didn't know how to react. But I did say that I didn't want to work for them anymore. I made the excuse that I wanted to stay in touch with them."

Sebastian said his head was spinning.

"And I wanted to satisfy them that I was not going to work for them—but that I was also not going to tell on them to the police. And I wanted to get myself out as smoothly as possible."

As soon as Doren left, a nervous Sebastian started talking about his moviemaking plans. He told Shinkaruk that they needed $200,000 to make the film. But he quickly added some surprising news—that they had found investors. So, Sebastian told Shinkaruk, he no longer needed the organization's money.

Shinkaruk was surprised by Sebastian's claim, but he didn't show it. Instead, he pressed Sebastian for more details about the film. Sebastian described it as "a sort of more gritty and brutal and sort of intellectually ruthless version of *Ferris Bueller*." When Shinkaruk continued to ask for more details about the movie, Sebastian clammed up.

Sebastian looked across at Shinkaruk—and saw the face of an enforcer for a criminal organization, someone who was obviously dangerous and might not be trustworthy.

Sebastian stuttered a little bit more about the movie plot—but after more cajoling, he finally told Shinkaruk that the movie was largely based on the fact that he and Atif were under investigation for three murders in Bellevue. This was the first mention of the murders on tape—and Sebastian was the one who'd introduced the subject. But Shinkaruk noticed what Sebastian didn't say: that they were under investigation for the murders they *did*. He told Shinkaruk that because of the investigation, he didn't want to risk getting a criminal record if he were caught doing any crimes for the organization.

"That's why I was so anxious last time about that thing with the car and, like, you know, I wanted everything perfect or whatever," Sebastian told him.

At this point, Shinkaruk was certain that Sebastian was a murderer. So to try to get him to open up, Shinkaruk wanted to convince the teen that he was "an outlaw-type character who is not offended by anything . . . We're crude to women, we're crude to minorities, whomever."

Shinkaruk told Sebastian that he'd done time in prison because he "fucking toasted a guy." He looked straight at Sebastian and continued, "You know how solid [Haslett] is? When it came time for fucking court, the person that could finger me, they're not around anymore; so I know that business gets taken care of."

This was the next phase of the plan to draw Sebastian further and further into the criminal world, and to plant two important thoughts in his mind: that Haslett was a powerful crime boss who could make the Bellevue murder investigation go away, and that he was willing to kill to achieve his goals.

23

Dead Serious

Instead of loosening up, Sebastian seemed to get more nervous once he heard about Shinkaruk's violent past. He repeated to Shinkaruk that he didn't want to work for them because he didn't want a criminal record, and also reiterated that he'd found other investors for his movie, so he didn't need their help anymore. This was all a lie. And the undercover operators had a clear advantage in this drama—because they were able to listen to everything that was said in Sebastian's house. So they knew when he was lying.

"Things right now may not necessarily be as worth the time because, um, like I'm a bit busy and once this movie thing is working out . . . I'm going to have to focus on that right now," Sebastian nervously said, as he tried once again to break away from Shinkaruk.

But then he said something chilling. It could have been fear, or bravado, or genuine evil that compelled Sebastian to say what he said next. He told Shinkaruk he might be interested in working with them in the future, if they needed "people getting killed or things getting blown up." Sebastian laughed after volunteering for murder. Shinkaruk asked him if he was serious, and Sebastian assured him, "Dead serious."

Sebastian was now sending mixed signals to the undercover officers. He wanted to pull away, but if they needed someone killed, they could give him a call. On the surveillance audiotape, Sebastian seemed to start to relax after his stunning offer. Shinkaruk realized that he had gotten Sebastian talking—and needed to keep this conversation moving. So Shinkaruk asked what kind of business Sebastian thought their organization was into.

"I don't know, I guess cars, guns, drugs . . . I don't know if you guys would be into homicide for hire, 'cause that's more of a policing element . . . I don't know, prostitution, maybe." Sebastian chuckled as he thought of all the possibilities. "I don't know . . . How many crimes can I think of?"

"You're looking at it wrong right there," Shinkaruk said. "Now you—this is what struck me about you before. 'Cause you're looking at it as crimes. They're not crimes—it's fucking opportunities."

Shinkaruk tried to get Sebastian to open up even more, now that he was starting to relax. He asked the teenager what he'd be willing to do, what he was capable of doing.

"What I would be willing to do totally depends on, like, on risk really," Sebastian told the mobster.

Sebastian then asked Shinkaruk to tell him about

money laundering—and what the likelihood of getting caught doing that was. He also said he probably wouldn't mind moving drugs. Shinkaruk, ever trying to get Sebastian to reveal his values, asked him a direct question.

"How would your conscience handle that?"

Sebastian didn't hesitate. "OK, conscience is not the issue here . . . OK, well, let, let me put it this way, OK? If you said to me, yeah, there's a family out there or there's some guy who we know, who screwed us around . . . and we'd like you to go and shoot him. Um, in no way would I have any dilemma about this."

But then Sebastian told Shinkaruk that even though his conscience wouldn't bother him, he'd choose not to kill anyone for the organization. He just wouldn't have the time or the technical training, he said.

"I'm quite busy; the issue would not be . . . that I'd feel bad about it afterwards."

In a *48 Hours* interview, Van Sant challenged Sebastian to explain his startling conversation with Shinkaruk, one that Sebastian claimed was the result of fear.

"You're afraid at this point?" Van Sant asked. "You sound like a willing participant. You're offering to become a hit man."

"I am not offering to become a hit man," Sebastian said. "And if you finish that quote, you'll see that I tell him that I wouldn't want to do that. And I think that anybody can see that that is just a plain lie and an excuse."

"You're saying, 'I'd do it, but I wouldn't do it.' You're saying, 'Yeah, I'd kill somebody. But you know, I guess I wouldn't kill somebody.' Is that what you're saying we should take from that exchange?"

"I was trying to satisfy him that I wasn't going to tell the police what he'd just confessed to me. And I also told him, however, that I didn't want to do it."

Once Haslett arrived, the conversation ended, and Shinkaruk started counting a stack of cash that Doren had left earlier. He got Sebastian to help him, and they counted out about $300,000 in cash. This was set up to be one more thing that would entice Sebastian into this world of beautiful women, fast cars, and piles of cash.

Then Shinkaruk said he was leaving on an errand, and Haslett and Sebastian were left alone. It was a nerve-racking time for Sebastian. He tried to cover his nervousness by putting on an even more arrogant air than usual.

Right away, Haslett told the teen he could tell he was unhappy after the last job, when he'd driven the stolen car to Vancouver. Sebastian stuttered about how he just didn't know what was going on, which he didn't appreciate; he just didn't know at that point if Haslett and Shinkaruk could be trusted.

"You're a smart man, but don't ever worry about that," Haslett told him forcefully. "If you're working for me, you're looked after one thousand percent. You have to decide if, in fact, you want to work for me. I have to decide if, in fact, I want you working for me."

Haslett asked Sebastian if he'd ever done any prison time. Sebastian said no, but told the crime boss he was being investigated for a triple homicide in Bellevue.

"What's your role in that triple homicide?" Haslett asked.

"They think that I am the murderer," Sebastian said.

"Why?"

"Because they didn't have anyone else, because . . . we were at the house for a few days, and they don't have any other leads. I'm not worried about it, because forensically or whatever they don't have, uh, a particularly big case."

One social constant among criminals is big shot banter, where a lowly grunt brags, hoping to impress the boss. Despite all the time Sebastian had spent with these wise guys, all the grooming he'd unknowingly endured, he hadn't really given them anything.

The two chatted about random topics for a while, and Sebastian told Haslett what he'd already told Shinkaruk, that he was going to be too busy with his movie during the next few months to work for them.

Haslett humored Sebastian but continued to bring the conversation back around to the Bellevue murders. This was the first time he'd gotten a chance to push Sebastian on the topic.

"What evidence have they got against you down there?" Haslett asked.

Sebastian shrugged. "They, as far as I know, they don't have shit."

Haslett kept changing the subject so that Sebastian wouldn't get suspicious. They talked about what Sebastian could do for Haslett's criminal organization, and discussed the possibility of selling cocaine. But after about twenty minutes, Haslett again went back to the murders. He told Sebastian he needed to know that Sebastian could take care of business for him. He needed to know the teen was "solid."

"What happens when these fucking bozos from down in Bellevue come fucking up here and grab you? Who's the first person you're going to give up?" Haslett stared at Sebastian. "Well, you're looking at him. That's what I want to be fucking sure of, you know what I'm saying?"

Sebastian got nervous again—Shinkaruk was back in the room now, and both men were staring at him, hard.

"Um—as if, well, whatever—I mean, fuck. First of all, I don't know shit to give up—and nor would I," Sebastian stuttered.

Haslett used this moment to push Sebastian harder.

"What went on down there, tell me what went on down there," Haslett said.

"What do you want to know?" Sebastian asked nervously.

"Tell me about it."

"OK, well, we came back in the house and saw the mom first, went upstairs, saw the dad and didn't bother with his sister because things were pretty screwed up by then . . ."

Sebastian was telling the same story he told Bellevue police. This clearly wasn't what the undercover officers wanted to hear. So Haslett switched tactics. He started joking around again and tried to put Sebastian at ease. Then he told Sebastian he had a lot of people working for him who could find out information on the Bellevue investigation.

"I got guys. I'm not going to say fuck-all to you right now, but I got people in different places that can do a lot of things."

Haslett told Sebastian that he was going to do some checking around in Bellevue to see what kind of evidence the cops had on him and Atif. Sebastian shrugged nonchalantly—but then said he would be interested in knowing if Haslett found out anything.

As Haslett kept trying to push him on details of the murders, Sebastian again reminded the two men that he didn't know if he could trust them—and Haslett came down hard on him.

"I'll tell you something right now: You will never—and I'll repeat this one more fucking time: never—be set up by me, or anybody that ever fucking works for me," the crime boss said. "I do two things: I make money, and I look after people who make money for me."

He told Sebastian he'd pull out that $300,000 they just counted—or three times that if he needed it—to bail Sebastian out of jail if he was ever arrested. Haslett made sure Sebastian clearly understood that if any of his mobsters went to jail, it became a risk to the entire organization.

" 'Cause the minute I get fucking names on people that are working for me, are going to fucking jail, you know something, I got two things to lose: a lot of money and a chance of me going to jail."

He stared at Sebastian.

"There's two things I ain't going to fucking do in my life, is go to jail or lose money. And you always remember that."

Sebastian nodded his head obediently. "K."

If he had thoughts of leaving, the teen now knew he couldn't.

24

One of the Most Intelligent
People in the World

This meeting on May 6 was the first time Sebastian realized that if he got arrested for the Bellevue murders, he could become a big problem for Mr. Big's organization—and it was clear to Sebastian that being a problem could be very dangerous. He now believed that the only way to protect himself was to make sure the two mobsters trusted him—and to avoid arrest for the Bellevue murders.

Sebastian was scared. He tried to act cool when Haslett revealed he'd been checking up on him, reading the newspapers about the murders in Bellevue. Haslett told Sebastian he was going to keep checking and find out through his sources what evidence the cops had. Haslett let Sebastian know that the ruthlessness they assumed he possessed made him an asset to the organization.

"You did that murder. And that's why you're here

today, because you're fucking solid," Haslett told the teen.

"Well, that's up to you, but uh, I'm curious about, uh, finding out anything that I need to know." Sebastian laughed nervously. "Or whatever."

Haslett told the teen he knew he and Atif had committed the perfect murder—and asked him how someone plans the perfect murder.

Sebastian said he should be asking Haslett that question. But then he thought about it for a moment, organized his thoughts, and logically laid out a strategy.

"I'd get a book on forensics, and I would get out the police manual on how to investigate a murder," Sebastian said. "And, you know, so I would become a master of forensic science and whatever the fuck else. Or I'd hire some guy who didn't know who I was. And from my perspective, it'd be perfect."

Haslett tried to push Sebastian to tell him more details about the Rafay murders, but Sebastian maintained that he didn't know anything. Haslett watched the teen carefully, deciding when to push for facts and when to back off.

Feeling he wasn't going to get much more out of Sebastian at that moment, Haslett changed the subject to a teenage boy safety zone: fast cars and women. The talk then turned to Sebastian and Atif's movie, and Sebastian got even more comfortable. He rambled on about his film project until Haslett steered the conversation in a different direction.

The topic turned to what Sebastian could do for

the organization—and Sebastian asked Haslett if people could tell he was a crook, just by seeing him walk down the street. Haslett acted offended. Shinkaruk pretended to calm him down. Haslett then turned the question back on Sebastian.

"How do you think people see you?" Haslett asked the teen.

Sebastian answered in that arrogant tone that had so irritated some of his teachers and classmates.

"People see me, and think, I want to give that boy a ride. Even though I've never picked up a hitch-hiker before in my life, this guy, he looks like a nice boy—and I think I should give him a ride to wherever he wants to go."

Haslett told him that was exactly the kind of person he needed in his organization—someone with an innocent look and the brains to use it. He turned to Sebastian's favorite topic: talking about himself.

"Tell me how smart you are," Haslett said. "Tell me how fucking smart you are."

This time, Sebastian didn't pause, didn't pucker his lips. This answer took no contemplation.

"I am one of the most intelligent people in the world."

Haslett asked Sebastian to rate him on the intelligence scale—but the teen sidestepped the question, scared to tell Haslett he didn't think he was as smart as Sebastian and his friends. Sebastian philosophized on how 95 percent of the people in the world were "sheep" and not nearly as smart as he was.

Haslett brought the conversation back to the murders, giving it one last try.

"You've got some problems in the States; I have no idea if I could ever fucking help you out down there . . . Till I know what's going on down there, I don't know," Haslett said. "You tell me what's going on down there, that's what I'm asking you."

"I don't fucking know," Sebastian answered back.

Haslett then played an old investigator's trick—lying about evidence.

"You left something behind down there," Haslett told the teen.

Sebastian looked up. "I didn't even know that."

"What went on down there, what went on down there? You tell me, I'll be able to fucking find out a lot more. Last thing I want to do is go fucking fishing around."

"Listen," Sebastian said, frustrated. "You know as much as I do, OK?"

"You were there, I wasn't."

"Yeah, there's nothing I could say that would, that would help one or the other because, as far as I know, they don't have crap."

Sebastian said he was certain Bellevue police were fabricating evidence, and he had no way of knowing what that fake evidence was. He then made reference to what had been in the papers—the boys' fascination with Nietzsche and the play *Rope*.

"Police say that, uh, this is a hate crime. They say that . . . they're trying to say that, you know, we're philosophers and all this shit and say that it gave us a thrill. But, uh, what does that tell you, I mean, they say read between the lines—that tells you that they don't have shit. That's the biggest load of shit I've ever heard."

Haslett pushed him a little more and realized he wasn't going to get anything more out of him at the moment. He decided to wrap up the day's meeting by playing to Sebastian's arrogant nature. He asked him about Atif, who was also mentioned as a suspect in the newspaper articles.

"This friend of yours, how much can you trust him?" Haslett asked.

Sebastian answered without hesitation. "Entirely."

"When it comes down to business, he's trust-worthy?"

"Absolutely."

"He's smarter than you or no?" Haslett asked.

Sebastian paused and smirked. "Um, he's . . ."

"If you're the smartest in the world, where does he stand in the world?"

Sebastian smiled. "Well, I said I'm one of the smartest, and he's up there as well."

Haslett decided to play with Sebastian's mind a bit.

"You still haven't told me where I'm at in the world. Give me a fucking graph from zero to a hundred. You're a hundred. Where am I then?" Haslett asked. "Be honest, you'll never fucking insult me."

"Yeah, I, uh, OK, if I'm say I'm a hundred, all

right—and I'm saying you're somewhere between fucking sixty-five and ninety-five."

Sebastian laughed with mock confidence. He realized what he'd just said took a lot of balls, as Haslett might say.

"You're a fucking prick—huh, you're scared to insult me, aren't you?" Haslett laughed. "You committed the fucking perfect crime here, haven't you? You're fucking—you're scared to insult me."

Sebastian looked at him, feeling, for one moment, superior.

"There, there's more to the world than, you know, the perfect crime."

They made plans to talk again—and Sebastian left.

25

A Turning Point

It was never Haslett's job to put the entire case together against the teenagers—he was not the lead investigator in this murder case. He was simply to use all of his years of experience, all of his manipulative powers, to get a confession. But in the back of his mind, it would give his mission a sense of higher purpose if he was convinced Sebastian was, in fact, guilty. That May 6 meeting was a turning point for Haslett and his undercover team. After the encounter at the Four Seasons, he was sure they had the right guys in their scope—and he was even more positive he'd get a confession to prove it.

"He never once denied ever being involved in those murders," Haslett said. "He discussed the topic, discussed different things in a roundabout way. But never once did he look at me and say, 'I have nothing to worry about because I am not responsible for those murders. The police are way out to lunch.' That was never said."

In his interview with *48 Hours,* Sebastian said the May 6 meeting was a realization for him as well—but in a very different way.

"At a certain point in the conversation, I'd been in a sheer panic that they were going to kill me right in the room on May the sixth. After that, I was like a piece of Silly Putty," Sebastian said.

"You even say, 'I would just assume that I would wake up one day with a bullet in my head,'" Van Sant reminded him, referring to a recorded conversation Sebastian had with Haslett.

"That's right. And that's what I believed. I believed that if I crossed them or if they weren't happy with me, or if they thought I was going to betray them, that they would have me killed."

"Why didn't you just say to them, 'Guys, I didn't do it.' You never deny it."

"Well, I don't think that's true, Peter," Sebastian said. "I'm affirming my innocence."

"Did you ever, in the thousands of hours that are on tape, say to those mobsters, 'I did not kill this family'?"

"I didn't say those exact words," Sebastian conceded.

"It's a pretty simply sentence."

"Well—I'm affirming my innocence."

Sebastian said he was trying to get away from the mobsters—telling them that he no longer needed them or their money. He was trying to convince them that he had other investors for his film and was too busy to work for them. But they made it obvious to him that people didn't dare walk away once they knew about the organization. So although Sebastian said he wanted to cut off all contact at that point, he didn't.

"This isn't an intellectual exercise. This is the difference between right and wrong," Van Sant reminded the teen. "And you kept making the wrong decisions, didn't you?"

"Well, in a way, you're right," Sebastian said. "But at the same time, I wasn't free to do what I wanted to do."

"You didn't walk away."

"No. But there is no walking away from Haslett. He's telling me that regardless of what I say to him."

Sebastian did seem frightened at times when he was with the two men, but there were other moments when he plainly seemed to be enjoying the perks of this new world. As he spent more time with the mobsters, he was drawn deeper and deeper into their very convincing world of make-believe crime. And as was his nature, Sebastian was not content to be just one of the boys in the organization—from that first stolen car scenario, he began using his intelligence and arrogance to get closer to the boss, even offering Haslett advice on future crimes. Sebastian was doing what he'd always done with his friends, in school—he was asserting himself, leading. As he got more comfortable, he came to want to impress Haslett. It wasn't enough for him to just follow orders; he wanted to be a part of the decision-making process.

And there was a youthful attraction to danger and adventure that kept Sebastian coming back, even when the mobsters weren't pushing him. On the one hand, he might have been fearful of them—but on the other, he was taking this thrill ride as far as he could, as long as the risks stayed minimal.

"Here you've been introduced to a world of money, women, fancy hotels, fast cars," Van Sant said. "You liked it, didn't you?"

"No, I didn't," Sebastian told him. "I didn't want to be a part of their organization. And I think they got that impression pretty clearly."

Haslett said Sebastian could have walked away at any time.

"He didn't have to return our calls. He didn't have to ever be available to us if he chose not to," Haslett said. "He wanted to be. There's no doubt."

And Haslett said every scenario they put into play during their operation came from an idea Sebastian gave them. Because the teen asked during their meeting on May 6 whether the organization did money laundering, the undercover officers decided to try it, as a way to draw him in.

"We had to have Sebastian Burns believe that, yes, he was dealing with the criminal element," Haslett said. "And that we had something that he wanted. And we had to make it believable."

The officers had to sit down with their counter-parts from the white-collar crime unit to get details on how to stage a money-laundering scenario, because they had never done it before. "We had to educate ourselves from the ground level," Shinkaruk said.

The RCMP was producing its own play. And just like in high school, Sebastian was the star.

26

Crime Is Cool

At their next meeting, on June 15, the RCMP picked a fairy tale setting. Victoria was the provincial capital of British Columbia and one of the top tourist destinations in all of Canada. Nestled near the southern tip of Vancouver Island, about forty-five miles across the Strait of Georgia from Vancouver, Victoria boasted Canada's warmest climate. It was founded in 1843 as a trading post for Britain's Hudson's Bay Company and named Fort Victoria, after the Queen of England.

Victoria grew to become a city of more than three hundred thousand. Its downtown was dominated by the majestic domed parliament building, which at night was illuminated with thousands of white lights that traced its outline. The architecture of the downtown was unmistakably English, true to its roots.

Victoria's main attraction was its spectacular setting, wrapped as it was around an inner harbor with a distant view of the snowcapped Olympic Mountains. The harbor area was a bustling place of water taxis,

seaplanes, and ferry boats, bringing tourists who arrived from Seattle and Port Angeles, Washington.
They crowded the harbor area, walking along streets
decorated with large floral pots hanging from antique
light posts. Tourists visited popular spots such as the
Royal London Wax Museum, with its chamber of
horrors, and the Undersea Gardens.

Just one block away from the throngs of tourists
was the quaint Royal Scot Inn, with its signature giant
carved wood bear out front, dressed in a kilt and with
one paw raised, welcoming all of the inn's guests.

Sebastian Burns scoffed at the bear as he pulled
into the inn's parking lot. This is definitely not the
Four Seasons, he thought. But the Royal Scot was
conveniently located just a short walk to every major
bank in downtown Victoria, making it the perfect
location for a money-laundering scenario.

Sebastian was not alone on this trip. He brought
his good friend from high school, and one of his cur-
rent roommates, Jimmy Miyoshi. He introduced
Jimmy to Shinkaruk and assured him that Jimmy
could be trusted. Once again, Sebastian didn't realize
that his conversations were being recorded.

The teens started talking about their movie project, on which Jimmy was now assisting, telling the
mobster that they planned to start filming in August.
The two teens laughed about how it would help them
get girls—"Hey, baby, you want to go in our movie?"
Jimmy said, laughing.

They talked about fast cars and girls, how their screenplay was geared toward the intelligent, "the elite." The teens were very relaxed, laughing and joking with Shinkaruk as they waited for Haslett to arrive.

When he arrived about fifteen minutes later, Haslett told them the plan for the day—the two teens would be laundering money for his organization.

"What I want you guys to do, which is no big deal, it's pretty straightforward—[Shinkaruk] is going to drive you around, just like you've done before, but he's going to take you to a few different banks. You're going to go rob them," Haslett said.

Sebastian and Jimmy stiffened. Haslett broke the tension.

"No, I'm fucking joking," he said.

Haslett told them they would be given envelopes of cash, each containing less than $10,000, and they would deposit the amounts at various banks around Victoria. (Any amounts exceeding $10,000 would have to be reported to provincial tax authorities.) Both boys got worried looks on their faces.

"You guys are young, good-looking kids, uh, you know, clean-cut," Haslett said. "No one's going to fucking give you any heat—this is no big deal."

Sebastian and Jimmy immediately began peppering Haslett with questions. What if the teller asked who they were? Did they need to show their IDs? Maybe they should do each deposit together, to make it less conspicuous, and because they did everything

Tariq and Sultana Rafay, just after they were married,
courtesy of the Bellevue Police Department

Tariq Rafay holding his children, Atif and Basma,
courtesy of the Bellevue Police Department

Sebastian Burns—with his sister, Tiffany—playing the cello, courtesy of the Burns family

Sebastian Burns—with his parents, Carol and Dave—during a Christmas at home in Vancouver, courtesy of the Burns family

Sebastian Burns in his high school graduation robes, courtesy of the King County District Attorney's Office

Atif Rafay in his high school graduation robes, courtesy of the King County District Attorney's Office

Jimmy Miyoshi in his high school graduation robes, courtesy of the King County District Attorney's Office

Sebastian Burns receives a Royal Air Cadet award from
the Duke of Edinburgh, courtesy of the Burns family

LEFT Sebastian Burns, singing during his high school years, courtesy
of the King County District Attorney's Office; RIGHT Sebastian Burns
and his girlfriend, Sarah Isaacs, during happier days in high school,
courtesy of the King County District Attorney's Office

The room where Basma Rafay fought for her life, courtesy of the King County District Attorney's Office

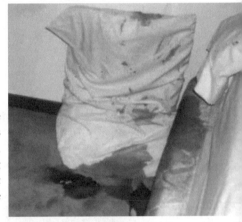

The room where Tariq Rafay was beaten to death, courtesy of the King County District Attorney's Office

This room in the Rafay house appeared to be ransacked—but police suspected a staged burglary; courtesy of the King County District Attorney's Office

LEFT Atif Rafay at the crime scene, just after discovering the bodies of his family, courtesy of the Bellevue Police Department; RIGHT Sebastian Burns at the crime scene, just after discovering the bodies of the Rafay family, courtesy of the Bellevue Police Department

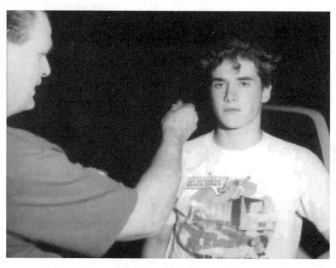

Sebastian Burns at the crime scene, where a police officer conducted tests on him to check for blood, courtesy of the Bellevue Police Department

Atif Rafay, leaving a memorial service in honor of
his family, pursued by the Vancouver media, courtesy
of the King County District Attorney's Office

Sebastian Burns, leaving a memorial service in
honor of Atif Rafay's family, pursued by the
Vancouver media, courtesy of BCTV

LEFT Atif Rafay arrested in Vancouver, courtesy of BCTV
RIGHT Sebastian Burns arrested in Vancouver, courtesy of the BCTV

Atif Rafay and
Sebastian Burns confess
to the murders of
the Rafay family in
undercover RCMP
video, courtesy of the
King County District
Attorney's Office

LEFT Atif Rafay, escorted into court, courtesy of CBS News; RIGHT Sebastian Burns, escorted into court, courtesy of CBS News

Sebastian Burns's initial defense attorney, Theresa Olson, standing in her office, courtesy of CBS News

LEFT Sebastian Burns testifies in his own defense, courtesy of CBS News; RIGHT Atif Rafay delivers a speech at his sentencing, courtesy of CBS News

Sebastian Burns delivers a speech at his sentencing, courtesy of CBS News

The defense team reacts to the guilty verdicts,
courtesy of CBS News

LEFT Atif Rafay reacts to the guilty verdicts,
courtesy of CBS News; RIGHT Sebastian Burns reacts
to the guilty verdicts, courtesy of CBS News

The prosecutors react to the guilty verdicts,
courtesy of CBS News

Peter Van Sant interviews neighbor Marc Sidell
in front of the crime scene, courtesy of CBS News

Defenses attorneys Amanda Lee, Song Richardson, and Jeffrey Robinson interview with *48 Hours,* courtesy of CBS News

Prosecutors James Jude Konat and Roger Davidheiser interview with *48 Hours,* courtesy of CBS News

Bellevue Police Department lead detective Bob Thompson interviews with *48 Hours,* courtesy of CBS News

Carol and Dave Burns interview with *48 Hours,*
courtesy of CBS News

LEFT Tiffany Burns anchors the *19 Action News* in Cleveland,
courtesy of CBS News; RIGHT Sebastian's girlfriend Sarah Isaacs
interviews with *48 Hours,* courtesy of CBS News

Atif Rafay interviews with *48 Hours*,
courtesy of CBS News

Sebastian Burns interviews with *48 Hours*,
courtesy of CBS News

The grave sites of Tariq, Sultana, and Basma Rafay,
courtesy of CBS News

together? Maybe they should go on their Rollerblades to seem more like teenagers?

Haslett shut them down.

"Don't bring no heat on yourself, don't bring no attention to yourself, just in and out, simple and easy."

Haslett told them to get going and page him when they were on their way back to the hotel—he would meet them back in the room.

Shinkaruk drove the teens around to a handful of banks, and they took turns going in and depositing the envelopes of money. It was summertime, and Victoria was buzzing with tourists. The teens moved easily through the crowds of people carrying shopping bags and cameras, as well as street musicians and actors, who gave a kind of Disney World feel to the tourist district. After about an hour of making deposits, they headed back to the hotel.

Once back in the hotel room Sebastian and Jimmy got themselves glasses of water, while Shinkaruk chided them for not waiting on the beer that Haslett was bringing. When Haslett showed up, he asked the teens if they would mind staying in the hotel room that night and doing a few more deposits in the morning.

Sebastian said that was fine—but he told Haslett that he and Jimmy had been thinking about this money-laundering thing. He said that they'd like to do the deposits together, rather than splitting up, because "that's how we're used to doing things, together." And they also thought it made sense to do them while wearing their Rollerblades because people tended to smile at them when they were Rollerblading.

Haslett patronized him and said that for now, they should do it the way he had planned—but next time, they could talk about Sebastian's ideas.

"You're a smart man, I told you that before," Haslett said. "I'll listen to someone if you got some different ideas that can, uh, make things run smoother for me, you know that. That's the bottom line."

They switched gears to the boys' favorite topic, their movie. Haslett asked how it was going.

"Filming is basically going to be in August, but the script is brilliant," Sebastian said. "The script is so good that it's . . . I'm confident that we're going make, like, quite a few bucks off this . . . Before I was expecting to get a bit of cash and sort of notoriety, but it's so bloody good that I'm, it's going to be unstoppable."

They talked some more about how much it would cost to make and some different movie companies that might be interested—and then Haslett changed the subject again.

"You guys good with computers?" he asked the two teens. "Obviously."

"Pretty good," Sebastian agreed.

Haslett told them he was thinking of taking a computer course, which Sebastian told him was a waste of time—he and his friends could easily show him how it worked. Haslett wanted a computer to keep track of where his money went, and Sebastian told him they could probably get him the computer and the software that would be right for that.

"We can get you a kick-ass one," Sebastian said.

"We'll get you a kick-ass computer, and you will be able to do things that you haven't been able to discover yet, kinda thing," Jimmy echoed.

The teens told Haslett all about the Internet and how he could use that, too—and how there were ways to set up deals so they couldn't be traced back to you. They explained to him how he could encrypt his messages so the police wouldn't be able to intercept them, although they reminded him there were always dangers involved. Jimmy Miyoshi wasted no time in trying to impress Haslett.

"Yeah, well here's an example of something," Jimmy said. "You're on the computer and you're doing some stuff or whatever, and all of a sudden crashing through the window is coming, you know, police agents or whatever—and, you know, you're really slow over there and you're too slow to, you know, either turn the computer off or you know erase the disk that's in the computer or something, whatever. That would be the only really critical time where, where you run into that kinda problem."

They talked about some other options, and the teens said they would do some research for Haslett. Since the banks opened at 10 the next morning, they planned that Shinkaruk would come pick them up around 11. Then Haslett would pay them for their work and they could catch a B.C. ferryboat back to Vancouver.

The two mobsters left, and Sebastian and Jimmy headed into town on their Rollerblades for the evening. They ate at a seafood restaurant and checked out some clubs, but decided they were all pretty lame. They talked to some girls from Holland for a while, then headed back to the hotel.

The next morning, the teens ordered room service—the most expensive stuff on the limited menu, Belgian waffles and "Eggs Marvelous"—and ate before Shinkaruk showed up to take them for another day of money laundering.

After an hour or so—and a few more bank deposits—the teens and Shinkaruk met Haslett back at the hotel room to debrief. Haslett handed a wad of money to Sebastian, who smiled from ear to ear. The mobsters then left, telling Sebastian they'd be in touch in a week or so. Jimmy grabbed the wad of money out of Sebastian's hand and started counting.

"Let's see what we got," Jimmy said, counting. "Two grand."

"Well, that's fantastic," Sebastian said.

"Well, oh, sorry, I thought I'd get like two hundred or five hundred. I was totally anticipating that. Like, well, you got three hundred the other day."

"Yeah, well, last time, they paid me the two hundred bucks, and I basically took a shit," Sebastian reminded his friend.

Sebastian looked at their stack of newly earned cash. He couldn't believe their good fortune.

"This is the world of crime," he told Jimmy.

"Wow."

"It's so cool. This has been the coolest thing ever. I couldn't ask for any more."

Sebastian appeared to have fully completed his transition from onetime air cadet and star student to full-time criminal. In his interview with *48 Hours,* he tried to explain why his claims of fear had now, apparently, given way to feelings of joy.

"The simplest answer is that, you know, it was—I couldn't help but be excited about having two thousand dollars put in my hand," the teen said. "And I hardly had to do anything for it."

"But also, it could be you're enjoying the life of a criminal," Van Sant told him. "The easy money."

"Well, for a few seconds, literally."

Haslett and Shinkaruk said Sebastian was free to go at any time. Whatever fear he was experiencing, they said, was the result of his own interpretations of their conversations. Both officers had never directly threatened to harm Sebastian if he walked away.

The cool side of crime was about to become a distant memory for Sebastian. The RCMP's play was entering another act, and Sebastian's fears would soon be focused south of the border—on the Bellevue Police Department.

27

A Wild Hair

Weeks of listening to wiretaps had led to nothing. Sebastian had been fully incorporated into the criminal organization, but that was anticipated; remember, the RCMP had said that anyone could be drawn into one of its scenarios. But what was most frustrating for investigators was that the boys never spoke about the murders—not a single word.

Back in Bellevue, Detective Bob Thompson finally got the DNA results of that coarse body hair found in Tariq Rafay's bed. This was the moment Thompson had waited for—the proof that Sebastian was in the man's bedroom on the night of the murders, the RCMP having provided a sample of Sebastian's DNA from that discarded tissue. Bellevue investigators also had the DNA profiles of the entire Rafay family, from hairs that had been gathered in the house.

Thompson opened the envelope from the lab and read the report.

"The coarse hair was analyzed—DNA analysis.

Did it match Sebastian or Atif?" Van Sant asked the lead detective.

"No," Thompson said.

"Any of the family members?"

"No."

"There's your killer."

"No," Thompson said. "That's an unknown hair. We don't know who it belongs to."

"How about the person who's swinging the bat?" Van Sant asked.

"That—that hair could belong to . . . anybody from the medical examiner's office, the firefighters that came into the scene . . . police officers," Thompson said.

"It was described as a coarse hair or pubic hair. That didn't come off the top of the head."

"It also could have come off of an arm," Thompson said.

"I don't know about in your bed. I know in our bed, I've never found strange hairs. Have you?"

"Well, I haven't looked," Thompson said. "And I'm sure you haven't either."

That once vitally important hair was now dismissed as irrelevant. It didn't fit Thompson's theory of the crime.

A couple of weeks after the first money-laundering scenario, Sebastian and Jimmy met up with the mobsters again. They went back to the Royal Scot Hotel in Victoria. As instructed, the boys got the key for room 142 and paged Shinkaruk to let him know they had arrived. They sat around talking about movies while they waited for Shinkaruk to pick them up.

Almost an hour later, no one had yet shown up to meet them—so Sebastian paged Shinkaruk again.

"Hi. Yeah, room one four two; this is the second time I'm leaving a message," Sebastian said. "I'm just calling a second time because, I guess, I was worried that maybe you didn't get the first one 'cause the wait has sort of been a while, so whatever."

They sat around for a while more, reenacting their karaoke singing from the night before and laughing about how badly Sebastian sang. About half an hour after that, Shinkaruk finally showed up—and they immediately headed out to make some more deposits, same as last time.

The three of them got back to the hotel room after the deposits were made, and Haslett arrived a few minutes later. He poured some wine for the boys. After some small talk, Sebastian revealed something for the first time. He said he was sure his home phone was tapped.

Haslett largely ignored the comment. He looked over at Shinkaruk and offered a strong suggestion.

"Why don't you and Jimmy go for a ride," Haslett said. "Go have a beer somewhere; I'll page you."

Shinkaruk and Jimmy headed out the door. Haslett wasted no time in bringing up the murders in Bellevue.

"Well, I read some interesting stuff out of the States," Haslett said, looking at Sebastian. "Really interesting."

"Like what?" Sebastian asked.

"Well, they have you in a pretty big fucking way down there, to the point when these murders took place, whoever did it—and not 'whoever' did it; the report I read knows *you* did it."

Sebastian just stared at him. Haslett went on.

"They have you with your hair samples in the shower, lots of them, about twenty, twenty-one or twenty-two are named in this report I read," Haslett said. "They're just about right around the drain. In with these hair samples, there is blood from the dead people, from the male and female dead person in that house, and it comes right back to you. They know the last person to take a shower in there had the blood from the dead people on them, 'cause they used some sort of light to scan it which shows the fucking droppings of the blood."

Sebastian was frozen, staring at Haslett.

"You're the only person mentioned in this whole report I read," Haslett told the teen. "It's your hair, their blood, in that shower. You said they haven't got your DNA, or whatever—they have got your DNA. They got it out of some fucking snot Kleenex up here, somewhere in a restaurant."

Sebastian finally reacted. "Up here?"

"In Canada, in a restaurant. You're the only guy mentioned in that whole report I read, Sebastian."

Sebastian started stuttering, asking where they would have gotten his DNA, which restaurant it was, how they got it. Haslett told him he only knows what he read, that they have the DNA. Sebastian was looking more disoriented by the second.

"And right now, they're culturing your DNA in some small lab, and it's down in the States. Private lab," Haslett said. "And there's mention of a fingerprint of yours in there."

"Where?" Sebastian asked.

"On a box, something to do with a box that was tipped over."

The box Haslett was referring to was discovered in the room where Detectives Thompson and Gomes felt a burglary had been staged. Boxes had been tipped over, but the contents had not been thrown about.

Sebastian was clearly frightened. He wondered why he hadn't been arrested yet.

"You're the only name mentioned in that report I read," Haslett said. "That's all I can tell you."

Haslett paused, taking in Sebastian's fear. He continued.

"If you want me to help you, I can help you. But you're going to help me," Haslett told him.

Sebastian ran his hands through his hair, agitated.

"OK, yeah—what the fuck—what do you want me to do?"

Haslett told him that he wanted Sebastian to continue doing money laundering, and he wanted him to run the organization's computers for him. Sebastian said fine, but he was clearly still thinking about the bombshell information Haslett had just given him. Sebastian contemplated for a moment, and then the conversation took a bizarre turn. He brought up the movie he wanted to make, *The Great Despisers*. With his imagination now moving at the speed of light, Sebastian speculated about how they could profit from his predicament.

"If there's a possibility in the world that it could be made so that I was, like, cleared, as in eliminated of these charges, then there's so much potential—because we've been slandered so badly by the press and whatever," the teen said, excited about the prospect.

Sebastian said that if Haslett could help him be exonerated of any murder charges, the resulting publicity could help his film earn millions.

"I mean, because basically, all of a sudden, 'Why don't you come on an interview with CNN and talk about your brutal experience with the police? Sebastian Burns and Atif Rafay, you know, why don't you guys come and talk on every show?' And . . . the film, with that kind of promotion . . . I mean, because as it is right now, it's like, 'Oooh, controversy,' right? Which in itself promotes, right? But this is like, 'Oh, you're heroes,' you know? And you know, it suddenly goes up to twenty-five, thirty million."

Haslett got it and smiled. The next phase of Project Estate was already taking shape in his mind.

"In other words," Haslett said, "I just make it look as though you're innocent."

28

A Bullet in My Head

Haslett told Sebastian that he'd be happy to use his underworld contact in Bellevue to get rid of the evidence that supposedly implicated Sebastian, but that before he acted, he wanted more information—information about the murders.

"What went on down there that I got to fucking worry about covering up for you and destroying for you?" the crime boss asked.

Sebastian became hesitant. He stuttered out an answer.

"Well, like, I really, I have no idea what they will have, like, you know, what kind of things they'll have."

"How did that hair get in the shower with blood and everything?" Haslett asked.

"Um . . ." Sebastian clearly didn't want to talk.

"Let's be straightforward with each other right now."

Sebastian had gone from being excited at the prospect of his film's making millions of dollars if he was proven innocent to becoming obviously nervous about Haslett's hard line of questioning.

"OK, tell me about the shower," Haslett said. "I want to know about the shower. Like, how did all this blood get in the shower?"

Sebastian didn't like the interrogation. He became guarded.

"Um, but, like, there's no percentage in, like, talking about this," the teen said. "You know what I mean? I can't say anything that will help, all right?"

Haslett kept pushing Sebastian—and Sebastian talked around the issue. He never gave a direct answer, but he never said that the reason he didn't know was because he was actually innocent. Haslett told him that he wouldn't send in his guy to destroy evidence against Sebastian until he knew exactly what he should be looking for. He grew more demanding.

"How did this blood get in the shower for starters?" Haslett asked him again. "Did you wash out the fucking murder weapon in it or what? That's what I want to fucking find out. Be straight with me, and I can fucking maybe look after you. Don't be straight with me, I cannot fucking look after you. I told you before, I'll look after everybody who works for me, and I'll spend money to look after them, as long as they're truthful and fucking straightforward with me. If they're not, I'm not going to stick my fucking neck in the dark."

Sebastian paused for nearly a full minute. Then every word was measured.

"Ah, the ways of the police are—are the way they've decided that I'm a murder suspect and things like that," Sebastian said. "Um, like, obviously, anything I say can potentially like . . . like . . . could be . . . end my life."

He looked up to see if Haslett comprehended what he was saying. Sebastian told the mob boss that he'd be happy to say what he'd heard from the police, or what he'd heard on television about what they supposedly had against him, but nothing more. Haslett was distressed.

"You were there, and I wasn't," he told the teen. "I don't give two fucks with what the police are telling you to fuck your head. If I'm going to go down there and fucking look after you so you'll be able to work for me and make me money, I want to know. 'Cause like I said, I will not be going fucking back—and I cannot fucking risk going back two or three times, start fucking asking for little bits of information every fucking week or two or three weeks. Now what the fuck went on down there so I can go look after everything fully? And once it's looked after, we'll talk again, and then you'll know you're clear."

Sebastian explained to Haslett that he and Atif were in the house for five days before the murders—so of course his hairs and fingerprints were going to be there. Haslett kept pushing—he pointed out that it still didn't make sense why Sebastian's hairs would be mixed with the dead people's blood.

"Well," Sebastian said. "I guess at some point, I must've been in the shower and, uh, at some point there was blood in the shower, and uh . . ."

Haslett interrupted him—he was visibly losing his patience. The interrogation turned dramatic. Sebastian paced the room while he listened.

"Forget about it fucking—you're fucking wrapped in circles," Haslett said. "I didn't come down with last night's rain. How did the dead people's blood get in the fucking shower with your hair?"

Sebastian shot back his answer. "How's the fucking answer to that question going to help you?"

They continued to talk at cross-purposes, both getting increasingly impatient. Finally, Sebastian had had enough—he tried to explain to Haslett that getting these details wasn't necessary, that the crime boss already wielded power over Sebastian and his friends.

"I just assume that, you know, with your connections and whatever, and all of your money and power and stuff, that if I were to fuck you around, OK, I would just assume that I would wake up one day with a bullet in my head," Sebastian said.

Sebastian brought up another fear, saying he had recently read an article in the *North Shore News*, a Vancouver newspaper.

"It's about a man charged with murder based on

boastful confessions to, they say, like police officers disguised as mafia and undercover bikers . . ."

The room got very still. Haslett lowered his volume.

"What are you accusing me of right now; first of all tell me, what are you asking me if I am?" Haslett asked.

"I'm not accusing you of shit," Sebastian said.

Although Sebastian didn't know it, Haslett already knew about that article—and he knew it was worrying Sebastian. When Sebastian read it at home earlier in the week, he mentioned to Atif that the guys in the article sounded a lot like Shinkaruk and Haslett. The RCMP heard this conversation on the wiretaps inside the house—and they wondered if their operation was blown. But Sebastian shrugged off his concerns when he read the article—and looking at Haslett, he seemed to do the same thing now.

29

Tell Me Anything

Project Estate had reached a critical juncture. Haslett continued to push Sebastian, hoping to hear something—anything that would incriminate him. But what struck Haslett as odd was that while Sebastian wasn't admitting anything, he wasn't denying anything either.

"Answer me this," Haslett said. "Why did you guys do this? Money? Answer me that, fuck, that's . . . for money or what?"

"Why do you want to know?" Sebastian countered.

" 'Cause I just want to know, I want to know what kind of guys I'm going to be working with. You can answer that. That's a simple fucking question, and I know who did it. Fucking so do the police. Let's fucking worry about you not going to fucking jail, but *why* you do it is for my peace of mind."

"Uhhh, there's really no gain in talking about that," Sebastian said.

Sebastian asked how intelligent these people of Haslett's were who read the police report—would they be able to catch subtleties that perhaps Sebastian himself might? And were the guys sure that the evidence report was complete?

Haslett told him the next report he got, he would let Sebastian look at before he burned it. But he was still seething that Sebastian wasn't opening up. And he let the teen know it.

"Hey, obviously, you fucking aren't going to fucking play straight with me," Haslett said.

Their meeting went on for nearly four hours, Haslett constantly badgering Sebastian.

"Was it for the money?" Haslett asked again. "Tell me, it's so fucking simple, answer, just tell me that. It's not as though—I know you fucking did it. You know you did it. The police even fuck know you did it. We'll take care of the police, uh, I want to know for the peace of fucking mind."

"I'm not a weirdo," Sebastian said. "I'm not some sleazy superviolent guy, I'm not some philosophical weirdo, dude. I'm kind of like yourself in many ways."

Haslett smiled inwardly, thinking Sebastian was finally beginning to incriminate himself. The pressure inside the hotel room continued to build. Haslett was a pit bull. Sebastian was like a pendulum, trusting Haslett one moment, suspecting him the next.

"Listen, you—the way you're asking me this, it's like you're a cop," Sebastian told the crime boss.

"Nah, I don't give two fucks what I'm like," Haslett brushed off his concerns. "It's on my mind, I want to know why."

Haslett kept asking whether money was the motive. Sebastian never admitted anything, but said that when Atif got the money from the Rafay family estate, it would be shared.

Haslett reminded him, however, that there was no evidence at the scene against Atif—so Sebastian could be left hung out to dry by Atif and Jimmy Miyoshi, who Haslett assumed knew about the murder plot.

"I fucking hope these guys are solid, man . . . because they got nothing to lose right now," Haslett said.

"What they have to lose is me—and that may sound like the biggest load of crap ever . . . The fact is that if they lose me, I guarantee you that the quality of their life from this point on would be shit," Sebastian said, confident of his friends' loyalty.

"OK, that's fine, but they'll also end up getting that fucking money."

"Whatever."

Haslett then asked Sebastian if he trusted him. Sebastian answered with a question, which led to Haslett's making an implied threat.

"What—do I trust you?" Sebastian asked.

"No, I don't give two fucks of whether you trust me or not," Haslett said. "I fucking—I got basically your fucking future in the palm of my fucking hand if I want it anyway, and you're going to make money for me, and I'm going to make your life happy anyway."

In his interview with *48 Hours,* Sebastian said the words were chilling.

"What was he saying to you?" Van Sant asked Sebastian.

"That I was dead if I didn't do what he said. And if you listen to the tape recording of that, you'll hear me choke on tape."

30
An Old Man

The pit bull technique finally came to an end. Haslett paged Shinkaruk and told him to come pick him up.

While they waited, Haslett casually asked Sebastian what this movie he was making was actually about—and how much of it dealt with the murders in Bellevue.

Sebastian said that only a small part of the film actually dealt with the murders—it was more about the three main characters and how they got through high school, which he described as "brutal," and then how they reacted to the murders.

"So the thing on Bellevue is like, the actual event of it, is like, it'll only be a little thing—and basically it will show how we kind of react to it, I guess," Sebastian said. "And also, it'll show all the police crap around it, kind of thing."

Sebastian got more excited and talked faster and faster as he described the details of the film. He, Atif, and Jimmy would be the lead characters, and would play their own parts. He then tried to tell Haslett, who looked as sophisticated as a beer can, about his favorite philosopher.

" 'Cause these are characters who, they're very Nietzsche, and I guess you don't really know about Nietzsche, but, for example, we're thinking of calling the movie *The Great Despisers,* which is actually an excerpt from a quote from Nietzsche."

Sebastian went on to say that at the end of the movie, two of the three main characters ended up getting executed for the Bellevue murders.

"Because basically we get framed or set up or whatever and get killed," Sebastian said. "Like these guys die basically, or two of them do, and one of them goes on to have a miserable life or whatever."

But, Sebastian said, that was all right, because the boys would have lived the lives they wanted to live—another Nietzsche philosophy, known as eternal recurrence. At this point, Haslett was staring blankly, hoping that Sebastian was revealing something about himself.

"Basically one of his little credos is people always talk about like afterlife and crap like that—and not only is this a bunch of bullshit, but it, it really fucks with the way that you live your life, right?" Sebastian explained.

The teen was in his element now, lecturing to a plebeian.

"Because you just live with this idea that there's some afterlife after, OK, and his suggestion is that you ought to live your life as though you will have to live every day over again, sort of thing—like you die and wake up and you live your life again."

Shinkaruk, where are you? Haslett thought as he listened to Sebastian ramble. He started to look away at objects in the room: the mirror, a lamp—anything.

Sebastian continued. "And you should live as though you know that that's going to happen kind of thing, so that you basically will do everything richly . . . but basically imagine that that thought didn't disturb you—imagine that you were rejoiced at the idea of living your life over and over again, like imagine that you lived such a life and that's like how the movie will end, I guess."

Haslett thought the lecture must be over. He was wrong.

"I guess seizing every moment—or rather it's just like living so that you would not regret having to do it over and over again," Sebastian said.

Sounding a bit drained, Haslett returned to the matters at hand.

"Could you, could you kill again, circumstances were right?" Haslett asked.

"Um, doubt it," Sebastian answered quickly.

"Huh?" Haslett couldn't believe the teen had answered directly.

"I doubt it, man."

"Why?"

"I just think that would be very unpleasant," Sebastian said. "I don't know."

"What if I needed it done and the circumstances were right?"

"I doubt it, man."

"Why?"

"Because I think that would be very fucking brutal," Sebastian said. "It's fucking making me an old man. And my hair falls out, and my face is aged."

Haslett held his gaze on Sebastian for an extra second. The lecture had been worth every word. Haslett believed he'd just got him, that Sebastian had finally admitted he was the killer. Haslett hid his exhilaration. He felt like the two of them had just connected—as criminal associates. Haslett asked Sebastian if he had any fear.

"Fear, well . . . Gee, lots of things, I guess," Sebastian said, thinking out loud. "I fear ultimately, I guess, I fear having a really shitty life—and I guess what I want is to have a really great life, and so I guess my fear is that I won't be able to do that. Yeah, a real kick-ass life, do tons of fucking great things."

"It takes money," Haslett said.

Sebastian laughed. "I know that's why I . . . ended up doing in Bellevue."

Sebastian had now made two references to the Bellevue murders, and it was all caught on audiotape. But were the references for real? Or had Sebastian just told Haslett what he so obviously wanted to hear?

Shinkaruk arrived to pick up Haslett, and they set the plan for the next day. Shinkaruk said he would pick the teens up for more money laundering between

10:30 and 11 the next morning. Sebastian and Jimmy were left alone for the night in the hotel.

Jimmy asked what Sebastian and the crime boss had talked about. The two spoke in a whisper, undetectable to the RCMP officers listening in the other room. Then the teens went to sleep.

Sebastian woke up in a foul mood. Atif had called in the middle of the night to announce that he'd gotten their new automobile—a black Mustang sports car. Sebastian was irritated because he'd left Atif with a long list of things to get done, and Atif had instead spent much of the day driving around in the new car.

Jimmy and Sebastian discussed how much money they were expecting to get from the Rafay estate—Sebastian thought it was a total of between $300,000 and $400,000. And he told Jimmy that the car cost them $20,500, but that they were having a few thousand more dollars' worth of work done to it to make it perfect. They were having the black leather interior changed to gray so it wouldn't be so hot during the day, and they were having a body shop lower it and put in a supercharger.

The three teenagers' lives were now intertwined. They lived in the same house. They shared whatever cash was raised. Soon, they hoped to be partners in a major motion picture about their lives.

Sebastian and Jimmy chatted a little more over breakfast. They then telephoned Shinkaruk, who told them to meet him down the street at a Taco Bell. The two teens happily headed out for another day of money laundering and quick profit. After making several more bank deposits, they couldn't have been happier as they caught a late ferry back to Vancouver.

Sebastian had no way of knowing that his next trip across the ferry would seal his fate.

31

A Scene to Remember

July 18, 1995. It had been just over a year since Sebastian Burns and Atif Rafay had called 911 to report the horrific scene inside the Rafay family home. No one had been arrested for the triple murders, which remained the most publicized unsolved case in both Washington State and British Columbia.

Sebastian and Atif remained the only suspects in the case. For more than three months, they had been the focal point of one of the most elaborate and expensive undercover investigations in British Columbia history.

During Project Estate, the RCMP had brilliantly used electronic surveillance, deceit, intimidation, improvisational scripting, and gifted acting to create a reality show in which Sebastian, Atif, and Jimmy Miyoshi had played—if obliviously—the starring roles. Despite their superior intelligence, the boys had been outwitted by men whom they saw as mere plebeians.

Friedrich Nietzsche would have been proud—of the RCMP officers.

Now, after thousands of hours of preparation, what Haslett and Shinkaruk hoped would be the final act of Project Estate was about to begin. Haslett laid the final trap. All his years of experience told him that Sebastian was ready to confess.

Early on the evening of July 18, Shinkaruk picked Sebastian up at his house, and they drove to the main BC Ferries terminal at Tsawwassen to catch a boat back to Victoria. This time, they skipped the kilted bear, heading instead to the Oxford Castle Inn. The hotel was actually built like a castle—and was located on a gorge overlooking a scenic water inlet, just minutes from downtown. After Sebastian got checked in, he and Shinkaruk drove over to the lush Ocean Pointe Resort and Spa—located on the waterfront of Victoria's Inner Harbor. This was where they would meet Haslett. It was yet another in the line of elegant, expensive hotels where the two make-believe mobsters had arranged their meetings with Sebastian. But this time, something was different—Haslett was so confident he would get a confession that he had arranged to have a hidden video camera placed in a room. A film was about to be made. But would the words and images captured be real? Or was Sebastian about to give the performance of his life?

Around 6:45 P.M., Sebastian and Shinkaruk arrived at the hotel. Haslett was waiting for them. The three men small-talked for a few minutes. Shinkaruk passed out bottles of beer. Haslett then got impatient and sent Shinkaruk away, telling him that he would be paged when he was needed again. He told Sebastian to check the door and make sure it was locked. They were in room 238. The camera was rolling.

Sebastian, dressed in a T-shirt and cargo-style shorts, sat down on the couch, while Haslett sat catty-corner to him in a chair. Haslett's first words were like a punch to Sebastian's gut.

"Well, I'll tell ya, they're fucking coming to lock your ass up. Yours and your friends. But there's, uh, things here that can be done very fucking quickly and very easy. Things, but they gotta be done quick. But you're going to want to do them, you're going to have to tell me you want them done, and you're going to have to play straight with me, 'cause things are fucking happening quick here now. And you and your friend, your fucking asses are going to jail."

Sebastian had had several weeks to think about what Haslett had told him during their last meeting—the evidence the Bellevue police supposedly had against him. He had decided Haslett was a man he could trust.

"Well, I want your help," Sebastian said.

"Yeah, you need my help," Haslett corrected him. "Not you want it, you need it."

"I know."

"I'm going to show you something. You never fucking saw this from me. What I'm saying, there is a lot of things are not answered, or answered here. Just read this piece of shit. That was fucking turned over to me with this. It's got to be destroyed."

Haslett handed Sebastian a memo on Bellevue Police Department letterhead that detailed the forensic evidence against Sebastian. The details were startling. The memo indicated that police would shortly be coming to arrest Sebastian for the Rafay family murders.

What Sebastian didn't know was that the memo was a fake, the product of a secret meeting between the RCMP and the Bellevue police.

Haslett repeated that Sebastian's arrest was imminent. But he had an eleventh-hour solution. Haslett offered to have his people destroy the evidence—for a price. Haslett demanded that Sebastian tell him all the details of the murders so that his people would know exactly what evidence to destroy.

Sebastian later told *48 Hours* that he was certain at this point that the Bellevue Police Department had fabricated evidence against him.

"Oh, at that point, I was almost certain of it," Sebastian told Peter Van Sant. "He had already told me that a scientist had come to the conclusion that I was the guilty party. And so the only possibilities were either that someone had fabricated evidence outright, or they were grossly misrepresenting evidence to convict us of something we didn't do."

As Sebastian was seen on video reading through the police memo, he was visibly confused. He couldn't figure out how some of the evidence got where it was. The memo said there were fibers from the red towels in the bathroom where the killer showered, and that the fibers were mixed with Sebastian's hair. He told Haslett he couldn't remember what color the towels were. The memo said that there were boxer shorts in the washer with stains on them; he said he had no idea whose those were. He searched his memory and then looked up at Haslett.

"I don't remember giving any of my clothing to be laundered there," Sebastian said.

The memo also noted there were bloodstains in the garage.

"Anyhow, bloodstains located in the garage, um . . ." Sebastian paused for twenty-four seconds, a lifetime during a conversation.

"I can't see how the fuck there'd be any bloodstains in the garage. Well, OK, but, I mean there, there, there is this possibility that there can be things that I don't know about that like they're basically fabricating to look like they count, you know what I mean?"

Sebastian looked at Haslett, seeking help.

"I don't believe they're sending a report to the lab or wherever this report is, asking to fabricate fucking evidence," Haslett said. "When you had blood on, were you ever in the garage when you had blood on you after? And it dripped in there? No?"

"No."

Gotcha again, Haslett thought.

Sebastian started arguing with Haslett that he didn't know any more details about the murders than what was contained in the memo—and that Haslett didn't need any additional detail to take care of this.

Haslett got angry. He said he spoke to his contact in Bellevue who had got this report for him.

"He said things got to be acted on fast if they're going to be acted on," Haslett said. "But I'm not fucking going and telling him to do anything else now, half the job and blind, because there's no time for any mistakes here."

Haslett became more forceful. " 'Cause I'll tell you right now, it's this close. Now, if you want my help, you have to fucking do as I say and things are going to be done proper. If you don't want it, you can tell me right now, and you're going to deny ever fucking knowing me."

Sebastian's head was spinning. He thought that if he gave Haslett the wrong answer, he could be killed.

32

The Straight Goods

Haslett stared at Sebastian, waiting for an answer. He didn't have to wait long.

"So, tell me what went on down there, and I'm going to tell you how I'm going to take care of your problem," he told the teen. "OK, and it has to be taken care of quick. Give me the straight goods, so I know exactly what I gotta take care of."

Sebastian would later say he was terrified at this moment—not only that evidence had been fabricated against him in the Rafay murders but that Haslett would have him killed if he was arrested and became a threat to the organization. But Sebastian said that based on the meetings leading up to this, he knew there was a good chance he was going to have to give Haslett the details he wanted to hear.

Atif backed up his best friend's story, telling *48 Hours* that Sebastian had called him panicked after the May 6 meeting and said they had to come up with a plan to appease the mobsters.

"Well, he certainly thought that if they felt that Sebastian was going to be arrested for the Bellevue charges, that they could kill him, and that they would kill him," Atif said. "Because they thought he would—he was capable of informing on them."

Atif told Van Sant that rather than advise Sebastian to stop seeing the mobsters, he went along with the plan.

"I think that we were actually remarkably vulnerable, especially at that point," he said. "I mean, we were essentially estranged from any kind of normal connection with a community. There just seemed no way to rectify the situation."

So the two teens claimed they researched various news reports to help them prepare a story they could tell Haslett, a story that would contain facts about the murder. They said that they met where they couldn't be overheard on any possible bugs in their house—on the roof of their house, at a nearby field, at a tennis court, and in restaurants.

"My plan was to claim to be the murderer that they insisted that they believed that I was," Sebastian said. "At that point, it seemed like the only safe choice. It seemed like the best choice."

Sitting comfortably on the couch, Sebastian looked across at the man he was thinking could order him killed in an instant. Captured on the videotape, Sebastian leaned back and started to answer Haslett's questions. His words, presented in a cold, matter-of-fact way, would soon end his freedom. It

was the confession Haslett and Shinkaruk had set out
to obtain—the confession Detective Bob Thompson
needed to make an arrest.

"Did you do this alone or is Atif there?" Haslett
asked.

"Um, Atif's like in the house but doesn't do anything," Sebastian said.

"Well, did he go see the dead bodies after?"

"Um, yeah. But I—I don't know, I mean, I don't
know about how blood clots or whatever like that, so
I don't know . . ."

"Blood on your clothes?"

Sebastian shook his head no.

"Why not?" Haslett asked.

"Because, um, they're gone," Sebastian assured him.

"Gone where?"

"They're disposed of, I guess."

"Well, where, tell me, 'cause they could have
them."

"Um, in uh, like a Dumpster downtown."

Haslett then asked what Sebastian did with the
murder weapon.

"OK, good. And whatever you used to fuckin' do
it with?" Haslett asked.

"In a Dumpster."

Sebastian was mumbling and giving clipped answers. But on video, he looked relaxed, leaning back
on the couch, taking occasional sips of his beer.

"What'd you use?" Haslett asked the teen.

"Uh, a bat," Sebastian said.

"How'd you fucking do three people at once?"

"Uh, not at once . . . it was one after the other."

"Well, how, why wouldn't somebody hear you?"

"Uh, 'cause the dad was sleeping and so was—"

Haslett interrupted, tried to get Sebastian to speak up so that the microphones would catch everything.

"Huh?" Haslett prompted him.

"They, they were asleep upstairs, the dad and the sister," Sebastian said.

"Well, what'd you, what'd, you and Atif just sit down and say let's go fucking do this to get the money?"

Sebastian shrugged. "Basically."

"Huh?"

"Basically."

Haslett asked if Atif could be trusted. Sebastian said yes without hesitation. Haslett took the opening Sebastian had just given him.

"I don't even know who he is, I gotta meet him before too long," Haslett said.

And what about his other buddy, Jimmy Miyoshi, Haslett asked. "Does Jimmy know what you guys did down there?"

"Oh, uh, yeah, he knows about that."

Sebastian assured Haslett that Jimmy wouldn't talk about any of this, that he was trustworthy and would never betray his friends.

Haslett again asked Sebastian how solid Atif was. In Haslett-speak, "solid" had a number of meanings, including trustfulness, toughness, and reliability.

"Solid, man," Sebastian assured him.

"Yeah? Where was he in the house when all this was going on, why wasn't he helping you?" Haslett asked.

"He's a little guy, he's little."

"Well, why wasn't he helping you, though?"

"What the fuck's he supposed to do?"

"I don't know, have another baseball bat or something," Haslett said. "Makes me think he's not solid. He's leaving you to do all the work. You were there, tell me what, I want to know why he wasn't there swinging a bat with you."

"Because it, it wouldn't have done any good, it was unnecessary."

On the video, Sebastian appeared to be even more comfortable now. If he was feeling fear, he was hiding it well. Haslett brought the conversation back around to motive.

"Well, both you guys woke up one day and said, 'Hey, let's go off your family and fucking get all their money'?"

"Basically," Sebastian said, laughing. "Essentially, yeah, I mean."

When Haslett asked how solid the boys' alibi was, Sebastian confirmed a theory that police had had from the beginning—that the boys snuck out of the movie theater in Factoria, drove to Bellevue, and killed the Rafay family, then cleaned up and went to Seattle to have ice cream and round out their alibi.

"You went to *The Lion King* for an alibi?" Haslett asked.

"Yeah, it was . . . We've seen the movie."

Sebastian said that after the murders were done, they drove into downtown Seattle and stopped at an all-night diner for a snack. They asked their waitress if there was a good club in the area. She gave them a suggestion of one within walking distance.

"She describes us as looking immaculate, like you know, perfectly paired," Sebastian said.

"So you cleared up and cleaned up and everything?" Haslett asked him.

"Yeah, well, yeah, like so it was like nice, nice-looking clean boys who don't invade houses."

After that, he told Haslett, they walked to the nearby nightclub, but the bouncer told them it was closed. They returned to the diner to use the restroom and then headed back to Bellevue.

"And uh, that's when we went back to the house and dialed 911."

33

"You Do It Naked"

Haslett's years of experience were paying off. He kept his cool as he kept Sebastian talking—drawing ever more incriminating details out of the unsuspecting teenager.

"So when'd you fucking, uh, do the dirty deed?" Haslett asked.

"Uh, during the movie," Sebastian said in a singsong voice.

Haslett chided Sebastian that he must remember to tell him all of the details, to leave nothing out, so that his contact could destroy all of that incriminating evidence at Bellevue police headquarters.

Sebastian had arrived at the Rafay home days before the murder. Detective Thompson had always believed that was part of the plan for the perfect murder—that it would explain why Sebastian's hairs would later be found in that downstairs shower. Remember, the killer had showered before leaving the Rafay house. Detective Thompson would soon learn that his hunch was right.

"So what's this about the shower?" Haslett asked.

"Took a shower to clean off—you know, blood and that kind of stuff—and um, yeah, I just . . . ," Sebastian said.

"And they're not going to find your clothes, 'cause they're going to . . . Is there blood on your clothes?"

"No, there wasn't; those clothes are going to be gone by now anyhow, but no, there was no blood on them."

"There was no blood on them?" Haslett asked again.

"No."

Haslett seemed perplexed. He pushed him a little.

"How do you fucking, uh, hit someone with a baseball bat, have to shower, and have no blood on you?" he asked the teen.

"You do it naked," Sebastian said.

Then Sebastian volunteered a quick correction.

"OK, actually, I just remembered one detail, sorry," Sebastian said. "Um, I had a gonch on."

A "gonch" was a Canadian term for underwear.

"And Atif was naked too?" Haslett asked.

"No, he was standing . . . he was just standing far away," Sebastian said.

"So, what'd you take your clothes off outside and walk in the house naked, in your shorts?"

"Um, no. I had clothes on outside and just undressed inside and whatever—because I didn't want to be walking around outside with no clothes on."

Haslett looked at Sebastian for a few beats. Sebastian took a swig of beer.

"I'm thinking this fucking guy has fucking planned this pretty smart," Haslett complimented the teen. "I'm still worried about little ol' fucking Atif, that he's standing back there with his clothes on while you're running around the fucking house in your fucking underwear, uh, using a baseball bat. Where was he when all this was going on?"

"Um, uh, first, just like, standing like fifteen feet away from me or something," Sebastian said.

Sebastian told Haslett that Atif watched his mother get clubbed with the baseball bat, but that he was around the corner when Sebastian killed his father.

"He didn't bother you hitting his fucking old man with a bat? Didn't bother him, I mean?" Haslett asked.

"Effectively, no," Sebastian said. "I mean, you know, he was anxious at the time or whatever, but, I mean, it didn't bug him."

"Who'd you do first?"

"Um, the mother."

"Then?"

"Then the dad and then the sister."

There was no emotion in Sebastian's voice. None. No regret. No conscience.

"Where'd you guys get the baseball bat from?" Haslett wanted to know.

"I think it was like just kicking around or something, I think," Sebastian said.

"Where, around the house down there?"

"Um, yeah."

Haslett then asked Sebastian when Jimmy Miyo-shi found out about the murders.

"He knew, um, before," Sebastian said.

"Why didn't he go help you?" Haslett asked.

"I don't know." Sebastian shrugged. "He was busy."

"Where'd you guys plan all this stuff, here or down there?"

"Um, a bit of both, I guess."

Haslett returned to the potential motive: money.

"Now all three you guys going to share the money?" he asked the teen.

Sebastian laughed. "I guess, well, whatever fucking money we get, it's like, we would invest it in our film, I guess."

Haslett asked Sebastian what Jimmy thought now that the murders had taken place.

"Well, yeah, personally, I think I'm a lot happier than, than if it didn't happen," Sebastian said. "And I'm sure he would feel that way, too."

"You're happier now, that it did happen?" Haslett clarified.

"Yeah."

"And he feels the same—yeah, well, fuck, sure, he's going to get rich. How about Atif, how does he feel?"

"Same thing."

Haslett felt it was time to give something back to Sebastian. He laid out his plan to destroy the evidence that Sebastian was worried about. He told him a foreigner he knew would go to the Bellevue police and tell them that he and a group of people were responsible for the murders. Then, Sebastian's hair in the evidence locker would be replaced by someone else's. After that a fire would be set that would destroy the lab—and eliminate all of Sebastian's concerns. The foreigner who'd "confessed" would then be whisked out of the country before he could be arrested.

But Haslett told Sebastian he needed some strands of hair from someone to use as a replacement for Sebastian's hair. He told Sebastian to take care of getting that tonight, and to make sure it was the right color.

"So did you think up this whole thing—this whole thing?" Sebastian asked.

"Doesn't matter who thought up this whole thing," Haslett said.

34

"What's the Highest IQ Possible?"

Haslett paged Shinkaruk to come pick him up. He knew Sebastian had just become his own worst enemy. As they waited, Sebastian started talking about his movie. Haslett showed a sense of humor.

"So you think you want to be an extra in a film?" Sebastian asked the crime boss.

"Extra in a film?" Haslett laughed. "Extra—I want to be the fucking star."

"Well, you're not going to be the star, but you can be an extra."

Haslett realized that he'd forgotten to ask Sebastian about an important detail.

"And the fucking, the bat, like, that bat's gotta have a lot of blood on it?" Haslett asked.

"Yeah," Sebastian said. "But it's long gone."

"How'd you wipe it off?"

"In the shower."

Like a student eager to impress his teacher, Sebastian added even more particulars.

"Oh, I'll tell you something else you should bear in mind," he told Haslett. "I also had gloves, and so there's no prints on the bat; the gloves are gone."

"With your clothes or separate?" Haslett asked.

"Everything separate."

"How many stops you make at Dumpsters?"

"I don't know—quite a few."

Haslett asked Sebastian who was driving. Sebastian didn't remember.

"How long did it take you to fucking whack these guys and get out of there?" Haslett asked.

"Maybe an hour and a half or something, I don't know," Sebastian said.

"And then you left there and went back, went to the restaurant?"

"Yup."

Haslett looked at Sebastian as if he was impressed. "And ate dessert and looked clean?"

Sebastian began to act downright cocky. He referred to his near celebrity status as a suspected murderer: "The fact that you know we're on fucking TV every day already and stuff, as it is," Sebastian said. "And, you know, the girls saying we're soooo handsome."

Haslett ignored that—and told Sebastian that he, Atif, and Jimmy might want to get out of town for a while once this fire happened in the Bellevue lab. Sebastian tried to remind Haslett of their brilliant minds.

"OK, well, we're not going to talk to any reporters or anything, OK, don't worry about that," he told the crime boss. "We're the only people, OK, who have avoided making a statement for an entire fucking year. We had press outside our house every day. We're the masters at eluding these guys, OK? We know everything about how to deal with the press."

Haslett's mind was working as they were waiting for Shinkaruk to show up—he was trying to make sure he had asked Sebastian everything they would need. He went back to the teenagers' alibi, asked if they'd planned it in advance. Sebastian said they pretty much knew where they were going that night and what would happen.

He thought of another detail he'd forgotten to ask. "Did you use a metal or a wooden bat?"

"Uh, metal," Sebastian said.

Not everything Sebastian said on the videotape was incriminating. Without using the word "fear," Sebastian still made it clear to Haslett that he considered him dangerous.

"I'd figured that you could always feel pretty confident that I would never fuck you around right from the start, because I would just assume that, you know, some guy with a gun, you blast me in the head," Sebastian said.

"No, I'm not a killer," Haslett replied.

This was the first time Haslett had ever said that to Sebastian.

"Everything, everything I do, I do for money," Haslett went on.

"Well, whatever, if I was you, OK, and, you know, some kid fucked me around, uh, he, he'd be one dead guy," Sebastian said.

Haslett told Sebastian that he shouldn't be worried. But he warned him not to do anything stupid.

"Think smart," Haslett told the teen.

"Yeah," Sebastian said. "I'm a pretty smart guy."

"What's your IQ?"

"I don't know. I don't know, man, what's the highest IQ possible?'

"Fuck, I don't know."

Around 9 P.M., Shinkaruk finally arrived, and Haslett told him to give Sebastian a ride back to his hotel. After Shinkaruk dropped Sebastian off for the night, the undercover officers met to discuss their good fortune—and their next move. They had one confession on tape, but they wanted another: Atif Rafay's.

35

The Code

The next morning, July 19, Haslett and Shinkaruk went to Sebastian's room at the Oxford Castle. They woke him up. It was about 10:40. Haslett told Sebastian to phone Atif and instruct him to catch the 1 P.M. ferry to Victoria. The officers had enough information to seek the boys' arrest, but they were hoping that Atif would verify Sebastian's confession from the day before. Neither had met Atif before—but they were counting on his following his friend's lead.

They stayed in the room, making sure Sebastian didn't warn Atif of what to expect. The call was not being monitored or recorded. Sebastian told Atif that he'd had a Rollerblading accident and needed him to come to Victoria to give him a ride. He gave him the hotel and room number. And Sebastian told Atif that he would leave a key for him at the front desk—but instead of leaving it under Atif's name, he would leave it under the name of a Star Trek character, Khan. Sebastian later told *48 Hours* that was his way of letting

Atif know that the plan was in motion—and that he should be prepared to tell Haslett a story.

Sebastian hung up, and Haslett told him to get dressed. He wanted the teen to go with Shinkaruk to collect some money for him while they were waiting on Atif. Sebastian went into the bathroom to change.

Ten years later, Sebastian would write a letter to *48 Hours* producer Jenna Jackson, telling her that while he was in the bathroom, he hurriedly wrote a note for Atif, with details of his confession.

He said the note was approximately this:

> *Trust Day*
> *{Haslett} is more paranoid of you ratting than ever.*
> *{Haslett} showed me a BPD memo with new info.*
> *Didn't know how to incorporate it, and he was mad last time for "holding out," so I dismissed whole memo.*
> *Recap—*
> *You: saw mom then larcened. You didn't use a bat cause you're little. Bkt-bvds + gloves +? violet scanner clothing? All stuff from Bellingham, all tossed in downtown Seattle separately, never find it. Bat in plastic, washed.*
> *J: knew, but no planning. Would have done himself. You and I planned before. Left during movie.*
> *Kobayashi Maru!*

Sebastian explained to Jackson that the expression "bkt-bvds" referred to "what we understood to be Detective Thompson's [Bob K Thompson] theory that we committed the crime wearing underwear." The "violet scanner clothing" referred to what the boys heard about a piece of Atif's clothing that was thought to have blood on it.

The expression "Kobayashi Maru" described their plan—it was from a scene called "The No-Win Scenario," from the movie *Star Trek II*. In his letter to Jackson, Sebastian wrote that the scene portrayed a "simulator test for officers in training, from which there is no correct way out. Atif and I had analogized our relationship to Haslett to this."

According to Sebastian's story, he folded the note and slid it down into a brown paper bag. He came out of the bathroom, and the three men headed out. They dropped Haslett at the Ocean Pointe. Sebastian and Shinkaruk continued on to Nanaimo, the second largest city on the Vancouver Island, just over an hour's drive north of Victoria.

During the drive, Shinkaruk told Sebastian that Haslett must really be starting to trust him to send him along on this job. He told the teen that they were heading to a hotel to collect some money from a person who was behind in paying the organization. The plan was that Shinkaruk would go in and collect the money while Sebastian stood guard, or "stood six," outside the door to make sure no one interrupted.

Shinkaruk would later say that Sebastian misunderstood and thought they were going up there to shoot someone. Shinkaruk corrected him, explaining he was only going to rough the guy up a little. Sebastian was excited. Shinkaruk said he seemed "very willing to participate." When they pulled up at the hotel, Shinkaruk pointed out the car that belonged to the person they'd be meeting. He knew it was the right car because it had an "Angel Acres" bumper sticker on the back. Angel Acres was a big party hosted every year by the Hell's Angels.

Sebastian stood guard at the door of the hotel room, which was slightly ajar, as Shinkaruk went inside. Sebastian watched the hallway. But in his peripheral vision, he could see what looked like Shinkaruk beating up the other guy. Shinkaruk was playacting like a good stuntman. He even scraped his knuckle during the fight, so he'd have a bloody hand to show Sebastian. Shinkaruk then grabbed the beaten man's leather jacket, which had some money stuffed in the pocket.

They headed back to Victoria, and Sebastian was in a good mood. He mentioned to Shinkaruk that Haslett now knew Sebastian's capabilities when it came to violence. They arrived back at the Ocean Pointe around 3:30. Haslett asked them how the money collection went. The videotape was rolling again.

"He had a fucking attitude," Shinkaruk told Haslett. "Plus that I fucking hurt my knuckle."

"Boo-hoo," Haslett mocked him.

"Did I tell ya, he fucking said, uh, he needed the money for something, a real fucking attitude. I told him, uh, next time it happened, I'd chop his fucking old lady's hand off. Fucking, ah, till he paid, she'd fucking sit there and bleed."

They counted out the money for Haslett—it was more than $20,000. Haslett told Sebastian to call Atif at their hotel and let him know Shinkaruk would be on his way to pick him up. Sebastian called and asked for room 213. When Atif picked up, Sebastian told him that Shinkaruk would be there in about ten minutes and to wait outside for him. He then told Atif something he would later say was vitally important.

"And can you do me a favor, can you bring— there's a little um, plastic bag there, it's a Save-On-Foods or something," Sebastian told his friend. "Um, OK, well, I think, I think there's like a brown bag there and my contacts or something in it. Hey, can you get, can you just bring it with you?"

It was the bag with Sebastian's note inside, and this was Sebastian's way of telling Atif to read the note before he came.

While they were waiting, Haslett quickly picked up where he left off the day before. He brought up Sebastian's fingerprint that the memo said investigators found on a tipped-over box in the Rafay house.

"About that print, I don't know what we can do about that," Haslett said.

"Print on the box?" Sebastian clarified.

"Yeah."

"Well . . ."

"Why is that there, though?" Haslett asked.

"Um, well, I mean like we kind of moved things around and like and whatever, and, and . . ."

"Why?"

"Well," Sebastian said, "I guess to simulate a break-in kind of thing."

Haslett asked him if they took anything from the house to make it look more like a break-in. Sebastian said they took the VCR, but buried it beneath garbage in a random Dumpster so the cops would never find it.

"Did you put it in the same Dumpster as the bat?" Haslett asked.

"No, man, all different," Sebastian assured him.

"The bat's gone, eh?"

"Yeah."

"And you say you had gloves on when you did that?"

"Yeah . . . kind of thick like garden-type gloves."

Sebastian said he thought they bought the gloves in Vancouver or Bellingham, Washington—and then said he thought they also bought the bat in Bellingham, which was different from what he'd told Haslett the day before. He said then that they found the bat at the Rafay house. Haslett either didn't pick up on the discrepancy or just didn't point it out.

He was focusing on something much more important, something that could make the case against the boys airtight—a confession from Atif Rafay.

36

"I'm Flattered by Your Attention"

Shinkaruk pulled into the Oxford Castle parking lot and spotted a short teenager with a gentle face. It was Atif.

On the drive over, Atif was very friendly. He volunteered to Shinkaruk, who he was meeting for the first time, that he hadn't had sex in a year and masturbated often. For the first time in weeks, Shinkaruk was speechless.

The two arrived back at the Ocean Pointe. They walked into room 231, which was like walking onto a movie set, although the boys didn't know it. In a nearby room, several RCMP officers, each wearing headphones, were listening and watching a television monitor that showed a wide shot of the room.

Sebastian was lounging on the couch, his head resting against the back. He was talking with Haslett about the best way computers and the Internet could help the organization, when there was a knock at the door. It was Atif and Shinkaruk.

Sebastian introduced Atif to Haslett, and the teenager sat down in the chair across from the crime boss. A coffee table separated them. Sebastian sat back down on the couch.

Haslett told Shinkaruk to leave—to have a cold beer and deal with the money he'd just collected. He said he'd page him when he needed him back. The two teens were left alone with the crime boss.

Haslett offered Atif a beer. Sebastian told him they had stout, which Atif said he was hooked on. Sebastian grabbed Atif a beer and sat back down, taking a swig of his own. Both teens seemed calm—but Atif would later say he was watching Sebastian closely, looking for silent clues as to how he should proceed.

"I don't know what Sebastian's told you about me," Haslett began.

"Um, well, when he introduced me," Atif said.

"Before that, before today."

"Um, that you're a businessman of some kind . . ."

After a little more nervous stuttering on Atif's part, he told Haslett that the suggestion from Sebastian was that Haslett's business wasn't "necessarily legitimate."

Haslett gave Atif a little speech on how they needed to be honest with each other or they wouldn't be able to work together.

"And I'm going to get you out of the trouble you're in," Haslett said.

Atif responded in a submissive, almost feminine way. "I'm flattered."

"Huh?"

"I'm flattered by your attention," Atif told the crime boss.

Haslett told Atif that he knew from reading the newspapers that the boys were in a bit of trouble.

"Yeah," Atif agreed.

"In fact you and him are so close to going to jail right now, it's fucking unreal," Haslett said, "and I know that because of different things I know and I've read—like, I don't know what Sebastian's told you."

Haslett looked at Sebastian.

"But you can tell him about the report you read yesterday," Haslett told Sebastian.

Sebastian explained to Atif that he'd read a memo from the Bellevue police the day before, and that it detailed the evidence against them. Sebastian listed all of the facts.

If Atif was surprised that Sebastian was speaking so freely about the murders in front of Haslett, he didn't show it.

"So, anyhow, as you may have gathered, uh, I've like, we talked about this, like quite a bit," Sebastian said.

"Hmm-mmm." Atif nodded in agreement.

"And, yeah, so I guess he's . . ."

Atif finished his friend's sentence. ". . . completely informed."

Haslett interrupted the conversation.

"I want to be sure he can trust you, and I fucking want to be one thousand percent positive that I can trust you," Haslett said.

"Umm-hmm," Atif said.

"Because it's pretty easy for you now to go and rat him out."

Atif didn't hesitate for a second. "That would never happen."

"Why?"

"I would never do it," Atif said.

Haslett kept pushing him. "Why?"

"Because Sebastian, well, he's my best friend, but apart from that—I guess he's so important to everything that I do that, there'd be no point in doing that, because I might as well rat myself out. I mean, I might as well, like, I'd be—I'd be fucked," Atif said.

Haslett asked Atif why he would be involved in killing his own family. Atif looked over at Sebastian, who didn't react to the question. Atif was on his own.

"Well, I guess the reason we did anything was to, I guess, set ourselves up so that we could, I guess, become richer and more prosperous and more success-ful," he explained, laughing.

"Hey, don't be embarrassed," Haslett told him. "Everything I do is for money . . . I don't give two fucks what you did with your family. My concern is, here, can you be trusted. You see what I'm saying? Can you understand what I'm saying?"

"I understand what you're saying."

Haslett next told Atif that Sebastian could be in more trouble than he because of what went on inside the house.

"What'd you do when you were in the house?"

"Stood around." he laughed. "Yanked out a VCR."

"Why didn't you fucking swing a bat?"

"I guess, uh . . ." Atif kept interrupting himself with quick air bursts of laughter. "I guess I, uh, I don't know, I just didn't have the nerve for it . . . and I guess, he was bigger and stronger—and I don't know."

"Did you see it happen?" Haslett asked.

Atif's voice got a little lower. "Yeah."

"All three?"

"No, only one."

"Which one?"

"My mom." Atif took a breath and exhaled.

"Did any of them fight?" Haslett asked.

Atif looked over at Sebastian. "Uh, um, yes."

Sebastian took over the story.

"Well, that's a story that hasn't really been told, 'cause—," Sebastian started.

Atif gently interrupted. His words throughout were mixed with soft laughter, almost an embarrassed, "aw shucks" kind of sound. "I don't think you want to tell anything about that."

"Yeah, I know that," but Sebastian continued anyway. "Well, basically, the father was really nothing—and the curious episode was the sister, who basically, yeah, was standing up and walking around and whatever . . ."

"Oh, God." Atif laughed louder now. His hand went up to his face.

Sebastian was laughing as well; it was as if the two boys were remembering a fun moment from their past.

". . . and took a little more bat work," Sebastian said.

Sebastian later said he actually said "effort," not "bat work," and that the transcriber had got it wrong. But to the ear, it sounded like "bat work." Either way, the brazen description, delivered with laughter, was disturbing. Atif later tried to explain his attitude on the tape.

"I suppose to even make a plan like that up, and to deliver those lines," Atif said, "to a certain extent, I had to essentially put the real events out of my mind entirely. So that I was really only thinking of the story that I was selling to Mr. Haslett."

If that was a performance, there was more drama to come.

37

"I Think of It as a Sacrifice"

Haslett was satisfied for the moment that Atif had sealed his fate. He turned now to the topic of the boys' other best friend, Jimmy Miyoshi.

"Jimmy's another guy," Haslett said. "What does Jimmy know all about this, what happened in the States? Tell me."

"He knows what happened and then he knows . . . that we did it and stuff, but he doesn't know any details," Atif said.

"It's the third guy we got to worry about. Sebastian guarantees me he's solid, what do you think?"

"He's solid."

Haslett said he wanted to talk to Jimmy at some point. He looked over at Sebastian and told him to go to the lobby and page Shinkaruk to come back. Sebastian looked a little uneasy but did as he was told and left the room.

Haslett looked at Atif.

"Can you see what I'm saying about trust? Eh, Atif?" Haslett asked.

Atif seemed comfortable being alone with Haslett. "I, for me, this was a big thing, because I, we didn't know that we could trust you for example, right?" Atif said.

"Don't ever worry about trusting me."

"I know that now. I know that now because Sebastian trusts you, and if Sebastian trusts you, that's cool."

Atif told Haslett that the boys expected to make more than $300,000 from the murders.

"How long were you guys planning this?" Haslett asked him.

"Not very long, actually," Atif said. "I was at the university for a year, and I came back, and right back then, it was just a little thought at the back of my head."

Atif later told *48 Hours* that he thought his life was on the line at that moment.

"Would he—would he think I was OK, or would he think that Atif's not solid, I gotta shoot him in the head?" Atif said he was thinking. "Would I pass muster or would I end up in a Dumpster?"

Haslett continued grilling Atif on the details. "When you guys left the house, how did you leave?"

"Uh, we left by a sliding door at the top of, uh, the top floor of the house."

Sebastian started impatiently knocking at the door. Haslett yelled at him to hold on a second. He wasn't done with Atif yet.

"How does it feel to kill your parents and knock off your sister?" Haslett asked.

"Pretty rotten, but it was tempered by the fact that I felt that it was necessary," Atif said matter-of-factly.

"Why?"

"It was necessary to, I guess, achieve what I wanted to achieve in this life. It was—I think of it as a sacrifice. I think of it as, I guess, a sort of injustice in the world that basically, basically forced me and Sebastian to have to do the thing."

If true, those were words from a true sociopath, someone who knew the difference between right and wrong, but didn't care.

Sebastian reentered the room, walked to the couch, and sat down, leaning back with his feet up on the other cushion.

The three men sat around and chatted a little longer while sipping their beers. When Shinkaruk knocked on the door, Haslett asked the two teens if they had any questions.

"Well, I'm a little overwhelmed, but other than that," Atif said.

"Why are you overwhelmed?" Haslett asked him.

"Well, I don't know, impressed, I, uh . . ."

"You happy?"

"Uh, moderately, yeah, I'm very happy—I'm pretty happy about your involvement, yeah," Atif said.

Shinkaruk walked back in, and the four of them had another drink and chatted about why Atif hadn't had sex in a year. Shinkaruk suggested Internet sex if he couldn't meet real girls. They talked about how to pick up women, and what the best and worst Canadian cities were for that. The two undercover officers knew that Atif's social life was about to become even more confined.

Within the hour, Haslett told Shinkaruk to give the two teens a ride back to their hotel room. It was all very friendly.

"OK, see ya guys, then," Haslett said.

"Yeah, see ya later," Sebastian called back as he left.

It was about 5:30 in the evening, and Shinkaruk drove the two boys back to the hotel built like a castle on the water. The teens were relieved that the crime boss seemed satisfied with their stories.

Haslett told *48 Hours* that he was satisfied as well.

"There's no doubt in my mind they didn't synchronize these stories," Haslett said. "These stories were told as it happened. As they knew it happened. As only they knew it could happen, because they were the only two that were there."

But the RCMP wasn't through listening. Officers gathered to hear what the boys had to say once they returned home. They wanted to make sure the confessions weren't prompted by fear. All they heard was random conversation mixed with laughter. The confessions appeared to be, as Haslett might say, solid. Project Estate was an overwhelming success.

But the RCMP wanted one more meeting—with the alleged third conspirator in the Rafay family murders, Jimmy Miyoshi.

38

"He's Just Being Clever"

Sebastian merged his car onto B.C. Provincial Highway 99 and 1A, heading toward downtown Vancouver from the North Shore. Directly in front of him was the spectacular Lions Gate Bridge, which spanned Burrard Inlet. At the center of the suspension bridge, Sebastian was driving two hundred feet above the water below. Completed one year after the Golden Gate Bridge, the Lions Gate had become a symbol of Vancouver.

Sebastian glanced out both sides of his car at the beautiful view, although his mind was in no mood for aesthetics. Sitting next to him was Jimmy Miyoshi. They were headed for the Landis Hotel in Vancouver to meet with the crime boss, Haslett.

Sebastian soon drove alongside Stanley Park, with its old-growth forest, hiking trails, and First People art. Vancouver was one of the great cities of North America, a combination of San Francisco, Seattle, and Hong Kong that could be breathtaking for a first-time visitor.

It had been one week since Sebastian and Atif had poured out the gruesome details of the murders. Some within the RCMP wanted to seek the boys' immediate arrests, nervous about the thought of having two killers living free around Vancouver. But with both boys still under surveillance—and still being listened to—officials decided to find out more about Jimmy Miyoshi's role in the murders.

At the Landis Hotel, Haslett met Sebastian and Jimmy in room 621, an apartment-styled unit with a feeling of privacy. The room was wired for sound, but there was no hidden video camera. Haslett quickly realized that Jimmy was the strong, silent type.

"Jimmy, the reason I want to talk to you is, I talked to Atif and Sebastian here over the last couple of days quite a bit—and the biggest thing I gotta be sure of is I can trust you," he told the teen.

It was Haslett's standard approach. But Jimmy wasn't taking the bait. He was very nervous about talking inside the hotel room. He answered most questions with a shake of the head. Haslett told Jimmy that he liked the fact that Jimmy hadn't ratted out Atif and Sebastian before the murders took place.

"There was nothing to rat out," Jimmy said, glancing sideways at Sebastian.

"Why? You could have ratted them out," Haslett said.

"I'm just saying that there's nothing to rat out."

Sebastian looked at Haslett. "He's just being clever."

Haslett reminded them both that this wasn't the time to be clever—he had to know he could trust them if he was going to take care of this problem.

Haslett tried again.

"Why didn't you go down to the States and help him?" he asked Jimmy.

"Pardon me?" Jimmy wasn't giving anything up.

"Why didn't you go down to the States and help them, ah?"

"That's just the way things were," Jimmy said.

Haslett told Jimmy he needed to be honest.

"Why didn't I go down to the States with them?" Jimmy said, repeating the crime boss's question.

"Yeah."

" 'Cause I didn't go down to the States with them."

"How much did you know about this ahead of time, what they were going to do?" Haslett asked.

"Pardon me?"

"How much ahead of time did you know what they were going to do?" Haslett asked again.

Jimmy looked at Sebastian like he was crazy. Sebastian laughed.

"It's OK," he told Jimmy.

"Hmm-mmm. Well, I mean, what do you want me to do?" Jimmy asked his friend.

"Well, he just, he basically just wants to know, like to confirm with you, I guess."

"Well, then you talk then. Well, then you talk for me then."

Haslett stood up and said this wasn't going to

work. Sebastian looked at Jimmy sternly. Haslett said he'd give them two minutes alone so Sebastian could explain things—and he pretended to leave the room. But Jimmy later said he could see Haslett standing just around the corner.

Sebastian turned to Jimmy, who was staring at him.

"I've explained to him, like, previously, what occurred in, in Bellevue," Sebastian said. "Like I, whatever, I mean because I guess I felt that, that was like a necessary kind of thing—and I, you know, trust [him] and like . . ."

"Well, I guess, I guess what I was getting at was like, um, kind of the opposite or whatever," Jimmy said. "Like why would that be asked, kind of thing?"

Sebastian tried to explain that he knew he could trust Jimmy with his life, but that Haslett didn't know that and wanted to hear it straight from Jimmy. Haslett came back into the room.

"Did you explain it to him?" the crime boss asked Sebastian.

"Yeah," Sebastian said.

"So how long did you know about this before it happened?" Haslett asked Jimmy.

Jimmy sighed heavily.

"Well, approximately, I mean," Haslett said.

"Um, I don't know," Jimmy said.

"Approximately, approximately, a basic estimation," Haslett said.

Jimmy finally broke.

"A month," he told Haslett.

"OK, do you know who killed the parents?" Haslett asked.

"Yeah," Jimmy said.

"Who?" Haslett asked.

"Is that what you want?" Jimmy asked.

Jimmy stalled some more—and asked Haslett to explain one more time why he needed to know this. Haslett explained, again, that it was for trust.

"OK, so, yes, I do know," Jimmy said.

"OK, so, who did it?" Haslett asked.

"Right there," Jimmy said, nodding in Sebastian's direction.

"When they came back to Canada, did they tell you right away what they did?" Haslett asked.

"Yeah," Jimmy said.

The icing was on the cake. Haslett had what he wanted.

"Jimmy was concerned about who we were and that these people [undercover officers] might have been talking to us," Haslett said. "By then it was too late."

"In some ways, was Jimmy Miyoshi the smartest of them all?" Peter Van Sant asked.

"He's not in jail," Haslett said.

Haslett told the two teens they could leave and that he'd get to work on taking care of that evidence in Bellevue.

"The wheels will be put in motion in the next couple of days, and we'll start doing what we got to do," Haslett said.

Before they walked out, Sebastian asked Haslett if he had any more questions.

"No," Haslett told the teen. "Like I said, I'm going to take care of what I gotta take care of and then you'll hear from me, ah, in the next three or four weeks."

Sebastian, Atif, and Jimmy would actually hear from Haslett much sooner than that.

Detective Bob Thompson was on vacation. Thompson and his family joined two other families for a trip to the Oregon coast. They rented a large house in Lincoln City, which boasted seven miles of sandy beaches. It was also home to the D River, which flowed from Devils Lake to the Pacific Ocean. The river was the shortest in the world, running the mighty distance of 120 feet.

Thompson had just gotten back to the house after a walk on the beach when his cell phone rang. It was Jim Dallin of the RCMP in Vancouver. Dallin was the overseer of Project Estate, and Thompson's contact. He was calling with good news: Sebastian and Atif had "given it up," he told Thompson, and they'd be arrested within twenty-four hours.

Thompson congratulated his RCMP counterpart and hung up the phone. He turned to his wife, Rebecca, who had been listening to the conversation.

"We got 'em," Thompson said. The two embraced.

"Great news! I'm so happy for you, honey," Rebecca said, knowing how the case had consumed her husband's life.

Thompson thought that it could take as long as a couple of years to get the boys extradited back to the States. On this point, he would eventually learn that his instincts had finally failed him.

PART III

THE TRIAL

39

"Good Morning, Boys"

July 31, 1995 was a beautiful summer day in Vancouver. The boys woke up typically late and were sitting around drinking coffee. Having just gotten out of bed, they were wearing wrinkled T-shirts and shorts, and their hair was uncombed. As they stared into space, they heard a knock at the door. As usual, the master of the house spoke first.

"Who is it?" Sebastian shouted. No answer. He heard people coming up the stairs outside and asked again, "Who is it?"

"It's the RCMP."

The officers poured in, separated the two boys, and cuffed them.

"You're each charged with three counts of aggravated murder in Washington State," an officer told them gruffly.

The officer was right. Charges had already been filed at the King County Superior Courthouse in Seattle.

Sebastian later said he was stunned and frightened. "I guess, in some respects, I felt like I had—I'd just died."

Looking dazed, the teens were taken from their home on Phillips Avenue in Vancouver in handcuffs and placed in the backseats of separate police cars, in front of a crowd of television cameras waiting outside.

A few minutes later, across town, Sebastian's long-time girlfriend, Sarah Isaacs, answered the phone at her parents' house. She sat down and cried.

"Did Sebastian ever tell you that he was involved with these underworld figures?" Peter Van Sant asked Sarah Isaacs.

"No. He didn't," Sarah said. "I only found out about it after he was charged."

"As his girlfriend, did you notice that suddenly—even though he didn't have a job—Sebastian had money in his pocket?"

"I didn't really notice it that much. I didn't notice him being particularly extravagant. And I assumed that Atif was getting some proceeds from his estate."

Then Sarah inadvertently helped solve something that for months had perplexed the officers involved in Project Estate: Why didn't the boys ever talk about the murders?

"Our phones were tapped—we knew—my phone was tapped, their phone was tapped," Sarah said. "We could tell."

"How could you tell?" Van Sant asked.

"There was all kinds of clicking on the line. It was really obvious."

"Did you have any rules when you got together inside a house or whenever you were on the phone, not to talk about certain things?"

"The only rule that I ever had was that we weren't supposed to say that we knew the phone was tapped," Sarah said.

Dave and Carol Burns were also shocked by the arrest of their son. Sebastian had never told them about his work with Haslett and Shinkaruk.

"We had no idea whatsoever," Carol Burns said. "I think Dave said to him, 'Keep your nose clean,' you know, that was it."

Dave Burns learned of his son's fate at 10 P.M., when an RCMP officer called him and told him that the boys had confessed and been arrested.

"I didn't sleep at all that night," Burns said sadly. "And Carol had gone to bed. I thought, Well, no point in telling her that now."

Burns paused. The memory was obviously painful.

"That was one of the most unpleasant nights I've had forever. That was really devastating."

That same day, the RCMP also tracked down Jimmy Miyoshi, who both boys said would never betray them, and arrested him. He was questioned separately. His pledge to his best friends would soon be put to the test.

Within a few days of their arrests, Sebastian again came face-to-face with the crime boss Haslett—but instead of at a swanky hotel, this time it was in the

North Vancouver RCMP station. Sebastian was in one of the interview rooms when an officer introduced him to the "crime boss" with whom he had spent so many hours—Sergeant Haslett of the RCMP.

Haslett looked directly at Sebastian, but didn't smile. Sebastian muttered something to him, and then turned his head.

"I don't recall exactly what he said. But he turned right away," Haslett remembered, "and I like to think then he just realized, Now the trouble begins."

"Did you feel like a fool at that moment?" Van Sant asked.

"Like a fool?" Sebastian said. "No."

Sebastian said that once he was arrested, he suspected the mobsters might have been undercover officers. He said he felt conned.

"I felt like I'd been subjected to a terrible injustice," Sebastian said of that moment of terrible clarity. "I mean, when I thought about all of the implicit threats that these guys have used, and the inducements, and the general unfairness of the entire situation, in getting me to say something that I didn't do. I felt like I'd been victimized by an unconscionable police method, which should not be allowable by law—which, in the United States, is not allowable by law."

Haslett and Shinkaruk were certain their undercover operation had netted the two *real* killers of the Rafay family. But this case was far from over. Within a month of their arrest, the King County Prosecutor's Office in Seattle filed extradition papers, asking the

British Columbia government to send Atif and Sebastian back to the U.S. to stand trial for the murders of the Rafay family.

The teens' Canadian attorneys immediately opposed the request, arguing that if the boys were convicted in Washington State, they would face the death penalty, which was abolished in Canada in 1976.

The extradition fight, which began in the summer of 1995, lasted for *nine years,* during which Sebastian and Atif consistently proclaimed their innocence.

"This has certainly ruined my life," Sebastian said. "I think about a lot of things. I think about my hopes for the future trial."

During his first year in confinement, Sarah Isaacs still considered herself to be Sebastian's girlfriend. She regularly visited him. After that, she moved on with her life, while still keeping in contact with her high school sweetheart.

While angry at their confinement, the boys knew what awaited them in the States. U.S. jails were notoriously dangerous. In Canada, Sebastian and Atif were housed in cabins instead of jail cells, where weekly family visits were allowed. Sebastian was even allowed privacy for conjugal visits.

Four years into their extradition fight, the boys were assigned American attorneys to begin preparing for a possible trial.

The Burns family decided it could not afford the hundreds of thousands of dollars it would take to hire a private defense attorney for what was expected to be a long trial. And Atif didn't have access to his parents' estate. So both boys were assigned attorneys from public defender agencies in Seattle.

Sebastian got a real firebrand as his attorney—Theresa Olson, considered one of the most eccentric and talented defense lawyers in Seattle.

Olson immediately traveled to Vancouver to meet with Sebastian. She filed a discovery motion, seeking all the transcripts of Project Estate. Once she reviewed the files, she became passionate in her belief in Sebastian's innocence.

Olson is a forcefully intelligent woman in her early forties. Her face isn't intimidating, but her hair is. It is a curly eruption of red that looks like it hasn't been brushed in years. It enters a room before she does. Her hair is as dominating as her personality: frazzled, yet purposeful. You can't keep your eyes off her.

Olson's wardrobe is created by her favorite designer—herself. After taking a sewing class one summer, she started making her own clothes, and always has some outrageous piece of clothing to top off her outfit, even in court. Olson especially loves the black-and-white cow print, having made herself cow slippers, a cow hat, and a cow coat. Her unconventional appearance sometimes belies her brilliance—and she was tirelessly dedicated to the boys.

Consulting with other attorneys on the defense team, Olson developed a strategy. The biggest point of attack for the defense team would be the confessions captured on videotape by the RCMP. *48 Hours* asked Sergeant Haslett about accusations raised by Olson that the confessions were coerced.

"Sergeant Haslett, you are with the best under-cover team in Canada and perhaps the finest un-dercover team in the world," Van Sant said. "Why shouldn't people believe that you, as a master ma-nipulator, simply manipulated two teenage boys to confess to a crime that they didn't commit?"

"Well, truth speaks for itself," Haslett said. "There's no way a confession like that is manipulated or programmed or rehearsed. Those were solid, strong confessions that only the individuals that were respon-sible for that murder would be able to sit down and tell it like it was."

But Olson knew the history of the Mr. Big scenar-ios, including that case in Rossburn, Manitoba, where a confession was later ruled unreliable.

The judge in that case wrote that while he recog-nized that police officers sometimes had to "resort to tactics which some may describe as unfair or dirty," they should also be aware that "as the level of induce-ment increases, the risk of receiving a confession to an offence which one did not commit increases—and the reliability of the confession diminishes correspond-ingly."

Olson was convinced that Mr. Big went too far with Sebastian and Atif as well, and she looked for-ward to confronting Sergeant Haslett in court.

40

The Fight Begins

Sergeant Haslett was proud of his team's professionalism and reliability.

"If these investigations are handled correctly, are monitored correctly, and the right people are doing them, these confessions are not false confessions," Haslett said emphatically. "We take great care to be sure we are not getting false confessions. And I am confident that we have never, ever received a confession, and taken it to our courts, which was false."

That included the case in Rossburn. In regard to Project Estate and the chilling videotaped confessions he got from Sebastian Burns and Atif Rafay, Haslett was unwavering.

"The truth speaks for itself. And that's it. You can't get away from that," he said. "If they were making this up, it would have been obvious to us in some way. We are confident they weren't."

Even Sebastian admitted that the way he and Atif appeared on those videotapes—relaxed, arrogant, laughing over three brutal murders—was devastating.

"When people don't know how much inducement and coercion was involved in this, when people don't know that I'd been with these guys for three months and that I had started out by telling them, though, that I was innocent. And they told me they didn't believe I was innocent. And that the only reason I was safe and why they trusted me was because they thought I was guilty. When people don't know that, then I suppose it is startling," Sebastian conceded.

But he maintained that the story was a lie, and his nonchalant attitude an act. Sebastian claimed his performance was the only way to be safe from the mobsters.

"And it wasn't overnight that we made the decision to just go along with it—and that I made the decision, just go along with it," he said. "It was after a good eighty or ninety days before finally, I just gave in and said what they wanted me to say."

Van Sant pushed Sebastian.

"Sebastian, aren't we looking at you on this videotape?" Van Sant asked. "The real—"

"No," Sebastian interrupted him.

"—Sebastian Burns, the person who planned this murder, killed these people, and has no conscience to the point where you can laugh about it?"

"No, that's completely wrong," Sebastian said. "No, you are never seeing the real me on any of these tapes, in my opinion."

After watching the videotapes, the people who knew Sebastian the best, his family, said they became even more convinced of his innocence.

"I saw Sebastian," said his sister, Tiffany. "He was just sitting around trying to be cool in a very bad situation, trying to bluff his way through some ridiculous type of undercover, mafioso-type setup where he's petrified that those guys are going to kill him. Or they're going to kill me or my parents."

And the nature of the Project Estate operation gave Sebastian and Atif's defense teams plenty of ammunition to say that the two teens were just playing along in this elaborate scheme.

There were a handful of statements made by the two teens to the mobsters that did not match evidence at the crime scene. And despite what the fake police memo indicated to Sebastian, the Bellevue police had no slam-dunk physical evidence linking the boys to the murders. The hair found on Tariq's bed was not Sebastian's—or any other member of the Rafay family's; its orgin remained unknown. And the discovery of Sebastian's hairs in the shower could be explained away by the fact that he was staying in the home for five days before the murders and had taken many showers.

There were also a couple of inconsistencies between Sebastian's and Atif's confessions, which their attorneys would say indicated they were making up a story to appease the crime boss—and that they hadn't gotten the story exactly straight. Sebastian told Haslett that they threw their clothes in Dumpsters in downtown Seattle, while Atif said they "hucked them out the window." Sebastian said they found the bat in the Rafays' home, while Atif said he and Sebastian bought it together at a store in Bellingham.

The two teens said the inconsistencies proved that they were lying. They said that in between the June 28 and July 18, 1995 scenarios with the make-believe mobsters, they devised a plan to tell Haslett what he wanted to hear. Sebastian said that Haslett assumed them to be killers from day one—and that he feared he and Atif would be killed if they didn't prove they were trustworthy by admitting to be killers. So they combed through newspaper accounts—and used their own memories of what they saw the night they discovered the bodies, in addition to what police had told them during interviews—and concocted a convincing story. The reason there were inconsistent details, the teens said, was because they had only a few conversations about it and just hadn't covered every base.

There were also several inconsistencies between the boys' chilling confessions and the crime scene. A prosecution expert would later say that no fewer than three people killed Tariq Rafay. But Sebastian and Atif both said in their videotaped statements that Sebastian was the only one involved in the killing of Atif's father.

The medical examiner would later say that wounds found on the victims were caused by a second weapon, something sharp. Neither boy mentioned a second weapon in his confession to the mobsters.

One of their alibis would also become crucial. Sebastian told Haslett that they killed the Rafays after they snuck out of a showing of *The Lion King*. Witnesses placed the boys at the movie theater until at least five or ten minutes after 10 P.M. But the neighbors on either side of the Rafay home initially told police that they heard pounding noises between 9:45 and 10:15—definitely not past 10:15 P.M. That would mean the teens were still at the movie theater when neighbors heard the Rafays being killed.

Sebastian told Haslett that he wore gloves during the attacks—he said he told the crime boss this so Haslett wouldn't worry that he'd left fingerprints behind. But the state's expert who looked at the crime scene says the murderers were not wearing gloves, as smudges consistent with glove marks were not found.

And one of the boys' biggest arguments would become that their so-called confessions didn't contain information that only the killers would know. They said that everything they told the undercover officers was information they could have gleaned from newspaper accounts, what they saw at the scene, or what detectives told them.

The legal machine continued churning ahead against the two boys, but it moved much more slowly than anyone could have anticipated. The extradition battle waged on for years. The two teenagers grew into men in a Canadian jail.

The fight finally reached the Canadian Supreme Court, and the Court ruled on February 15, 2001, that the boys could not be taken back to the United States unless the U.S. agreed it would not pursue the death penalty.

Prosecutors in Seattle had no choice but to agree to take the death penalty off the table. If the two teens were convicted in a Washington State court, they would face life in prison, without the possibility of parole.

And on March 29, 2001, Sebastian Burns and Atif Rafay—now twenty-five years old—were finally brought back to Seattle, escorted before a sea of television and newspaper cameras and reporters, and booked into the King County Jail.

41

A Defense Begins

Once the teens were back in Seattle, the system began to move. Lawyers on both defense teams realized that the most damaging evidence they had to overcome were Sebastian and Atif's own words.

Theresa Olson worked tirelessly for Sebastian's cause—and she became a fixture on local media, expressing her belief that the two teens had been falsely accused and imprisoned. She rifled through every crime scene picture, looking for more inconsistencies. She became as much an investigator as she was a lawyer—and she was determined that by the time she was finished, the boys would be acquitted.

Olson might have been supremely confident, but Atif's lawyers were not. They tried to convince Atif to testify against Sebastian in exchange for a plea deal. Atif rejected the idea.

In April 2001, shortly after Sebastian and Atif were brought back to Seattle and booked into the county jail, *48 Hours* producer Jenna Jackson called

Theresa Olson. It began a journalist-source relationship that lasted for several years, and grew to include Sebastian Burns himself.

Jackson traveled to Seattle to meet with Olson. Jackson had built a reputation as someone who could land big interviews. It was a high compliment in television news—a person whose charm and professionalism could secure exclusive access to a source that scores of other journalists were pursuing.

It was a chilly Seattle day in April as Jackson walked from her hotel to a tall, imposing building on Third Avenue. She took the elevator up to the eighth floor, and through a glass window told the receptionist who she was there to see.

The public defender's office was a secured area. Attorneys there dealt with some of the worst crimes—and defendants—in King County. They could never be too careful.

The receptionist spoke to Olson on the phone, and then directed Jackson to her office. The suite of offices was decorated in dark leather and hardwood. Jackson pulled open a heavy door and walked up some stairs that resembled an old fire escape. As she rounded the corner, she stepped into an entirely different world— the world of Theresa Olson.

Olson called out from the top of the stairs, "Keep coming." Jackson reached the top of the stairs and saw a large closet on her right, which she'd shortly find out was filled with Olson's sewing projects, many of them made out of her favorite black-and-white cow print. She got to the door and looked inside at a large room that must have once been some sort of attic. With windows on two sides, it had great views of the Seattle Mariners' ballpark and much of downtown Seattle.

Olson's office was a lot like her hair. It looked like it had just been hit by some kind of explosion. Files, videos, and pictures were scattered on the floor, her desk, and shelves. The mess represented the last seven years of Sebastian Burns's and Atif Rafay's lives.

The two women greeted each other. Olson noticed Jackson's signature dark-rimmed glasses. Jackson noticed Olson's hair. They immediately hit it off.

In the far corner of the room was another desk with a dark-haired, good-looking man sitting behind it: a former model, and now Olson's colleague, Mark. He wasn't involved with the Rafay/Burns trial, but he knew all the details—Olson was not shy about her views on this case. Her entire life, and her hyperactive energy, were now focused on saving these two boys' lives.

After an agreement was struck that no interviews would be broadcast until after the trial was over—and that everything was off the record until that time—Olson excitedly began to tell Jackson snippets of her defense strategy. She played portions of the video-taped confessions, and pointed out moments where she believed coercion was taking place. This was the first glimpse Jackson had gotten of these videos, so it was difficult to get past the boastful, laughing confessions and see the underlying tactics being used.

Olson suggested they walk to get a milk shake at a local coffee shop. While they walked, Olson explained that for their relationship to continue, it would take a lot of people signing off on it—her bosses, for one, and Sebastian. He was very intelligent and had clear opinions about how he wanted the case run, she told the producer. The key, Olson said, would be getting him to trust Jackson.

It took two months of back-and-forth negotiating to get Olson's bosses to sign off on an agreement that would let *48 Hours* follow Sebastian Burns's case in detail. Now came the moment Jackson had been working toward—she would get to meet Sebastian for the first time.

42

Meeting Sebastian

On her return flight to Seattle from her home in Houston, Jenna Jackson looked out her window as the 737 began its final approach. Below her, a ferryboat was pulling into the dock at Vashon Island. Looking up, she saw the snowcapped Olympic Mountains in the distance. Ninety minutes later, she and Theresa Olson were entering the King County Jail, where Seattle's most notorious best friends were being held.

They were checked through two security points. Soon, they passed through a heavy steel door, which slammed shut behind them. Jackson shuddered at the sound. She often got that feeling in jails—a sensation that she was a prisoner, too. Jackson couldn't imagine not being able to walk out at the end of the day.

Eventually, Jackson and Olson were seated in a tiny concrete room. Jackson didn't know what to expect. Sebastian had already spent seven years behind bars, awaiting trial. She knew he hated the news media.

Sebastian was led inside. Jackson introduced herself. She shook his hand, which was cold. He looks pale, she thought. He was tall, still good-looking, and charismatic, although toned down from his teenage years. His sandy brown hair was curly, just like in the pictures Jackson had seen, and he still spoke in a formal manner. Jackson noticed that he occasionally smirked and had a discomforting way of staring intensely while waiting for an answer.

The three talked. Sebastian seemed quite intelligent, and said he was a voracious reader. He was definitely different from the inmates Jackson was accustomed to interviewing. He still had a hint of the arrogance you could hear during the RCMP scenarios, but that youthful confidence had given way to insecurity over the years. He still had a need to control what he could, probably prompted, at least in part, by the fact that he'd been sitting in jail for seven years.

The more they talked, the more comfortable Sebastian became. His questions started to veer into the personal realm, and Jackson felt it was only fair to answer most of them. What kind of books did she read, where did she go to school, what were her religious beliefs, was she married? Jackson sensed some trust beginning to build.

Sebastian used detailed knowledge of obscure things to make Jackson feel uncomfortable and inadequate during these early conversations. He was testing her, and she knew it. He could be extremely warm and charming—and, in an instant, the emotion could completely go from his face if he heard an answer he didn't like.

Sebastian was extremely curious about life on the outside especially popular culture in the United States. He was constantly asking questions about politics and celebrities. Jackson sent him magazines such as *Newsweek* and *Time*—and *People,* which he seemed almost embarrassed to read, but also mesmerized by.

In July 2001, after dozens of intense meetings, Sebastian gave Jackson some great news—he agreed to be interviewed and to let *48 Hours* follow his case. He and his lawyers were now spending hours together putting together their defense. The trial was set for less than a year away—May 2002.

Olson worked doggedly on the case. In nearly sixteen years as a lawyer, she had developed a reputation as an obsessive advocate who would do almost anything to win a case.

In August, she finally got a copy of the 911 call to police made by Sebastian on the night of the murders. She also got copies of both boys' statements to the police in the days after the murders happened. "They are good for us," she e-mailed Jackson.

Theresa Olson's obsession with the Rafay murder investigation was uncovering some fascinating details. She told Jenna Jackson that Tariq's wallet was not found at the scene, and that no one knew what had become of it. She assumed that the killers stole it, but said the police never checked to see if his credit cards or ID had been used. She started the process of subpoenaing Tariq's bank records, going back six years, to see if she could learn more.

She also talked about fingerprints found in the Rafays' home that were never identified by police. After she pushed the issue, she said, the prints were run through the national fingerprint identification system, NCIC—and one fingerprint was matched to a man with a criminal record. She wouldn't give more details at that point, because she and her team were digging deeper into the lead.

In October 2001, she put together a memo for Jackson that laid out the crux of the defense case— that when the neighbors on either side of the Rafay home heard the murders happening, Sebastian and Atif were at the movies. "I have prepared a memo which will outline some of the expected testimony from witnesses in this case who support our strong belief that the murder happened at a time when the boys had an unimpeachable alibi," Olson wrote.

She laid out the time line of the night the murders took place:

8:30—According to the boys, they leave the house.
Shortly after 8:30—Neighbors see Tariq and Basma leave in car. Nobody knows where they went and/or how long they were gone.
8:45—Boys arrive at Keg (verified by independent witnesses).

9:30—Boys leave Keg (they are there the whole time and do not leave; verified by independent witnesses).

9:50—By that time, boys have purchased tickets to movie and are there until 10:15 or so (verified by independent witnesses). The witnesses say their hair is not wet, they are not acting weird or like they just got done killing three people.

8:50 to 10:30—When the only weird noises are heard in the neighborhood that night. Amazingly, by the people who live on either side of the Rafays. I cannot believe that if these people got killed after 10 and before 11:45 that nobody would have heard anything.

Olson revealed another piece of information that could help set the time of the murders as a time when the boys had a clear alibi. She said there was only one reason that Sultana would have been in the basement that night: "There is no other explanation for why she is in the basement, facing Mecca, with her glasses off, other than to pray. And, she had to do this before sundown. This firms up a finding that the murder happened before 10:00."

Olson also found a neighbor who remembered Marc Sidell calling his cat that night. The man said that his Chihuahua started barking, which was very unusual. His memory of when it happened was the same as Sidell's, bolstering the boys' alibi.

Olson e-mailed Jackson, laying out her main

arguments. The case was set to begin in just a few months.

"My closing argument theme is 'The evidence is the clearest is that which is the simplest—the evidence is the simplest is that which is the truth.' (I am crying when I say this.) It is so true here. Why they refused to see that is beyond me."

Olson now believed that she could overcome those videotaped confessions and leave a jury with enough reasonable doubt for an acquittal.

43

"The Role of Second Fiddle"

Although Jackson had met with Sebastian numerous times at this point, she had not met with Atif—his lawyers wouldn't yet allow it. But they had exchanged a couple of letters. He was very polite and proper in these letters—and indicated he knew she was meeting extensively with Sebastian. Atif said whether or not he granted an interview would largely be up to his best friend.

Atif had grown unhappy with his attorneys. He claimed they had lied to him, saying that Sebastian had agreed to testify against him. He asked the judge for new representation, but the request was turned down. Atif then threatened to represent himself at trial. Eventually, the judge reconsidered and granted Atif's request for new lawyers. The trial was delayed an additional two months.

While all of this was going on, Atif at one point agreed to meet Jackson. "He is very sweet, and you will adore him," Olson wrote Jackson. "He is so small." But that meeting didn't materialize until months later.

As everyone readied for trial, the boys' old friend Jimmy Miyoshi became a key figure in the case. After his arrest in July 1995, Jimmy was given an ultimatum: Either he cooperated with authorities, or he would be charged with conspiracy to commit murder—and would be jailed along with his two best friends.

After initially denying he knew anything about the murders, Jimmy eventually accepted an immunity deal that would allow him to go free if he gave a statement implicating Sebastian and Atif. He gave the RCMP officers a detailed statement. The man who said he would never betray his two best friends had done just that—but Sebastian and Atif wouldn't learn of his betrayal for years.

After striking his deal, Jimmy went on to go finish college—which he'd begun with Sebastian the semester before the murders—at the University of Western Ontario. He got his bachelor of arts degree in business administration—then basically disappeared.

During a hearing in March 2002, prosecutors told the judge they hadn't been able to locate Jimmy. Theresa Olson was angry but not surprised. She e-mailed Jenna Jackson that the prosecutors were saying Jimmy likely didn't want to testify. "They claim it is because the boys have threatened him," she wrote.

"I think they do not want to find him so they can say he is 'unavailable' and get his extradition transcript in. They know we would eat him alive. I think he knows that, too, and that is why he is hiding."

Prosecutors said they thought Jimmy might be in Japan, where his family originated, and they would try to subpoena him.

Olson asked her investigator to locate Jimmy. They got a lead that he might be in Tokyo. Unable to find a phone number for him, the two decided to hop on a plane to Japan to track him down in person.

As soon as she arrived back in Seattle, Olson wrote of her adventure to Jackson. She was elated. "Let me begin by—oh my god! This is a long story, be ready."

When Olson and her investigator had arrived in Tokyo, they had an address where they thought Jimmy might be. Language was a big problem. "Nobody can find it on the maps, they just circle a general area," she e-mailed. "We take off. At 7 a.m., it is 85 percent, 1 million percent humidity."

They walked for a couple of minutes—and saw his apartment building right across the sky bridge from the Westin Hotel, where they were staying. "We check it out and figure out how many people live there and how many entrances (1)." They staked out the building, by sitting on the Westin side of the sky bridge and watching the entrance. After about an hour and a half, they saw him walk out. They decided not to talk to him that first day—and, instead, watched through the window of a room at the Westin that faced his apartment building . . . "binoculars, smoking, the whole deal."

Olson said she wrote him a letter—and included with it letters from Sebastian and Atif so that Jimmy would know she was legitimate. They waited the entire afternoon for him, with no luck.

The next morning, they started again at 7. And again at around 8:20, he walked out, in a white shirt, tie, and dark pants.

"I jet down the sky bridge," Olson wrote of what happened next. "My heart is racing, this is a key moment in the case, in my life! I turn the corner as he gets there.

"Theresa: 'Jimmy?'

"Guy in white shirt: 'yes.' (I'm in heaven now.)

"Theresa: 'Hi, I'm Theresa Olson, and I am one of Seb's American lawyers. I came to Tokyo to talk to you.'"

Jimmy looked scared, she said, but took the letters and said he would probably call.

"[The investigator] and I are stoked," Olson wrote. "Even if we do not hear from him again (which we did not expect to do), we had found him. He was not 'unavailable' like the State said."

They headed back to the hotel room—and two hours later, the phone rang. "Hi, Theresa, it's Jimmy. I would like to meet with you today, at lunch." While they were waiting for him to arrive in the lobby, he called back to say he had to delay the meeting to that night at 8. Jimmy and his wife showed up at the hotel just after 8 P.M.

"We go into the bar and had one of the most interesting meetings I have had," Olson wrote. "I really felt like he was testing me. He told me he wanted to hear what I had to tell him, so I went into all of the evidence of innocence etc. . . . he watches his words very carefully."

They met for about an hour and a half, and Jimmy left. The next morning, they were in Olson's room working when the phone rang. "Between 10 and 11 (now called the 'Jimmy hour'), he calls. He wants to see me again, and he wants to see the immunity agreement [that he signed with the RCMP in 1995]."

They took a cab to the Tokyo Tower and waited for Jimmy to arrive. Once he did, Olson showed him the immunity agreement he'd signed. She said she also showed him a letter that the RCMP officers got from Canadian prosecutors, before he gave his deposition against Sebastian and Atif. The letter said that the prosecutors in Canada did not feel they had enough evidence to charge Jimmy with conspiracy.

Jimmy told Olson that he had been talking to the prosecutors in the last few days—that they had finally convinced his mother to tell them where he was living. They told him they had a solid case against his two former best friends—but that as icing on the cake, they needed him to come give a deposition that they would be able to admit into evidence. They weren't sure his earlier deposition would be allowed in front of the jury, because the Canadian defense lawyers at the time hadn't been given much opportunity to cross-examine him.

"He then told me that he had been led to believe that the government had such a strong case that, no matter what he did, they were going down," Olson wrote. "So, the fact that he saved himself by getting immunity did not change the boys' fate. But now he realizes that it was different."

Jimmy told Olson that under Japanese law, he didn't think that the prosecutors could force him to come to the United States to give a deposition. "He wanted me to know that he would tell the State that he would not cooperate, and he wanted me to know that he hopes the judge rules his deposition cannot be used," she wrote. "He is on our side!!!

"You can tell his conscience is there, and he does not want them to be convicted of something they did not do—and he knows that if he does not testify and his deposition does not get used, that is the best way to make that happen."

They headed back to the United States the next day, and when she arrived back at her office on Friday, August 9, Olson had a message from the judge's bailiff. Jimmy had called the judge—and was expected to call in for a hearing that next Wednesday.

"Can you believe it!!!" she wrote. "This little red head has managed to get to him and talk to him. This hearing is going to be wild. There is so much more."

Olson was ecstatic at their big break—she had

managed to locate a key witness who, up until now, had been missing. And she was hopeful his testimony might help Sebastian and Atif, rather than condemn them. She couldn't wait to tell Sebastian all of the details about her Tokyo trip. On the morning of Saturday, August 10, 2002, she went to the jail to visit Sebastian. What happened next turned the case—the entire trial—upside down.

44

A Shocking Delay

Theresa Olson had just flown twelve hours nonstop back to Seattle. Instead of heading for home to sleep, Olson headed straight to the King County Jail. She was bursting with excitement as she made her way through the security checkpoints and into a small meeting room, where she was left alone with Sebastian.

But according to several witnesses, what started out as a conversational encounter quickly turned conjugal.

Back home in Houston, Jenna Jackson got a late-night phone call from one of Atif's former lawyers. The news was stunning: Guards at the jail announced that they had caught Theresa Olson and Sebastian Burns having sex in the visitation room. They revealed very few details, as the judge ordered most of the records sealed.

Here is what they did release in one redacted report from a jail sergeant.

"Officer {blank} looked into the room and said, 'They're still doing it Sarge.' I looked through the window and observed Ms. Theresa Olson and inmate Burns holding each other. Ms. Olson was standing facing the door {blank, for the next four lines} . . . I said to Ms. Olson 'What's going on!' . . . She said 'I was giving him a hug and it got a little out of hand.'"

A few details emerged from other jail staffers' reports.

"I could see Ms. Olson facing the window in the door of the side interview room {blank, two lines} and I could see that inmate Burns was {blank, several words}."

"When we were on the upper tier . . . I was able to see Ms. Olson facing the window {blank, one line} and inmate Burns {blank, several words}."

"As Officer {blank} opened the conference room door, I observed the dress which was worn by Theresa Olson {blank, several words}."

"{An officer} observed both inmate Burns and Ms. Olson {blank, maybe five words}. As Sgt. {blank} entered the room, both proceeded to cover themselves."

Olson immediately and publicly denied that they were having sex. She sent Jackson an e-mail two days after the incident.

"Jenna—if you watch the news, I am sure you will see what has happened in the case. I am no longer defending Seb."

In future e-mails throughout the week, she maintained that the accusations were untrue. "This is very tough," she wrote. "I am glad I have a great husband and friends. It is hard to believe that I went from case savior to pervert adulteress in one day. It is great to see the people who are rallying around me and who are helping me.

"I am about to watch the late news and hear how I supposedly had sex with Seb. [My husband] is watching it with me. It is almost funny because it is so ridiculous, but it is going to change my life—and end my ability to defend Seb."

Olson didn't want to discuss it on e-mail, but she wrote that "the summary is that what 'they' say happened did not."

The incident garnered huge headlines in Seattle and Vancouver. And if Theresa Olson wasn't humiliated enough, her jailhouse romance even ended up becoming a joke on the *Tonight Show with Jay Leno*.

"And a female lawyer in Seattle is in trouble for having sex with her client who is a murderer," Leno said to the audience. "How creepy is that?"

He paused with that smirk on his face.

"Hot sex with a lawyer. Ooooh."

It was hilarious to everyone except those who still supported Sebastian Burns. Theresa Olson was immediately suspended from her job while the matter was investigated. She was removed from the case. This was a huge blow to the boys. Olson had spent years preparing for trial.

It would take nearly three years for Olson's disciplinary case to be formally decided by the State Supreme Court. Her law license was suspended for two years. During her hearing, Olson admitted that she had developed romantic feelings for Sebastian. She said that she enjoyed the passionate hug he gave her that morning—and that she should have resisted.

But she continued to deny having sex with him and said she did not know he had dropped his pants. Her unplanned, unprofessional visit was devastating to the defense. No one knew Sebastian better or had a better command of the evidence. In many ways, she was irreplaceable.

45

The Dream Team

While the judge searched for new attorneys from the private sector who were willing to take on the mammoth case, the trial was delayed. But it didn't take long for a team of new attorneys to sign on to defend Sebastian—convinced, in part, by Theresa Olson, who was an old friend and fellow attorney.

Sebastian's new dream team was made up of a team of Ivy League graduates: Jeffrey Robinson, Song Richardson, and Amanda Lee, from the prestigious Seattle firm Schroeter Goldmark & Bender.

Robinson, forty-six, led the team. An African-American who was considered one of the top defense attorneys in the state of Washington, he once represented a State Supreme Court justice who had been arrested for drunk driving.

Robinson was raised in Memphis. As a boy in 1968, he was inspired by the lawyers who came to town to represent blacks who had been arrested during a Martin Luther King march. He realized then that he wanted to be a lawyer when he grew up. His hard work earned him entry into Harvard Law School.

Robinson is handsome. His fashion sense is impeccable. His suits are understated yet elegant, much like his personality. Robinson wears an earring. On the wall of his office, he has a framed poster of Underdog, a cartoon hero from the 1970s—and an appropriate metaphor for his client, who was about to go into trial having confessed on videotape to the Rafay family murders.

Co–defense counsel Song Richardson is young and beautiful. She has shoulder-length black hair, which she wears in ringlets, parted to the side. Brown-skinned and exotic-looking, Richardson commands attention wherever she goes, including the courtroom.

Richardson also attended Harvard. She received her law degree from Yale. After graduation, Richardson went to work for the Racial Disparity Project, which provided legal help to low-income defendants.

Robinson and Richardson reviewed Theresa Olson's case file and also met with Sebastian Burns. They became so convinced of his innocence, they agreed with King County to be paid at public defender rates, far below their usual fees.

While Jeff Robinson's courtroom style was understated, Song Richardson wore her passion on her sleeve. When not practicing law, Richardson focused her attention on the violin, where her skills were so highly regarded, she could have been a classical concert violinist.

The third member of the defense team, Amanda

Lee, was described by her colleagues as the brains behind the operation. Amanda has light skin and long, curly brown hair that frames a pretty face that can quickly become intense when discussing this case.

Lee rarely argued in court during this case, but she was responsible for writing many of the motions submitted by her cocounsels. She was quiet, a thinker— and a vital force behind Sebastian's new legal team.

Judge Charles Mertel set the date for an important hearing, one that could decide the fate of this case, set for less than a year away—a very fast turnaround time—and the attorneys buried themselves in the thousands of files that made up the case. The hearing was in response to a defense motion asking the judge to throw out the entire undercover investigation.

Just after he was assigned new attorneys, Sebastian wrote Jenna Jackson another letter. It was filled with overly formal, British boarding school kind of language. "I am certain, barring any crisis with my personal health, that I shall be speaking with you at some point; however, in these uneasy times, I am unable to specify when," he wrote. "My hands, regrettably, if not literally at this precise moment, are tied."

He told Jackson that he'd understand if she no longer wanted to send him books to read while in jail. Over the many months, he had made several requests for dictionaries or works of Shakespeare. He also told her that he needed to get her e-mail address again; he sometimes had friends or family members send her an e-mail, rather than taking the time to send a letter.

"It has been a pleasure knowing you and I am eager to meet with you again as soon as possible," Sebastian wrote. "But as I'm sure you know, in my predicament the vivisection of the word 'soon' is a feat at the complete mercy of a villainous clock, who with all the bitterness of age had felt unobliged to hold his arms with any particular rectitude since my arrival at this side of the looking glass."

Jury selection was set to begin in mid-October 2003, and opening statements were slated for November 17.

Going up against Sebastian's new dream team were two of King County's most gifted prosecutors. James Jude Konat is a charismatic presence in the courtroom. Handsome and articulate, with a wardrobe torn from the pages of *GQ* magazine, Konat could easily star in a TV drama. He has medium-length dark brown hair, which is perfectly combed straight back. He is tall, lean, and athletic, averaging about twenty-five miles a week in jogs along the shores of Lake Washington. Despite Seattle's famous gray skies, Konat always looks tan.

Konat grew up in Omaha and Grand Island, Nebraska, one of eleven children. His father was a dentist and his mom a nurse. He rolled his eyes a bit when asked if his Midwest upbringing imprinted him with stereotypical Midwestern values. But it did.

"What I love about being a prosecutor is that truth is always on our side," Konat said in a Boy Scout manner. "It's always on our side."

Konat was used to hard work. As a young man, he worked as a railroad "gandy dancer," repairing rails and ties in sweltering Nebraska summers.

"It was a thankless existence," Konat said.

Preparing for trial, Konat smiled when he thought about the strength of his case—those videotaped confessions.

"The worst thing you can do is talk to the cops," Konat said. "There's a reason it's the worst thing you can do: because it uncovers the truth."

Konat believed that Sebastian Burns would have to take the stand at some point during the trial.

"I think he'll have to explain why he bragged and admitted to the murders to an undercover officer and his best friend, Jimmy Miyoshi," Konat said confidently.

And if Sebastian did take the stand, he would open himself up to cross-examination by the prosecutors.

"We would relish the chance," Konat said, nearly salivating.

Working alongside Konat would be his most trusted colleague, Roger Davidheiser.

Davidheiser is the opposite of Konat in almost every way—he is slightly bulkier, blond, with light, Irish skin. He is quiet and blushes easily, particularly when he gets angry. He methodically prepared all of their motions. Where Konat had the dramatic presence in the courtroom, Davidheiser supplied the ammunition. And where Konat could sometimes ruffle feathers, Davidheiser smoothed them. They made a formidable team.

Konat began working with the RCMP officers to get them ready for trial. Because procedures were so different in the United States than in Canada, he ended up spending a lot of time making sure Sergeant Haslett and Corporal Shinkaruk knew what to expect on the stand. Through all of the preparations, he ended up getting to be their friend and occasional drinking buddy—these three men, especially, were determined to get a conviction.

Despite the fact that RCMP officers never spoke to the press in Canada, Konat managed to convince them to at least meet with the *48 Hours* team. The producers and correspondent met the two officers for the first time in downtown Seattle; they were headed to a baseball game that evening and agreed to meet at a sports bar before the game for a drink.

The television team could immediately see how convincing the two men must be at their roles as mobsters. They shook their hands without a word, sizing them up with suspicious glances. No one felt particularly comfortable. Once everyone was sitting, Shinkaruk turned his attention back to a Stanley Cup Finals game on TV. Haslett took turns staring at each of the *48 Hours* people. It would take many more meetings before the two officers loosened up some. But they remained wary throughout. No one from their RCMP unit had ever granted an on-the-record interview.

46

A Case Hangs in the Balance

The most powerful and incriminating evidence against Sebastian and Atif was their videotaped confessions—and the biggest issue now at hand was whether a jury would ever see those tapes.

The undercover tactics used in Canada to get them weren't legal in the United States. Police in the U.S. are not allowed to impersonate criminals and use violent scenarios—like the ones used against Sebastian and Atif—in order to acquire a confession.

The law that governed whether the confessions could be used in this particular case stated that if the Canadian undercover officers conducted the investigation on their own—and not as an arm of the Bellevue, Washington, police force—then the confessions could be admitted. But if the judge found that the Bellevue police were simply using the RCMP to do their investigative work for them, he would have to throw out the confessions. The judge would also have to look to past precedent in his decision. At play was a well-established tenet that lawyers called "the Silver Platter Doctrine." Basically, it meant that if a foreign investigation was legal in the country where it occurred, it was admissible in a U.S. court, so long as extreme measures, such as torture, were not utilized. The results could then be handed over on a "silver platter" to American prosecutors.

Daily pretrial hearings began in the case in June 2003. Judge Charles Mertel presided over the courtroom, a quirkily handsome man in his sixties who wears a signature bow tie and brings a cup of tea to court each day. A former tennis pro, he has a contagious sense of humor, and he is unfailingly polite, even when he gets aggravated, which is rare. Mertel's voice was folksy yet authoritative. He told lawyers and members of the media to drop off motions or notes for him at his favorite coffee shop down the street from the courthouse, where he had tea each morning. But Judge Mertel had a difficult job ahead of him on this case—beginning with the pretrial hearings, during which he would decide several vital issues.

Without the videotaped confessions, prosecutors would have little more than a weak circumstantial case against the boys. Remember, there was no forensic evidence that concretely linked them to the crime scene. The prosecutors knew this, as did the defense lawyers. The single most important battle of this case would be waged before a jury was ever chosen. Both sides dug in over whether the RCMP tapes should be allowed or thrown out.

"The State rests its entire case against Mr. Burns and Mr. Rafay on the statements the two young men made to undercover officers in Canada," the defense lawyers wrote in a brief to the court. "These undercover officers were posing as violent international gangsters, who after months of cajoling and threats of violence, and after a sophisticated campaign of press manipulation, were able to extract incriminating statements from Mr. Burns and Mr. Rafay.

"As will be documented in other pleadings, these statements were coerced and untrue and were the result of undue pressure that was brought to bear on the two young men."

The RCMP officers, Haslett and Shinkaruk, traveled to Seattle. They testified at the pretrial hearing for weeks. Sitting across from them in the otherwise empty courtroom were Sebastian and Atif. This was the first time they had been in a room with these men for an extended period of time since learning their true identities. It was also the first time the two teens would hear themselves on tape, captured both in the undercover scenarios and at home by hidden microphones.

As the officers were testifying, the defendants sometimes glared directly at them, visually challenging what was being said. At other times, Sebastian and Atif refused to make any eye contact with the men whose brilliant undercover scenarios had landed them in jail.

Sebastian realized how important this hearing was—if the judge refused to allow the confessions into evidence, the case against him and Atif could be thrown out altogether. And he felt that the coercive nature of the scenarios had elicited "confessions" which were not true, and that no jury should ever be able to watch them.

"There were clues that I was getting that for me to be safe in this situation, I had to say something that would make me seem like a trustworthy criminal," Sebastian told *48 Hours* of the scenarios. "They are never going to make an explicit threat. Because if they do that, everybody knows it won't be admissible. So they make an implicit threat. And for some reason, this doesn't count.

"If they were uniformed police officers and they made the kind of implicit threats that they made to us in this undercover role, then there is no question that these statements wouldn't be admissible in court."

Sebastian's attorneys grilled the officers on every detail of the undercover scenarios. They asked and reasked the officers to go through every step they took to lure the boys into their world. Haslett was shown a statement from the extradition hearing in which he seemed to admit that his mission from the beginning was not to determine whether the two teens had committed the murders, but to get them to confess.

Peter Van Sant asked Haslett about this later.

"Sergeant Haslett, you said during the extradition hearing, 'The direction from my superior was to meet the targets and attempt to get a confession from them regarding the murder they did in the States.' Defense attorneys have looked at that statement and said the undercover officers didn't care whether they were getting the truth or not, their mission was to get a confession."

"That's just a play on words there," Haslett said. "When we start these operations, we want the truth, there's no doubt. We have throughout our undercover duties, not only myself but another—other undercover operators—we have sat down with targets and proven that they are innocent. We do both."

But Sebastian's lead attorney, Jeff Robinson, said he thought Haslett was actually telling the truth during the extradition proceedings.

"I think it's an honest and direct statement of what they were up to," he said. "The Bellevue police, when they first went to the RCMP to ask for help, had already made up their minds that Sebastian and Atif were guilty. And they passed that belief to the RCMP like you'd pass a virus.

"And the RCMP bought it hook, line, and sinker."

47

Roll the Tape

Sergeant Haslett maintained the RCMP was only after the truth—and that the confessions they got from the two teenagers were just that.

"Does it trouble you that if this investigation had been run in the state of Washington, those confessions would not have been admissible? Under U.S. law?" Van Sant asked Haslett.

"Yeah. That's the law down there . . . unfortunate that that's the way it is," Haslett said. "We're fortunate up here to be able to. And we take great care in running these investigations so that our courts continue to allow them to be entered in."

While under oath, Haslett was challenged by defense attorneys. If he was really interested in the truth, they asked, why didn't he ever ask Sebastian directly if he was guilty?

"Well, if we had did that at the outset of meeting him, obviously, I'm confident it would never have worked," Haslett said. "Because he isn't going to come and tell anybody that right away, a total stranger off the street.

"We had to meet him in such a way that he obviously thought he was dealing with someone that could help him with his situation. And we had to build up to that."

The defense team hammered Haslett and Shinkaruk about the fact that they used the F-word frequently in the scenarios, one more way to appear as threatening as possible to the teens.

"I mean, I don't go around threatening anybody," Haslett said. "I use the F-word a fair bit to let him maybe realize that, yeah, I can have a temper at times or can be aggressive at times. But openly ever threaten anybody, never."

"You used the F-word a lot in these scenarios and in your conversations with Sebastian," Van Sant later said to Haslett. "Why is that?"

"It's a powerful word," Haslett answered. "Used properly, it—in different contexts, it has a number of various meanings. And it's a very strong word to use when dealing with an individual.

"We learned a lot of these techniques from dealing with the actual, real criminal element."

The defense attorneys pointed out during the pretrial hearing that the scenarios were set up to convince Sebastian that he had entered a world of guns and violence, that these men would kill people who crossed them.

"Do you believe that Sebastian Burns ever feared you? Ever feared for his life?" Van Sant asked Haslett.

"From us, no, never. There's never once throughout the entire time dealing with him did I ever feel that," Haslett said. "What he was more fearful of was when he was involved with us in some of the scenarios, that he would be brought to the attention of the police. And then what he was doing for us may then become headlines. He wasn't fearful of anything we were doing. It was more of being exposed in that manner."

Haslett conceded that the scenarios were designed to leave a lot up to Sebastian's imagination. During one scenario, Sebastian was shown a gun and told it was still "warm."

"What was the purpose of showing Sebastian those guns?" Van Sant asked.

"That was another undercover operator that Shinkaruk and I brought in to show that we are of a wider nature than just what Sebastian Burns saw with us . . . that was to show him we have connections other than just in the Vancouver area," Haslett said. "And again, it goes to Sebastian Burns's imagination. Let him sit back when he goes home at night and imagine whatever he chooses to."

"Didn't that moment communicate to Sebastian Burns, 'We kill people'?"

"If his imagination wanted to and if he let it go that way, we have no problem with that. I have no problem with that."

The defense attorneys said that was precisely the point. This was a nineteen-year-old boy who was ostracized from the community. The expert undercover officers played him.

"And it's amazing to me that Canadian undercover officers take such pride in forty-year-old men being able to manipulate and trick nineteen-year-olds into confessing something that they didn't do," Robinson said. "As I believe the undercover officer admitted himself, he said, and this was one of the most chilling quotes I've ever heard: 'We can get anybody involved in our scenarios. Anybody. All we have to do is push the right button or pull the right lever.'"

The defense argued to the judge that the tactics used by these skilled undercover officers set up a perfect recipe for a false confession. But prosecutors said that the two teens had no reason to give false confessions, and that their demeanors, as they kicked back and laughed while talking about the murders, didn't indicate they were in fear for their lives at all.

Lead prosecutor James Konat agreed that the undercover officers "did a masterful job of setting these two up." But, he said, what they got out of Sebastian and Atif was the truth.

"When those words finally came out of their mouth . . . it confirmed years of confidence, yet not one hundred percent confidence, that we had the right people," Konat said. "And when you hear that tape and you see the way they act when they describe beating these three unsuspecting people to death, there can be no doubt in anybody's mind that they're the real killers.

"And at that point in time, when Sebastian Burns realized that he really, at long last, forever and ever, could possibly get away with this, he couldn't help himself. He just couldn't help himself."

After weeks of compelling testimony, Judge Mertel ruled that the police technically followed the law in gaining the confessions—and that the jury would be allowed to hear them.

And he handed down two other blows to the members of the defense team: They would not be allowed to call an expert to the stand to testify about how false confessions could take place. And they would be very limited in telling the jury about any other suspects that they felt should have been further questioned by the Bellevue police. In fact, they would not be allowed to tell the jury at all about Douglas Mohammed, the man who came in and said he knew that the Rafay family had been killed as part of a religious hit, by a baseball bat—before that information was ever made public.

"Bellevue had simply determined that they already knew who committed these murders," Jeff Robinson said. "And so they went about building a case against Sebastian and Atif instead of trying to track down leads that might have brought us to a very different place."

And with the court's ruling, the members of the jury would never be able to decide for themselves whether or not the Bellevue police failed by not following up on what could have been important leads.

The only advantage to come out of these hearings for the defense lawyers was that they'd now heard much of Haslett and Shinkaruk's testimony—and they would be able to use some of it to show a single-minded goal of getting a confession at all costs, regardless of the fact that Bellevue police had no damning evidence against the two teens.

48

Betrayed

Another key part of the case played out before a jury was ever selected. As soon as Theresa Olson located Jimmy Miyoshi in Tokyo the previous August, prosecutors had issued him a subpoena. He didn't respond to the subpoena until prosecutors met with his bosses at the U.S.-based company where he worked in Tokyo. Prosecutors say that after that meeting, his bosses let him know that if he didn't go to Seattle to cooperate with prosecutors, he would be fired.

When Jimmy got to town for his pretrial hearing, he checked into his hotel, arranged and paid for by the prosecutors. But he immediately called Jeff Robinson, Sebastian's new lead defense attorney. Jimmy had arranged to meet with prosecutors the next day before he gave his deposition in court—but he asked Robinson what would happen if he testified on the boys' behalf instead. Robinson told him that he couldn't give him legal advice, because it would be unethical. But the attorney smiled as he hung up the phone. A crucial witness for the prosecution appeared to be having second thoughts.

When Jimmy took the stand the next day, it was to give an official deposition in the case. A camera was rolling to film his testimony. This was done because both sides were convinced that this would be their last shot at Jimmy Miyoshi—once he walked out of the courtroom, he would likely disappear again. His video-taped testimony would be shown to the future jury.

Jimmy walked uncomfortably up the witness stand and sat down, completely avoiding eye contact with Sebastian and Atif. A local attorney, who would be representing him during the deposition, pulled up a chair near the witness stand and took a seat.

James Konat began by asking him what he preferred to be called—Jimmy Hiroshi Miyoshi or James Hiroshi Kira, the name he went by in Tokyo. Jimmy said he preferred Miyoshi.

Jimmy said he had been living in Tokyo for the last three years, working for a financial company that was based in New York. When asked how he knew the two teenagers on trial, he said, "We were best friends. I would classify Sebastian and Atif, both of them, as my best friends."

As Jimmy began to weave an intriguing tale that could mean life in prison for his two former best friends, Sebastian intensely stared at him, rarely blinking and never wavering. Atif appeared emotion-ally crushed. There were no tears, just a series of painful expressions. Atif took turns looking back and forth between Sebastian and Jimmy.

Jimmy said that he met Atif during middle school and Sebastian during high school, either grade ten or eleven. They were friends, he said, based on "the ability to speak freely with each other."

"From grade twelve on, my circle of friends were myself, Sebastian, and Atif," he told the prosecutor.

After high school, he and Sebastian went to Capilano College in North Vancouver, while Atif went away to Cornell in New York. When Atif came home for the summer, though, after his first year, he spent much of his time in Vancouver with Sebastian and Jimmy—even though his family had moved to Bellevue by then. Jimmy said that was because Atif preferred his friends' company over that of his family.

It was early that summer of 1994, Jimmy said, that Atif brought up the idea of killing his parents. Jimmy was in Seattle to drop off his then girlfriend (and now wife) at the airport. After he dropped her off, he went to nearby Bellevue to have dinner with Atif and his parents. Then he and Atif drove back to Vancouver together. During the drive, Atif brought up the "notion" of killing his family, Jimmy said.

"I didn't take it as a joke," Jimmy admitted, but said he was "neutral" to the idea.

A few days later, Sebastian asked Jimmy if Atif had mentioned to him the possibility of killing the Rafay family. Jimmy said yes, and they talked about it a little. He didn't hear any more about it for a few weeks—and then Sebastian and Atif came over to Jimmy's parents' house, where he was still living at the time. They told him they needed to have a private conversation, so the three teens went down to a creek near Jimmy's house.

"They brought up notions, ways of killing Atif's parents," Jimmy said. He remembered that Sebastian did most of the talking, and they discussed only two possibilities that Jimmy could remember. They would either gas the family, by leaving the gas on in the kitchen while they were sleeping, or use baseball bats to beat them to death.

Jimmy said he thought Sebastian came up with the idea of using baseball bats, "because it was a quick and painless way of killing someone."

"I don't remember bringing up any new ideas," Jimmy said. "But I do remember asking questions about the ideas."

Jimmy did come up with a suggestion of how the boys could explain away any DNA they might leave in the house: They should just go down to Bellevue a few days earlier, so that their hair and skin cells would naturally be in the house.

"If they had been living in the house previously, whatever hair samples collected after wouldn't mean they had done it," he said, matter-of-factly.

His two best friends came to him again just before they carried out their plan, Jimmy said on the stand. He said that Sebastian and Atif had gone to Bellevue to stay for a few days, and came back unexpectedly.

They came to visit Jimmy where he was working at the time, as a lab assistant at an environmental company. Jimmy said he couldn't remember the exact details of the meeting, but said the teens told him they had bought the baseball bat or were about to, and that they were "going to Bellevue."

The two friends also told Jimmy that they planned to use *The Lion King* as part of their alibi, and that they would also go to various other restaurants and public places.

"They were going to attract enough attention that someone could recognize or remember that they were at these particular locations," Jimmy said.

A few days later, he said, he heard from a friend that the Rafay family had been murdered.

49

"No Going Back"

When Sebastian and Atif got back to Vancouver a few days after the murders took place, Jimmy testified, they each spoke to him about what had happened.

He spoke to Atif first. "He told me how he lured his mother into the basement and Sebastian struck her from behind. He was fairly distraught or upset at what had occurred."

Jimmy said that Atif told him that once he saw his mother killed, he was more shaken than he expected. So he concentrated on unhooking the VCR to make it look like a robbery—while Sebastian went in to kill his father. Jimmy remembered Atif's telling him that when the teens left the house, his sister was still alive.

He then had a conversation with Sebastian about the murders, Jimmy said under questioning from the prosecutor. Sebastian told him that there was a lot of blood in Atif's father's room, and that Atif was pretty distraught, but that after hitting the mother, "there was no going back."

"He said it was not the easiest thing to do or the most pleasant, but he guessed he had to do it," Jimmy recalled.

After a few weeks back in Vancouver, the three boys got together and talked again about the murders, and they agreed this would be the last time they'd discuss them.

"Because it wouldn't be a safe thing to discuss. I guess we were concerned about police surveillance," Jimmy said.

Within a month after the murders, the three boys moved in together at 2021 Phillips Avenue in North Vancouver. Robin Puga, another high school friend of theirs, also moved in with them. Jimmy says Robin only lived there for a few months, until the other three decided they no longer wanted him to live there. They did something to force him to move out, Jimmy said, but he couldn't remember what it was. Jimmy lived with his two best friends for another eight months or so.

"Robin Puga did not know anything about the crime that we know of," said lead detective Bob Thompson. Thompson said that Puga was not considered one of the "intellectual elite" of the group—and that he wasn't told of the plot to kill the Rafays either before or after the murders.

When asked by Konat if Sebastian ever had a job while living at the Phillips Avenue address, Jimmy said that keeping up with the details of the investigation became Sebastian's full-time job and that neither

Sebastian nor Atif worked while living there. They lived on public assistance, the equivalent of welfare in the United States, for the first six months. Then the Rafay family estate began to pay out, so they had funds to use. He said the first few months living at the house were stressful because reporters and police officers were constantly coming around. But he said this only made the teens' friendship stronger.

"I saw the media and police and people outside our house as antagonists of our situation," he said. "It was the three of us."

After a few months, Jimmy and Robin headed to Bellevue as a favor to their two friends. Atif said he need documentation of what was in the Rafay house for insurance purposes—and his two friends agreed to go take pictures. Sebastian and Atif couldn't go do it because they might get arrested if they crossed the border back into the United States. Almost as soon as the two boys showed up at the Rafay house, a neighbor called police—and the police took them into custody. Jimmy said the police questioned him and Robin separately. Jimmy refused to talk.

"At the time, it was in my interest to not say or have anything adverse happen to Sebastian or Atif," Jimmy said. "If I were to give info, like I'm doing right now, it would be something that could be used against them."

Jimmy said that by July 1995, he had moved out of the Phillips Avenue house to live with his then girlfriend. But he was visiting Sebastian and Atif at the house one day when Sebastian used a code to let Jimmy know he wanted to talk about something sensitive. They went up on the roof, because they suspected all along that police had secretly wired the house. Sebastian told Jimmy that he wanted him to meet with Haslett, the crime boss, and tell Haslett that he knew about the murders before they took place.

"I was to do this to enhance our relationship with [Haslett]," Jimmy said Sebastian told him.

Jimmy said he warned Sebastian that maybe these two guys weren't really criminals but undercover cops instead. Sebastian told him that he and Atif had already confessed to their parts in the murders—but that if the two men did turn out to be cops, Sebastian and Atif would simply say they'd gotten all of their information from the newspapers. Sebastian again asked Jimmy to meet with Haslett, "to curry favor" with the mobster. Jimmy went and met Haslett at the Landis Hotel, but didn't say anything that was too incriminating. He nodded his head when Haslett asked him whether he knew about the murders beforehand, instead of answering verbally, so that his answers wouldn't be caught on tape.

A few days after that meeting, Sebastian and Atif were arrested at their house. Jimmy was also arrested that day. He was taken to the North Vancouver RCMP station—where Haslett, the make-believe crime boss, was waiting for him in an interview room. He was interrogated by Sergeant D. G. Rinn, and refused to even say that he recognized Haslett.

"Do you recall speaking to Corporal Haslett, who is seated over in that chair?" the RCMP investigator asked.

"No," Jimmy answered.

"OK, do you recall having a conversation with him?"

"No."

And throughout the statement, he refused to say anything to incriminate himself or his two best friends.

"So when did Sebastian and Atif tell you about the murder and their involvement in the murder?" the investigator asked.

"When?" Jimmy answered. "They never did."

"Come on, Jimmy, now look at it, I know it's hard to do, it's hard to tell something about your good friends or you think who are your good friends. But I'm telling you and I'm asking you, that we've got three people in Bellevue, Washington, that were cold-bloodedly and brutally murdered. And I know that the people responsible for that were Atif and Sebastian Burns. And I know that you know that, Jimmy, and I know it's a hard, difficult thing for you to do to give up your friends."

Jimmy still refused to acknowledge having any information about the murders, but the RCMP officers continued to push him.

"If that's what you want to do, you want to be associated with those two, I'm telling you if push comes to shove, Jimmy, and it's either them or you, butter your forehead, pal, 'cause you're toast," the investigator told the teen. "They would get rid of you that quick, whether it took hurting you, whether . . . whatever it took.

"Come on, think about it for a minute, my friend. Don't worry about your two so-called friends or who you think are your friends at this point, they're not worth it, they're dirt, they're trash. They've done something so despicable that I don't even like talking about it. Their time will come. They'll meet their maker. They'll face a jury of their peers, and you'll see what those peers will do to them. They'll crush them like bugs. They'll put them where they belong. Do you want to be part of that, do you want to be associated like that?"

50

"I Think They Are Capable
of Doing Anything"

It didn't take long for Jimmy to switch sides, however unwillingly. Although Sebastian and Atif didn't realize it right away, the friend they believed would never betray them had done just that. The RCMP told Jimmy that if he didn't cooperate, he'd be facing charges of conspiracy to commit murder—and could be imprisoned along with his two best friends. Less than a month later, on August 24, 1995, Jimmy Miyoshi gave a detailed statement telling police that he knew about the murders beforehand—and that Sebastian and Atif had confessed to him after the murders were done. He followed up by giving another statement on September 26 of that same year. He hesitantly went through the details, again under questioning by Sergeant Rinn.

He talked about how Atif first brought up the idea of killing his parents, and how the three of them then discussed it in more detail at a couple of other meetings.

"Did you take them seriously?" the RCMP investigator asked.

Jimmy paused for several seconds. "I guess, like, with the fact that we were talking about it, yeah."

"Did you think they were capable?"

"I think they are capable of doing anything."

Jimmy described how the three teens discussed different ways of killing the family, but in the end decided to use a baseball bat.

"We talked about what would be an easy way to kill somebody," Jimmy said. "And, uh, they decided that it would be the baseball bat because there'd be kind of last-minute pain."

Jimmy told the officer that when his two friends got back to Canada after the murders, they weren't themselves.

"When they came back? I asked them . . . I was concerned about how they were themselves," Jimmy told the investigator. "Like, how they were feeling or whatever . . . I guess. I spent lots of time kind of driving them around, basically doing whatever I could do to cheer them up or whatever. They were pretty worn out, I guess. Umm, they never, they never talked about it. They never wanted to talk about anything. It was—it was more of a thing where we did anything but that, kind of thing."

"But they must have . . . given you some sort of detail," the investigator prompted him. "They must have discussed something with you as to what happened down there."

"They didn't want to talk about it. They didn't want to do that. They didn't want to talk about anything basically. They didn't want to talk about the situation."

But Miyoshi told police that eventually, Atif and Sebastian did each speak to him about the murders.

"Who actually did the killing?" the investigator asked.

"It was Sebastian," Jimmy said.

"What did Atif do, then? Did he watch them?"

"I'm pretty sure he saw his mom, but I don't know about the other two."

On October 27, 1995, less than three months after his arrest, Jimmy signed an immunity agreement with the Canadian government—and became the star witness against his two best friends. The immunity agreement would protect Jimmy from being prosecuted for conspiracy to commit murder in Canada. In return, he had to "make full and frank disclosure" of any information he had relating to the murders of the Rafay family. He also had to submit to interviews anytime the police asked, and to "attend court to give full and truthful testimony."

If he failed to fulfill any part of this agreement, the Canadian government would be free to prosecute him on a charge of conspiracy to commit murder, and his own statements would be used against him.

In his cross-examination, Jeff Robinson aggressively focused in on a new detail that had emerged in Jimmy's testimony, something that wasn't in any of his previous statements. Jimmy testified during his deposition that Sebastian had once told him that if the two mobsters ended up being cops, they would just say they had gotten their details about the murder from the newspapers.

Robinson pointed out that this was the first time in at least five different statements to police that Jimmy had said this, implying that Jimmy was making it up as he went along.

"Well, the real question is why would the prosecution put a person like that on the witness stand and ask a jury to believe him?" Robinson told *48 Hours*. "I am disappointed in that. And once again, I am disappointed if we are about the business of sending people to prison based on the word of someone under the kind of pressure Jimmy Miyoshi was under."

But prosecutor Konat said that even though Jimmy had changed his story in some ways over the years, he was the only witness who knew the *real* Sebastian and Atif.

"They were three peas in a pod as they have been described," Konat told *48 Hours*. "Jimmy Miyoshi certainly was on the inside, while everybody else was on the outside looking in. After he realized that he could be on the line in some smaller ways for the murders of the Rafay family, and only then, did we start to see Jimmy Miyoshi's true colors."

Although Jimmy at times came across as flaky and

unsure of himself, what he said on the stand was devastating to Sebastian and Atif's case.

Before he left the witness stand, Jimmy finally looked straight at Sebastian, returning his stare for the first time. Jimmy's face was blank. He then got up, walked out of the courtroom, and got on the next available flight back to Tokyo.

When Jimmy returned to Japan, prosecutors say he was fired from his job.

51

"This Is Going to Be a War"

It was November 2003. After nearly a decade, Sebastian Burns and Atif Rafay—now twenty-seven years old—were going on trial for what remained the worst murders in Bellevue history. Attorneys on both sides were brilliant, talented—and ready.

"This is going to be a war," said lead defense attorney Jeff Robinson.

"I have no doubt we're going to win," said lead prosecutor James Konat.

After nine years of sitting in a jail cell, Sebastian was looking forward to telling his story. He was more excited and determined than nervous, and was certain he would be able to convince the jury of his truth—that he and Atif had been railroaded for these murders and had spent nearly a decade in jail for something they didn't do.

Jenna Jackson went to visit him at the jail a few days before his trial began. He had sent her a letter several weeks earlier, so she knew he was feeling a little off-kilter.

"I'd like to be able to say I'm doing well; I'm certainly doing as well as one could and shall continue undoubtedly to do so," he wrote.

This time, because she was not with an attorney, Jackson was separated from Sebastian by a glass window, covered in crisscrossed wire mesh. She sat down in a metal chair, encased on two sides by stone walls to help keep the conversation relatively private. When jail guards brought Sebastian in, he looked down the row of booths to see who had come to visit him. His face lit up when he saw Jackson. He sat down on the other side of the glass and the guards unshackled his hands. Both Jackson and Sebastian picked up their telephones.

Sebastian was extremely jittery. The recent testimony of the RCMP officers and of his former best friend, Jimmy Miyoshi, had him on edge. He was afraid to say anything out loud, convinced the jail guards were listening for any piece of incriminating information they could pass on to prosecutors. So, instead of talking, he wrote notes to Jackson with the tiny stub of a pencil the jail allowed him to have. When he finished writing, Sebastian held the notes up to the window for Jackson to read.

Once she had read them, Sebastian tore them up into little bitty pieces. This became a long, tedious process—but he was determined not to say anything before trial that would hurt him or tip off the other side to his strategy. The notes mostly pertained to his version of how the RCMP scenarios unfolded, and what he said Jimmy was lying about to save his own skin.

Sebastian was worried about what lengths lead prosecutor James Konat would go to in order to get a conviction. But he stressed to Jackson that he was convinced he and Atif would be vindicated.

Sebastian saw Konat as his archrival. In his mind, he and Konat were the game masters on either side of this case. And in some ways, James Konat and Sebastian Burns were alike. They were both good-looking, confident, and accustomed to getting their way. Konat scoffed at this comparison and said that there was one clear thing that separated them: Sebastian's psychosis.

In November 2004, the jury began hearing, in painstaking detail, the case against Sebastian and Atif. Nearly ten years in the making, the trial lasted six long months. Hour after hour of undercover audiotape was played. More than eighty witnesses were called to the stand, including Sergeant Haslett and Corporal Shinkaruk.

One of the dramatic high points in the trial came when prosecutors played those chilling videotaped confessions. Jurors were riveted as they watched the teens laugh while Sebastian described how he had to chase Basma around the room to beat her to death.

The jurors also heard from the neighbors who lived on either side of the Rafay home. The neighbors testified that the pounding sounds from the Rafay house ended a little after 10 P.M., a time when independent witnesses saw the boys at the movie theater.

Lead detective Bob Thompson took the stand to tell the jury that everything in his investigation led him straight to Sebastian and Atif. Defense attorneys attacked him for not following up on other possible leads, but they were not allowed to raise Douglas Muhammed specifically.

After nearly six grueling months of testimony, the trial was down to its final days. Jeff Robinson met with Sebastian. He was not sure it was such a wise idea for Sebastian to testify. But Sebastian overruled him, demanding that he be heard.

For months, jurors had occasionally shot glances over at the boys. They were often puzzled at how indifferent the two seemed to be when listening to court testimony. Even when graphic photos of the murders were shown in court, the two boys sat stoically in their chairs.

But now, the man they all wanted to hear from was about to step onto the most important stage of his life. His own words had got him into this mess. He now believed his own words would save him.

Sebastian Burns was called to the stand.

52

Sebastian Tells His Story

The courtroom was packed on the day Sebastian Burns was scheduled to testify. He was led into the courtroom dressed in a plain navy blue suit. He nervously walked to the witness stand after his name was called. The large courtroom was absolutely silent, except for the sound of Sebastian's footsteps.

After he was sworn in, his lead defense attorney, Jeff Robinson, acknowledged the tension that now dominated the room.

"Are you scared right now?" he asked his client.

"Yes, extremely," Sebastian said.

Sebastian explained to the jury that he hadn't had a chance to speak socially for the last nine years because he had been in jail. He was afraid of the expressions on his face not being appropriate; he was afraid because he'd been wrongfully accused.

Robinson immediately asked Sebastian if he had anything to do with the murders. Sebastian looked at the jury and firmly said no. Then, Robinson asked him, why on earth would he confess to something he didn't do? Sebastian explained that "there was no recourse with [Haslett] but diplomacy." He told jurors that he and Atif had realized early on that they were a threat to Haslett—and that they had to play along or he would kill them.

Sebastian told the jury that when he first arrived back in Vancouver after the murders, he tried to get a job—but no one would hire him because of his notoriety. Even on his first day of college, Sebastian said, literally hundreds of people were staring at him. He never went back.

He described to the jury how he had been isolated at home for months when he met Shinkaruk outside Crimpers Salon in April. He was "just a nineteen-year-old kid," he said, and he was thrilled by the attention that Shinkaruk was paying him. But after the Whistler scenario, when Sebastian drove what he thought was a stolen car back to Vancouver, he told the jury he wanted out. He went to the next meeting with the mobsters, on May 6, with the intention of breaking ties with them.

"I was going to make excuses for why I couldn't work with them," Sebastian told the jury. "Number one that I was under investigation and didn't want to get in trouble, and number two that I was busy with the movie."

But, he said, when he actually met with them, he was intimidated by the "warm gun" he was shown, and he felt his excuses for not working with them were being "bulldozed." He told the jury that this meeting confirmed his worst fears about Haslett, that if he considered a person a threat to his organization, he could have him killed. Sebastian said he didn't want to be seen as "someone who would drop a dime on" Haslett.

Sebastian went on to talk about the next big meeting with the mobsters, on June 15, when Haslett began questioning him in detail about what had happened down in Bellevue.

"Were you giving evasive answers to [Haslett]?" Robinson asked.

"Yes," Sebastian said. "[Haslett] wanted an A-to-Z story of what went down so he could sabotage the case, and I couldn't do that because I didn't do it. I didn't trust myself to give him a story that quickly."

It was clear Sebastian had studied every transcript of each scenario—he quoted from them and pointed out details he wanted the jury to notice. While he was composed and clear on the stand, he came across as slightly arrogant and controlling. As Robinson was questioning him, Sebastian frequently interrupted. He seemed to be trying to take control of the questioning. It was clear he was uncomfortable. He also tried to look at each individual juror as he answered, and seemed to be trying to figure out how they were responding to his testimony. To jurors, his glances seemed more intimidating than inquisitive.

Sebastian said that when Haslett told him about

the Bellevue police memo in June, it confirmed his suspicions that the detectives there had been fabricating evidence against him and Atif. He and Atif talked about how they would deal with Haslett.

"I decided to give [Haslett] a story," Sebastian testified. "We decided we would give [Haslett] information from the media and information from indirect reports."

But Robinson pointed out to his client what the jury must have been thinking—that Sebastian seemed very relaxed on that video.

"Well, in some ways, I was very relaxed, because I thought I was taking the safest course of action," Sebastian said. "I was being cooperative, and I didn't think [Haslett] was going to kill me right then and there. I was nervous about screwing up the story, but by July nineteenth, I was pretty comfortable we didn't have anything else to worry about with [Haslett and Shinkaruk]."

Sebastian explained that after he gave his confession to the crime boss, he called Atif—at the mobsters' direction—and told him he needed to come to Victoria because Sebastian had fallen in a Rollerblading accident. He told Atif he'd leave the hotel key for him under a *Star Trek* code name at the front desk.

"I did it to prepare Atif for what was to come. The name I used, Khan, was an allusion to a joke we had about what we were going to say to [Haslett]."

Sebastian looked directly at the jury.

"We had discussed on June twenty-ninth saying

that we had done the crime in our underwear. . . . We had heard this from our probate lawyer, who said that Bob Thompson had told her that . . . When we had discussed the prospect of telling this to [Haslett] as part of our story, we discussed how we'd be in our bare chests, and Khan is a bare-chested character. So Atif was saying, 'I know who I am,' as in, 'I know what role I have to play.'"

"On July twelfth, were you inside the Rafay home between the hours of nine P.M. and two A.M.?" Robinson asked.

"No," Sebastian said.

"Did you have anything to do with the murders of these people?"

"No."

Robinson looked at the judge and said, "Your Honor, I have nothing further."

Sebastian looked dissatisfied, as if he didn't get to tell his whole story. He looked over at James Konat, expecting his nemesis to stand and begin his counterattack. The jurors looked at Konat as well. But surprisingly, the mild-mannered Roger Davidheiser stood up. He asked the judge for more time to prepare his cross. Judge Mertel granted him forty-eight hours. Sebastian stepped off the stand and headed back to the defense table.

He did not look pleased.

53

The Cross

Before Sebastian's cross-examination began, Davidheiser asked the judge to allow to be admitted as evidence several items that he said incriminated Sebastian and were important to the state's case: the yearbook entries that Sebastian and Atif made their senior year; details about the play in which Sebastian starred in high school, *Rope;* a video from the memorial service in Vancouver where Sebastian and Atif ran away from the mosque, laughing; and some e-mails from Atif's computer regarding murder as an act of morality.

The judge denied all of these things—but said the prosecutor could bring up what Davidheiser described as a previous attempt by Sebastian to "manipulate evidence and witnesses," in connection with a car crash where he'd used watching a movie as his alibi. This took place when Sebastian was sixteen and wrecked his father's car. Prosecutors said Sebastian took pieces of the car to the parking lot of a movie theater and filed a fraudulent claim with the insurance company, saying someone must have hit him while he was in the movie.

"The relevance and importance is that it directly rebuts what he testified to . . . that the only reason he said he committed the murders during the movie was that it had been suggested in the press," Davidheiser argued to the judge, while the jury was out of the room.

Robinson said the comparison was ridiculous.

"Mr. Burns had one car accident and didn't want to tell his father about it—it is so remote and different from what happened in this case. Wrecking your car and not wanting to tell your parents, or even asking your friends to lie about it, is completely different than killing three people and using a movie as an alibi."

But the judge decided that Davidheiser could question Sebastian about this incident.

Once again, Sebastian had become his own worst enemy. If he had taken his attorney's advice and not testified, the story of using a movie to cover up an accident could never have been introduced. But by taking the stand, Sebastian opened the door to new details that could doom him.

Sebastian looked extremely annoyed. His defense team was obviously upset. They realized this would be a big blow to their client's credibility.

Atif's attorneys told the judge they wouldn't decide whether their client would take the stand until they saw how Sebastian's cross-examination went.

The next morning, the prosecutor called Sebastian back to the stand.

"Mr. Burns, I'd like to invite you back to 1995," Davidheiser began.

The prosecutor started in about how arrogant Sebastian and his friends were at the time of the murders. He asked Sebastian if he remembered a conversation the teen had, captured on undercover audiotape, with Jimmy Miyoshi about hubris being "a tragic flaw which eventually brings about your downfall."

"At the time, did you believe you had this quality of hubris you described to Mr. Miyoshi?" Davidheiser asked.

"No."

Davidheiser read to Sebastian another clip from the undercover tapes: "I and my friends are among the smartest people in the world. I have no use for people of lesser intelligence."

Atif was watching intently, his gaze shifting between Sebastian and Davidheiser.

"I did have arrogant beliefs about me and my friends," Sebastian said. "I liked being arrogant, but as far as believing I was one of the smartest people in the world, I don't know if I sincerely believed that."

"Did you find it fun to act on your arrogant beliefs?" the prosecutor asked.

"I don't know what you mean."

Davidheiser continued to grill Sebastian about

the various arrogant comments he had made—and insinuated that he had acted on those beliefs in killing the Rafay family.

"I didn't do it. I did not murder the Rafay family. I did not commit this crime," Sebastian said.

"You did confess to these murders," Davidheiser pointed out.

"Those confessions were false," Sebastian said, looking at the jury.

"Mr. Burns, I understand you want this jury to believe those were false confessions, but you do admit to making the confessions?"

Sebastian nodded yes.

As Davidheiser asked another question, Sebastian interrupted him and went back to a question the prosecutor had asked him much earlier about who his best friends were at the time.

"By the way, Mr. Davidheiser, when you asked me about my circle of friends, I didn't mean to say that Jimmy and Atif were the only people I socialized with," Sebastian said. "I'm not sure if that was implied in your question. And I can't remember if you said 'confession' or 'false confession,' but I want to reiterate that these statements are false."

Davidheiser smiled and nodded. Sebastian's attorneys, sitting at the defense table, looked resigned.

Davidheiser moved on.

"The next statements you made about the murders of the Rafay family were recorded by the undercover operation—"

"Those statements were false," Sebastian interrupted.

"I understand you want this jury to believe those statements were false, but that was you, wasn't it? It wasn't someone else?"

Clearly flustered, Sebastian refused to answer directly, instead repeatedly arguing that his statements had been false. Sitting at the prosecution table, Konat smiled. Atif buried his head in his hands.

Davidheiser started asking Sebastian about his two best friends, Atif and Jimmy. He asked if Sebastian remembered telling Haslett that all three of them would share in the proceeds from the Rafay estate. Sebastian didn't answer directly.

"Are you saying it was a false statement that you were going to share in the proceeds from the estate?" Davidheiser asked.

"Yes," Sebastian said.

He asked the teen who paid for the Mustang they bought, and a trip they took in the new car to Sweetgrass, Montana.

"So it was Atif who was footing the bill for the trip and the car . . . ," Davidheiser said.

"Yes he was footing the bill, no I didn't commit the crime, no we weren't sharing in the proceeds from the estate," Sebastian said.

"Why are you now trying to distance yourself from Atif?"

Sebastian began blinking rapidly, a sign that his mind was in overdrive and that he was getting aggravated. He tried to explain his answer but only ended up getting more confused.

Davidheiser asked Sebastian about what happened once he and Atif got back to Canada after the murders.

"What efforts did you and Atif and whatever other friends you may have enlisted make to track the activities of the Bellevue police?" Davidheiser asked.

Sebastian started to get sarcastic. He repeated Davidheiser's question in an exaggerated manner.

"'Track the investigation'?" Sebastian asked. "Didn't do anything to 'track the investigation.'"

Atif's arms were crossed across his chest, as though he was bracing himself. Robinson looked frustrated as he watched Sebastian on the stand.

Davidheiser took Sebastian back to the undercover scenarios. He asked about the teens' screenplay, *The Great Despisers*—and the fact that it was Sebastian's hope for funding from Haslett that had led him to get involved with the criminals. Sebastian played down the importance of the movie project.

"Are you saying you and Atif were not serious about making a feature-length film called *The Great Despisers?*" Davidheiser asked.

"I think there are different components to your question," Sebastian said. "At one point, we were serious about the film."

"At what point?"

"I'd say in June. In April, I didn't expect to get any money from [Haslett] for the film."

"Isn't it true, sir, that your plans to make the

movie progressed at an identical pace to [the under-cover operation]?"

"Maybe."

Sebastian wrung his hands, which were sitting in his lap. Davidheiser continued to grill him on how much the movie was going to cost and how much money they were expecting to make out of it.

"You thought this movie was going to be pretty successful, didn't you?"

"I certainly hoped so. As far as my actual beliefs, I don't know."

Davidheiser read back to Sebastian some of the words he said to Haslett during the undercover operation—about the movie making them rich and famous. Sebastian tried to backtrack and said they didn't really even have a completed script done, even though they told Haslett they did.

"There was no script, no specific plan for the scope of the production . . . Saying we had a script when we hadn't even begun a script is perhaps the greatest exaggeration."

But Davidheiser reminded Sebastian—and the jury—that he and Atif were calling prospective film-makers as well, trying to find someone to shoot this film that they thought would be profitable. And they told filmmakers that they had a budget of $200,000 to $300,000 to make the film.

"Can you tell this jury where you expected to get the two or three hundred thousand dollars for the budget of this film?" the prosecutor asked.

"Our only source of money was Atif," Sebastian said. "We also thought of getting a grant . . . but our desire to make the film was not dependent upon having a two-hundred-thousand-dollar budget."

Davidheiser started questioning Sebastian about the various times during the undercover operation when he chose to indulge in criminal activity. Sebastian argued that he went along with this life of crime only because he was scared the mobsters would kill him if they didn't think they could trust him. But Davidheiser thought that wasn't Sebastian's real motive in getting close to the two criminals.

"But you weren't going to drop a dime on [Haslett], were you?" Davidheiser asked.

"No," Sebastian said.

"And you weren't going to drop a dime on [Shinkaruk]?"

"No."

"Because if you dropped a dime on them, they wouldn't invest in your film."

He kept pushing Sebastian to make the point that the real reasons he chose to be involved with the mobsters were the benefits—they could pay him well, and they could take care of his problems in Bellevue.

Davidheiser started asking Sebastian about all of the times during the undercover scenarios that the teen bragged about how close he was to Atif and Jimmy, and about how neither would betray him. The prosecutor was making it clear to the jury that

Jimmy Miyoshi was in a position to know the details of the murders—because he was best friends with the two teens who committed them.

Davidheiser asked Sebastian to read from a statement he gave to Haslett about his friends during the June 28 undercover scenario. Sebastian read it so fast that his own attorney, Robinson, asked him to slow down. Sebastian was flustered.

"If I die now, it would fucking wreck their lives," Sebastian read. "[Atif] would be miserable in the process . . . the whole thing would really suck and be meaningless. I am an integral part, like they are an integral part of me."

"That wasn't part of the story for [Haslett], was it?" the prosecutor asked.

"No, I was just boasting."

"Mr. Burns, can't we take away from that your feelings for Jimmy and Atif?"

Sebastian admitted they were very close—but he argued with Davidheiser and tried to play down how close they were.

Davidheiser reminded Sebastian of another statement he made to Haslett about his two friends: "If they were girls, I would probably marry them."

"You told Haslett numerous times that Jimmy Miyoshi knew about the murders before they happened," the prosecutor reminded Sebastian.

"Yes," Sebastian said.

"And you described for [Haslett] how it felt, in great detail, how it felt to kill the Rafay family."

"I remember [Haslett] asking me how it felt, and I remember giving him a solid answer."

"You remember telling [Haslett] that you were happier that it happened than if it hadn't happened?"

"That's right."

Davidheiser brought up Miyoshi's testimony that Sebastian had a plan in case he and Atif got arrested—they would just say that everything they told the undercover officers came from the newspapers.

"And that's your defense now, isn't it?" the prosecutor asked.

"That's the truth," Sebastian said forcefully.

"Just as Mr. Miyoshi said it would be."

Sebastian turned from the prosecutor and looked at the jury. And he repeated, "That's the truth."

By the end of the day, Sebastian was exhausted and on edge. And Davidheiser told the judge he had more questions for tomorrow.

54

A Recycled Alibi?

Into a second grueling day on the stand, Sebastian began to buckle under the pressure. He frequently interrupted Davidheiser to ask him questions about his testimony the day before—and to clarify his answers. It was clear he had spent the entire night in his cell going back over every single thing he said during his first day of cross-examination.

Davidheiser let him ramble on and got Sebastian even more rattled. Then, he brought up the topic that Sebastian and his attorneys had tried to keep out of evidence. Back in 1992, two years before the murders, Sebastian was with a friend and got into a car accident. Because he didn't want his father to get angry at him, Sebastian moved parts of the car to a parking lot at a nearby movie theater. He then went in and watched the film. When he and his friend came out, they acted as if they had just discovered the accident. Sebastian called the police and reported that someone had hit his car while he was watching the movie.

"You got into a car accident," Davidheiser reminded Sebastian. "It was kind of a dumb little accident, wasn't it? Doing what sixteen-year-olds do?"

"Yes," Sebastian said, knowing what was coming.

"But you didn't own up to it . . . you did something very similar to what you told Haslett you did in this case?"

"We told Haslett we committed a murder, which is a very different thing."

"In March of 1992, you picked up the pieces of evidence, took them to an entirely new location, and staged a scene. And this location was the parking lot of a movie theater, am I right?"

"Correct."

"You have told this jury that everything you told Haslett was a lie, didn't you?"

"Yes."

"It was not the first time you used a movie as an alibi, was it?"

Sebastian didn't answer. Davidheiser moved in for the kill.

"What you want this jury to believe is that in the first case it was true, in the second case it wasn't," Davidheiser said.

"The difference is in the first case, I was responsible for the car accident," Sebastian answered. "In the second case, I wasn't. The second difference is that the first one is a car accident, and the second was a murder."

Davidheiser moved on. He began describing the

crime scene for Sebastian, taking him through what each victim looked like after they had been beaten to death.

"It was a pretty horrible scene," he reminded Sebastian.

"That's right."

Then the prosecutor played a clip from the July 19 videotaped confession, where both teens were laughing while describing the murders.

"Was it part of your plan to giggle about what happened to Basma?" Davidheiser asked.

Sebastian sighed. "It was not a plan to giggle."

"Did you find it funny then? After having experienced this?"

"I wasn't focused on what had happened to Atif's family. I was focusing more on what I was telling [Haslett]. I was focusing on lying."

Davidheiser then switched to another line of questioning the defense team was hoping to keep out of evidence. He asked Sebastian if he remembered an old girlfriend of his from Vancouver, Nazgol Shifteh— and if he remembered telling her something to the effect of "I'd like to kill someone. I'd like to know what it feels like. I think I'd find it pleasurable."

Sebastian sighed heavily and admitted he made that statement.

"I do remember making an ironic comment about murder."

Davidheiser said he had no further questions, and defense attorney Jeff Robinson stood up. Robinson brought to the witness stand with him several letters between Nazgol and Sebastian. In the letters, it was Nazgol who sarcastically talked about killing people.

"So as a seventeen-year-old, did you really mean you wanted to murder someone?" Robinson asked.

"No," Sebastian said.

The defense attorney moved on to the earlier movie alibi. He asked Sebastian to explain what had happened.

"It was a mess," Sebastian said. "My parents found out . . . It was a shameful mess."

"So after this mess, did you, two years later, decide to use a movie as an alibi in a triple homicide?" Robinson asked.

"Absolutely not."

He asked Sebastian about the plan to tell the two undercover officers that he and Atif committed the murder.

"Was Jimmy Miyoshi present when you talked about using information from newspapers to concoct a story for [Haslett]?" Robinson asked.

"Yes," Sebastian said.

He asked Sebastian why they would confess to these murders if they weren't guilty.

"Hearing [Haslett] tell me that I was the guilty party based on scientific evidence was like hearing a nightmare that had been in my head that was now true," Sebastian said.

Davidheiser got back up to ask more questions of Sebastian. He asked Sebastian again whether the three of them—he, Atif, and Jimmy—were all in on planning the story they would give to Haslett. Sebastian said yes.

"So you want the jury to believe that Atif was sticking to the story, right?" Davidheiser asked. "But Jimmy wasn't cooperating at the Landis Hotel."

Sebastian said there was some miscommunication with Jimmy about that meeting—and that he was surprised when Jimmy wouldn't cooperate with Haslett at the Landis Hotel meeting.

"Jimmy thought [Haslett] might be a cop, didn't he?" Davidheiser asked.

"Yes," Sebastian said.

"And he told you he thought you made a grave error in judgment, didn't he?"

"Yes."

"You stated [to Nazgol] that you'd like to know what it felt like to kill someone, and that you might enjoy it, right?"

"Yes, I said something like that."

"And you'd like us to believe that this was youthful banter, right?"

"Yes."

He asked Sebastian if his hubris had led to his downfall. Sebastian admitted he had been young and his attitude had been based on "arrogance, immaturity, stupidity."

"So didn't your arrogance, immaturity, and stupidity lead to your downfall?" Davidheiser asked.

Sebastian's attorney objected—and Davidheiser

said he had no more questions. He'd gotten his point across. Sebastian stepped down from the stand and went back to sit down at the defense table. He looked like Superman after being exposed to Kryptonite.

Sebastian wasn't exactly sure how he'd done, he told Jenna Jackson later that day, but he felt like some jurors—he named specific ones—were definitely on his side once he was done testifying. He admitted that it seemed like other jurors had hated him from the beginning. But he thought that he'd won some of those over as he'd testified. And he thought that, over all, the jury believed his story.

Atif's attorneys were confident there was significant reasonable doubt in the prosecution case. They advised Atif not to risk taking the stand. He agreed, and the defense rested its case.

Judge Mertel told the jury that closing arguments would begin on Tuesday, May 18, and to have a good weekend. The attorneys headed out to prepare the most important arguments of the case.

55

Hubris Did Them In

Closings are similar to what you see on television—dramatic and full of controversy. What is unlike television is that, in the real world, closing arguments can sometimes last for hours. And, in this case, they did.

Lead prosecutor James Konat was up first. He was in full Armani mode: a dark blue suit, perfectly tailored, with a gray tie. Konat glanced at his notes on the prosecution table and then took a runway walk up to the jury. He'd sensed long ago that he had really connected with these people. Most had slight smiles of relief as he approached, knowing that the end of their long commitment was in sight. Konat paused for effect and began with some sarcasm.

"Ladies and gentlemen of the jury, almost ten years to the day, an Ivy League intellectual, Atif Rafay, and his *very best* friend in the world, Sebastian Burns, an incredibly annoying, and if ever it was possible, perhaps even more arrogant individual lived, the two of them conspired in the spring of 1994 to act on a plan of theirs," James Konat told the jury. "And ultimately capture that sense of entitlement that they believed belonged to them."

Konat led the jury through what he said Atif and Sebastian did: They planned the murders for four to six weeks, they went to Bellevue and carried them out, and then they fled to Canada, missing the family's funeral.

"This was a plan. They fled," he said. "Make no mistake about it: They didn't simply return to Canada—they fled to Canada. They fled to Canada because they knew there would be a safe haven from the inevitable series of questions that would follow from detectives like Bob Thompson at the Bellevue Police Department."

There were many motives, the prosecutor said. For Atif, it included freedom from his devoutly religious family and the fame the two boys would later gain from their movie.

"Tariq Rafay's life was worth fifty-nine thousand dollars a year. Dead, he was worth over a half a million dollars," Konat told the jury. "On two conditions— that Sultana is dead with him and that Basma is dead, too. We're not suggesting that Sebastian Burns and Atif Rafay wiped out this family just for the five hundred thousand dollars or so in proceeds. That was just part of the plan. They were going to make a movie. And it shouldn't surprise you to know that Sebastian Burns told Haslett the stars of that movie, the subject of that movie, were going to be Sebastian Burns and Atif Rafay."

He compared the level of violence used in the Rafay murders to the recent beheading of an American soldier in Iraq. The soldier was gagged and bound and beheaded as a video camera captured everything. Robinson leapt out of his chair to object, telling the judge this argument was "completely inappropriate." The judge allowed Konat to continue.

"I bring this up because, as grotesque and as horrible as that notion is, what these two did to Tariq, Sultana, and Basma Rafay is even worse."

Using an overhead projector, he showed them photographs of the crime scene: Sultana on the family room floor; Tariq lying nearly decapitated in his bed.

"This is the horror that they left behind, ladies and gentlemen," the prosecutor said.

Reminding jurors of the brutality of murder is always a psychological ploy. The idea, prosecutors believe, is that jurors will want someone to pay for the carnage they are witnessing. Konat said that Basma's murder was the worst—and the most like the soldier's beheading.

"Gagged and caged by her disability, she was in her bedroom while Sebastian Burns and Atif Rafay were systematically executing her parents," Konat said. "And all she could do, much like the man who was executed last week for the whole world to see, was wait. What we know, though, is you must imagine what was going through the mind of Basma Rafay when her killer opened the door to her bedroom."

He said that the defense attorneys had tried to throw jurors off track by making the lead detective out to be "the evil Bob Thompson," arguing that he didn't do his job because it was his first murder investigation, and that in his eagerness to make an arrest he'd focused on the wrong guys. But Konat told the jury they didn't have to believe him or Detective Thompson—they could believe Sebastian and Atif's own statements to undercover officers.

"They want you to believe that they were somehow in the wrong place at the wrong time in Bellevue in 1994," Konat said. "And that a year later, when they confess on video to committing these murders, they were again at the wrong place at the wrong time, and were only there by—through no fault of their own, but rather by virtue of nothing more than bad luck."

He played clips from the teens' videotaped confessions in which they are laughing about how they killed the family—and how it took more "bat work" or "effort," as Sebastian claimed he said, to kill Basma.

Konat then went back to what initially made detectives suspicious of the two teens: how they acted. They didn't remember much about what they had done during the day of the murders, he told jurors, but they remembered every single time and place related to their alibi that night.

"It isn't just the times that strikes a person, as they listen to this testimony, as being odd. It's the vivid detail. The way that they could describe the hostess who seated them. The way they could describe the sundress she was wearing. The froglike glasses that one waitress was wearing at either The Keg or Steve's Broiler later in the evening."

But, Konat said, from around 10 that evening to 12:50 in the morning, no one saw Sebastian and Atif. The prosecutor told jurors that this time frame is when they snuck out of the movie theater, drove back to the house, and murdered the Rafay family.

Konat did try to cover himself, however, in case the jurors believed the boys had stayed for the movie. "Even if you believe, for some reason, that they actually stayed for the entirety of that movie and left at eleven-thirty that night, I'm not suggesting that they wouldn't have had time to kill this family, even if they did."

Konat's comment was a surprising backtrack on the state's theory throughout the trial that the murders took place during the movie.

He argued that the two sets of neighbors on either side of the Rafay house—the defense team's strongest evidence of the boys' innocence—must simply be mistaken about what they heard.

"What I'm suggesting to you is neither Marc Sidell nor Judy Sidell nor Julie Rackley can tell you that anything they heard was, in fact, the murders," he said.

This was difficult to believe, given the fact that police did sound re-creations for the neighbors using an aluminum bat and had them retrace their steps that night.

Konat returned to an easier topic for the prosecution: the boys' odd behavior. He reminded jurors how little time it took for the teens to call 911 once they arrived back at the Rafay house around 2 that morning: It took them only about three minutes to discover the bodies and call. And it wasn't just how fast the call was made—it was what Sebastian said on the call that piqued suspicion. He told the 911 operator it looked like there had been some sort of a break-in. The teen would later tell Haslett that they tried to make the scene look like a burglary had taken place. These things, Konat reminded the jury, told them "loud and clear that this 911 call was contrived."

He reminded jurors that Sebastian and Atif acted oddly at the scene of the crime—that although they were emotional when the first officer arrived, they turned their emotion off "like a light switch" once he told them to calm down. Shortly after that, Atif told the detectives that he thought his Discman might be missing.

"I'm suggesting to you that Mr. Burns and Mr. Rafay on July twelfth and July thirteenth, 1995, were up to the same thing Mr. Burns was up to a couple of years earlier," he told jurors. "They're staging a crime scene, ladies and gentlemen, to put the Bellevue police off on an opposite trail. They're trying to put them on to a trail of a breaking and entering and the suggestion that somehow someone else was responsible for a murder that only Atif Rafay could commit and collect on."

Their odd behavior continued, Konat said: The night after the murders, after the two teens had been dropped off for the night at the Bellevue Motel, they walked to Blockbuster and rented a VCR and three movies.

"This is telling," Konat said. Instead of calling his relatives to tell them about the murders, Atif was watching movies.

Konat told jurors that the murders were an elaborate, well-thought-out plan by Sebastian and Atif. And he reminded them that this wasn't the first time Sebastian had tried to use a movie as an alibi—he'd tried it before in 1992, when he'd wrecked his father's car.

Konat told the jury that ironically, despite masterful planning, it was the boys' own statements in the undercover operation that did them in.

"And ultimately, the words that came out of Sebastian Burns's mouth led to his demise. His hubris led to his demise. And Jimmy Miyoshi is the one person who knew these two teens well—and shared this hubris," Konat said. "That's why his testimony was so important and can be believed. Jimmy Miyoshi was their other best friend in the world."

Konat used a full six hours during two days for his closing argument, sometimes jurors were dozing off and courtroom spectators were fidgeting. He jumped around from topic to topic quite a bit—and at times was rambling, unorganized, and seemed a little desperate.

But he finally wrapped up his argument with passion.

"Ultimately you will have to decide whether or not each of these two defendants is guilty of premeditated murder in the first degree, as they are charged," Konat said. "Mr. Burns and Mr. Rafay acted in tandem to extinguish—to systematically destroy, wipe out, if you will—the Rafay family in July of 1994. Whether it was just Mr. Burns's arrogance or just his hubris. Or whether it was the idea of Mr. Rafay thinking that they could get away with it, and they could use the cameras at Cornell University to make the movie about themselves, with the proceeds from these murders."

He paused and looked at each juror.

"The only answer we haven't given you is whose idea it was—and that doesn't matter. It's for all those reasons that we implore you to consider all of the evidence in this case . . . and you will come to the conclusion that we have proven beyond any reasonable doubt that these two are responsible for the murders in Somerset in July of 1994."

56

The Road to Hell

The next morning, the courtroom was once again filled with spectators, including Sebastian's parents, his sister, and his former high school sweetheart, Sarah Isaacs. All realized that Sebastian and Atif's fates now rested with the eloquence of lead defense attorney Jeff Robinson.

Two King County sheriff's deputies escorted Sebastian and Atif into the courtroom. Their handcuffs were removed, and they were directed to sit. Sebastian took a quick look back at his family.

Judge Charles Mertel entered the courtroom and sat at the bench. He told Robinson that he could proceed.

Robinson removed his glasses, stood, and slowly walked toward the jury box.

"'Arrogance.' 'Hubris.' 'One of the smartest people in the world.' 'Annoying,'" Robinson said, looking at each juror. "Within the first fifteen minutes of the state's closing argument, those were the references that you heard about Sebastian Burns. And those references shouldn't be surprising, quite frankly, because they're a continuation of some of the very first things that you heard during opening statements, almost six months ago. Chilling admissions. A beer in the hand. Laughing while talking about the murders."

It was a gutsy move. Robinson knew the boys were not likeable, that they seemed cold and disconnected from the murders. He'd all but acknowledged that. But he wanted the jury to go beyond appearances and focus on the facts.

"Folks, you are being given a not-so-subtle invitation by the state to judge this young man not on the evidence, but on appearances, on personality. On the concept of 'Doesn't he look guilty?'" Robinson said. "And when you start down that road, you head down the road to Hell. You head down the road to innocent people being convicted of crimes that they are not responsible for."

Robinson told the jury that the only evidence the state had against these two boys was circumstantial, and that the confessions presented in court were simply the products of skilled manipulation.

"The job that [Haslett and Shinkaruk] did on Sebastian Burns was masterful," Robinson reminded jurors. "And it shouldn't surprise you. Haslett has been manipulating people in scenarios like this for longer than Sebastian Burns has been alive."

He reminded jurors that the message from the two mobsters to Sebastian was obvious from the beginning.

"Sebastian, Bellevue is coming to lock your ass up. And we are the only people that can help. And the message was clear: You're a murderer, Sebastian. I only trust you because you're a murderer. If you get arrested, you're a threat to me. And threats to me, they get taken care of."

Robinson told the jurors that Sebastian was young and naïve and had been ostracized from the community since the murders—he was vulnerable, and got "*Rope*d" in by the wrong people. He was also afraid that the Bellevue police were fabricating evidence against him, which played right into the hands of the undercover operators.

"Sebastian Burns was in over his head," Robinson said. "And in order to avoid conviction for a crime he did not commit, in order to avoid putting himself in the situation of getting arrested and becoming a threat to the crime boss, Sebastian chose to lie. And that's how he ended up on a couch, sipping a beer and claiming responsibility for something that he did not do."

The way these undercover Mr. Big scenarios were designed, Robinson said, reduced their credibility.

"The problem with these scenarios is that the way they are designed and the manipulation that they use—it's a recipe for a false confession. There's a reason we don't do that kind of stuff down here. And the reason is, the results are unreliable."

He reminded the jurors that there was no forensic evidence that proved the boys murdered the Rafay family. If they had committed the murders, wouldn't it be likely that they'd have at least a speck of blood on them when officers checked them at the scene? Would it be possible, he asked the jury, for these two young men to commit the perfect forensic murder, but then be unable to pull it off because they couldn't act appropriately?

"And after six months of evidence, if we are willing to face the truth, the truth is, we still don't know who committed these murders," Robinson said. "But if we are here to do justice, and to judge on the evidence, one thing is clear. And that is that your verdicts should be not guilty."

Robinson's closing was theatrical, smart, and passionate—he clearly laid out the defense team's case without boring the jury. And as he talked, spectators began to think he could win this case.

Robinson reminded the jury members that they needed to judge the boys on real evidence—not on whether they liked them or on whether they thought the two teens behaved appropriately. And, he said, there was no real evidence that pointed to their guilt. The only evidence the state had brought against them, Robinson said, were the videotaped statements by the boys and the testimony of a known liar, Jimmy Miyoshi. And Jimmy had only given statements that incriminated his two former best friends after he was threatened with being sent to jail along with them.

"He couldn't keep his story straight," Robinson

said. "There is a lack of corroboration for any information he gives. It was all known to the public."

And he wouldn't let the jury forget that the boys had a solid alibi—given to them by neighbors who would rather have been helping the prosecution.

"What did Marc Sidell and Julie Rackley hear on July twelfth, 1994, if it was not the murders? Folks, they canvassed every house in the neighborhood, every single one," Robinson reminded the jurors. "And no one in any house in that neighborhood was doing anything to cause the sounds that Marc Sidell and Julie Rackley heard. They did hear the murders. That is something that has been proved beyond a reasonable doubt."

He told jurors with growing intensity that they couldn't even judge this case by Sebastian's demeanor when he took the stand. He admitted that Sebastian had an odd way of expressing himself and might not be the most likeable person, but that didn't mean he was guilty of murder. Robinson pointed toward Sebastian and Atif.

"You take a nineteen-year-old, any nineteen-year-old. Have them discover their best friend's family slaughtered. Have them become a suspect in that triple murder case. Have them become the target of an undercover operation by experienced and manipulative undercover officers, so that lies and manipulation and deceit are a part of this nineteen-year-old's life, for about six months. Then have that nineteen-year-old arrested for three murders. In jail, at nineteen years old. Social and psychological growth? Stunted. Development of communication skills, normal communication skills? Warped. 'Cause once that nineteen-year-old steps into jail, to everyone he meets, he's the triple murderer.

He stopped and looked at the twelve jurors.

"Now take that recipe and boil it. For nine years."

Robinson told the jurors that the state wanted them to judge Sebastian on his strange persona—because it had no real evidence. He continued in a mocking tone.

"Judge him on personality. Judge him on character traits. Judge him on arrogance. Judge him on hateful things that he said on some of these tapes. Judge him on that," he said. "Take a shortcut and judge him on those things. The question 'What has the state proved beyond a reasonable doubt?'—that's a complicated question. The question 'did he look guilty?'—that's an easier question."

He pointed to another way the state was trying to use a circumstantial action to make Sebastian look guilty in the murders—the incident where he used a movie as an alibi after crashing his dad's car.

"If he's so brilliant and so smart, do you really think he's going to use a movie as an alibi to kill three people when the investigation, when it starts looking at him, will reveal that he's tried to use a movie as an alibi before?" Robinson asked. "The state can't have it both ways."

He reminded jurors that the state's own expert

testified that there were at least three people in the room when Tariq Rafay was killed and that more than one weapon was used—and that the hair found on Tariq's bed didn't belong to either Atif or Sebastian. Robinson then mocked the police and prosecutors again, spelling out their thought processes.

"When it might help us, it's significant. When it turns out to be in conflict with our theory, just ignore it. Take a shortcut around it—it's not important anymore. The evidence is speaking loudly and clearly, trying to tell us that what Sebastian Burns and Atif Rafay talked about in their statements to Haslett is just not the truth."

He acknowledged that Sebastian's hairs were found in the shower drain, mixed with the blood of the Rafays, but insisted that proved nothing. Sebastian had showered there for five days, he pointed out, so of course his hairs were going to be there—and that was the only forensic evidence the police had.

"All you need is an accusation to prove guilt," Robinson said. "'Hey, there's no physical evidence I did this.' 'That's OK, we don't like the way you acted at the crime scene. You're guilty.' 'But, hey, wait a minute—I was at a movie theater. I couldn't have done this.' 'That's OK, you could have snuck out of the movie theater, you're guilty.'"

Robinson's Memphis roots, his memories of the civil rights movement, of people persecuted because of their appearance—it all coalesced into his heartfelt argument.

"Justice, the law, and common sense tell you that the presumption of innocence is where you have to start," he said. "If the history of the criminal justice system has taught us anything, it's that when we start talking shortcuts around the law, around the presumption of innocence and the burden of proof, we start sending innocent people to prison."

He told jurors that the Bellevue Police Department—and Detective Bob Thompson—didn't do their jobs on this investigation.

"Someone has got to check the facts from the crime scene, against the confession, to make sure it's the truth. Somebody has got to do that," he said. "And up until this day, nobody has done it. It wasn't done by the Bellevue Police Department. And now that job falls to you. You can't wake up three days after your verdict and say, 'You know, there was no physical evidence that these guys did the crime.' It's too late then."

Robinson was clearly moved by his own words—and by the responsibility he knew he carried for Sebastian and Atif. He concluded by sharing with the jury a conversation he had with a close friend just the night before.

"I was told, Jeff, just do the best you can," Robinson said. "You know the publicity that these jurors were exposed to before they ever walked into this courtroom. You know that the state is giving them invitation after invitation to judge Mr. Burns on personality as opposed to evidence."

Robinson took a step closer to the jurors. He seemed on the verge of tears.

"And I was able to look at my friend, and I was able to say, 'I know something you don't. I've looked into the eyes of this jury.'"

Robinson paused and cleared his throat.

"'Thank you' doesn't begin to express what I need to say to you. But it's the only words I have left."

Late into the afternoon of May 20, 2004, the case was finally placed in the hands of the jury. The bailiff called out "All rise" as the jury walked, single file, out of the courtroom. It was as though the entire courtroom had had the wind sucked out of it.

The jurors' faces had offered no hint of what they were thinking. The long wait for a verdict began.

57

The Wait

Both sides told *48 Hours* they were confident of victory. Deliberations stretched into four long days. Lawyers on both sides kept their cell phones turned on—and court watchers lingered around the courthouse—just in case. The longer the jury deliberated, the more reporters began to talk about an acquittal.

Sebastian's high school girlfriend, Sarah Isaacs, had been in Seattle during much of the trial.

"To tell you the truth, the trial was an exciting time for me, because, finally, all the myths were being shattered," she told Peter Van Sant. "All the evidence that was helping the defense was being exposed. I was becoming increasingly optimistic. And . . . this whole lie and this whole nightmare was finally coming to a close."

After she heard Jeff Robinson's closing argument, Sarah was ecstatic. She walked out of the courtroom with Sebastian's parents. "We were all very moved by what he said, and we all had the feeling that this was finally going to end."

Day after day, she waited at a nearby hotel with Sebastian's parents and sister for the verdict. Sebastian's father, Dave Burns, was nervous—his son's life was in the hands of twelve strangers.

"I'm going to have to listen to 'guilty' or 'not guilty,'" Burns said. "And I just don't know right now what it's going to be. I don't know what those people are thinking."

As their case hung in the balance, prosecutors James Konat and Roger Davidheiser talked to Peter Van Sant.

"If the jury believes these initial reports that Marc Sidell and Julie Rackley gave to police that the sounds ended at ten-fifteen, the case could be in trouble," Van Sant said.

"Absolutely," Roger Davidheiser admitted. "You can't be in two places at one time. There's no debating that point."

"Could you lose this case?"

"I never like to predict what juries are going to do. I can only say this—that I believe and I trust that we've provided this jury with all of the tools they need to come to the right decision. Ultimately, it's their decision."

Van Sant turned to James Konat, whose confidence didn't waver.

"James, what if you lose?" Van Sant asked.

"I can't imagine it," Konat said.

It was May 26. The *48 Hours* team was waiting to speak to the defense attorneys, sitting in their office lobby, when the phone rang.

"We've got a verdict," Robinson said as he hurried out of the office with the rest of the defense team. They speed-walked to the courthouse, which was just a couple of blocks away.

"It's time to go get the verdict," defense attorney Song Richardson said. "Every lawyer is going to be incredibly nervous when you know that a verdict has been returned."

Everyone piled in and sat on the hard, wooden benches of the courtroom. Sebastian's family sat together in nervous silence. Both the prosecution and defense teams sat with stunned, worried looks on their faces. It was the moment both sides had waited six months to hear, but the moment seemed oddly terrifying for everyone.

All heads turned as deputies brought Sebastian and Atif into the courtroom in shackles. Sebastian was smiling, and there was a bounce in his step. He glanced at Atif, who smiled back at him. They were the only people smiling in this tense courtroom.

In their last public moment before the verdict was read, the boys were, once again, acting oddly.

"I was excited," Sebastian said. "I thought we were going to get acquitted. After the closing argument of Jeff Robinson, I thought, at worst, it'll be a hung jury. I thought there's no way that all twelve of them will convict us."

Judge Charles Mertel called the attorneys to the bench and let them know that the jury had sent a note, along with its verdict form, asking when the sentencing would take place. He looked intensely at each attorney to make sure they were getting the message about what verdict to expect. Judge Mertel's look seemed to say, "Don't react to what you've just read."

But as the defense team walked back toward Sebastian and Atif, it was clear that something was wrong. They whispered to the two young men just as the jury filed back into the courtroom.

Sebastian quickly turned to his family, appearing confused, and mouthed the words, "It's not looking too good."

The *48 Hours* team was sitting one row behind the family and could see Sebastian shaking his head from side to side. Everyone in the courtroom seemed to be holding their breath.

58

The Verdict

The last of the twelve jurors took his seat. None of them was looking at Sebastian or Atif, a bad sign for the two young men.

"Has the jury reached a verdict?" Judge Mertel asked. The foreman stood and said, "We have, Your Honor."

He handed the jury form to the bailiff, who handed it to the judge's clerk—who briefly scanned the paper before impassively reading the verdicts on each of the three counts of murder for each boy.

"Guilty. Guilty. Guilty."

"Guilty. Guilty. Guilty."

Each word was like a body blow to Sebastian's family. There was a soft burst of shock, as if everyone had finally exhaled. A human sound was then detected—the sobs of Sebastian's sister, Tiffany.

As the verdicts were read, Atif stared straight ahead in utter disbelief. His chin dropped to his chest. Sebastian didn't look at his family or his attorneys. Instead, he was focused on the jurors, his mouth slightly open, with a look of shock—and what Van Sant and Jackson saw as menacing anger. He went down the line, seat by seat, of the jury box—focusing his threatening stare on each individual juror. He shook his head back and forth.

"Sebastian sneered," one of the jurors would later say of that moment. "He had an evil look on his face. He kept shaking his head at us, like, 'How dare you find me guilty? I told you I didn't do it.' It was eerie."

But Sebastian said he simply couldn't believe that they'd convicted him, because he was so certain he would finally be vindicated.

"I was just looking at the jurors because I couldn't believe what they had done," he said. "I was looking at individual jurors, just to see if they . . . I don't know, I guess I was looking for some kind of answer. But absolutely not threatening."

One row behind him, Tiffany was inconsolable.

"I was kind of thinking about how we'd all be going home to Vancouver that day," Tiffany said. "I'd be sitting in the backseat with my brother again."

She started to cry.

"And it didn't work out."

By this point, Tiffany was shaking uncontrollably and wailing. She tried to reach for her little brother, who was frozen in place at the defense table—but guards stopped her from touching him. She collapsed back on to the bench.

Sarah Isaacs, Sebastian's high school girlfriend, also broke down. "I became completely hysterical," she said. "I've never been so devastated."

Even the defense attorneys, who had been through dozens of verdicts, were shocked.

"I felt sick," Song Richardson said.

Jeff Robinson agreed.

"It was horrible. I disagreed with the verdict with every fiber of my being."

Sebastian's family was quickly ushered out of the courtroom.

At the prosecution table, Detective Bob Thompson was standing with Konat and Davidheiser. The three men maintained their poker faces until the jurors filed out. Then they began smiling and embracing. This case had dominated their lives for three long years. They had gone up against three of Washington State's best defense attorneys and two brilliant defendants—and won.

There were more hugs, some eyes welling with emotion and a strong sense of justice having been served. They patted Detective Thompson on the back, he couldn't stop smiling.

"It's a verdict that has been coming for a very long time," Konat told reporters gathered in the hallway.

59

The Aftermath

In the days that followed the verdict, the emotions of Sebastian, Atif, and their supporters ranged from disbelief, to anger—to a steely determination.

About a week after the guilty verdict, Peter Van Sant went to the jail to speak with Sebastian and Atif.

"Twelve jurors listened to the evidence, listened to your testimony, and found you guilty," Van Sant said. "Isn't it time you accept responsibility for these murders?"

"We didn't do it," Sebastian said. "We didn't do it. And I'm baffled by the verdict. I—I never believed this jury was going to convict us."

Sarah Isaacs wouldn't accept the verdict, either. She and Tiffany went on to create an extensive Web site that laid out the case for the boys' innocence.

"I decided that the jury made a terrible mistake," Sarah said. "Some of them are going to realize that they did make a mistake, and they're going to have to live with that. But I decided that we weren't going to live with their mistake. That we were going to overcome it."

Sebastian became convinced that some jurors who he sensed supported him during the trial must have been bullied by their colleagues. He immediately began to formulate an appeal in his head.

But several of the jurors agreed to speak to 48 Hours—and said they were comfortable with their verdict. They were now terrified of Sebastian, though, and only agreed to be interviewed if their names weren't revealed.

"How many of you are convinced these boys tried to plan the perfect murder?" Van Sant asked the group of jurors.

Every juror's hand went up, and voices chimed in.

"I am."

"Yes."

"All of you?" Van Sant asked.

"Yeah."

"Undoubtedly."

"In some ways, do you believe these boys are brilliant?" Van Sant asked.

"Very smart," one juror said.

"Smart, but not brilliant," another jumped in. "I think Sebastian was too smart for his own good. Actually, it was his overconfidence in himself that brought him down—his loose mouth is exactly what got him."

Many of the jurors planned to go to the sentencing because they wanted to see the boys sentenced to life in prison without the possibility of parole. They said they needed closure to the six long months they'd spent in the courtroom.

"I think about it," one juror said. "You know, you wake up in the middle of the night, and Sebastian and Atif are—you're thinking of them. Thinking of Basma, Tariq, and Sultana."

The sentencing took place five months after the verdict—on October 22, 2004, more than a decade after the Rafays were murdered. Sebastian again tried to take some control of his future. This was his last public opportunity to address a courtroom—and he took it. For an hour and a half, he gave a lengthy speech about specific pieces of evidence he felt weren't adequately explained to the jury during the trial.

He continued to adamantly insist that he and Atif were innocent—and that they were trapped, through fear, into giving false confessions. "The story [of the murders] freaks you out," he told the judge and the crowded courtroom. "If you look for the evidence, you won't find it, because we didn't do it, and that's the truth."

After Sebastian sat down, Judge Mertel spoke sternly to him. "It's chilling, your recitation of what you feel has occurred over these many years. You're not immoral, Mr. Burns, you're amoral."

Atif spoke for less than ten minutes. For the first time in public, he began to cry.

"I'm tormented by the fact . . . that my parents' killers walk with impunity."

He described what he missed about each of his slain family members.

"I'm going to continue to struggle for truth in this case," he said. "I won't betray their hopes and expectations for me."

Judge Mertel told Atif that he thought he was "genuinely remorseful." But, the judge told him, it was his and his family's misfortune that he ever met Sebastian, because their friendship "cost you years in prison and cost your family their lives."

He sentenced both boys to life in prison without parole.

They were sent to separate prisons in Washington State. Both were assigned new attorneys, and they filed appeals, arguing that the undercover operation was unconstitutional and the case should never have been allowed into a U.S. court.

"Do you have any hope left, Sebastian?" Van Sant asked.

"Yes, yes, I do," he said. "Yes, I hope we will win a new trial, and I hope we will be acquitted in a fair trial, as we deserve to be."

"Is this case over, Atif?" Van Sant asked.

"I suppose I'm not the one who will have the last word on that."

Initially, Sebastian was sent to a prison in Walla Walla, Washington, which he said was the toughest in the state. He was made to stay in isolation for many months; he was only allowed to leave his cell for one hour each day and never came into contact with other inmates. Prison officials said this was for his own protection.

Atif was housed in a different prison, across the state—and the two boys would never be allowed to see each other again. They did remain in touch via letters. Despite their guilty verdicts, neither man had ever betrayed the other.

They were best friends, forever.

In *The Great Despisers,* the screenplay that Sebastian and Atif wrote about the Bellevue murders, the story ended with the two best friends getting wrongly convicted and executed. In the boys' version, it was a great injustice.

But the case investigators saw it differently. They said it may have taken a decade, but that justice had finally been served—and that the two brilliant best friends had brought it on themselves.

Haslett, the RCMP "crime boss" who persuaded the teens to confess on videotape, said it was Sebastian's arrogance that did them in.

"Based on all the time you spent with Sebastian Burns, is he one of the most intelligent people on earth?" Van Sant asked the make-believe crime boss.

"No," Haslett said, "not by any means or stretch of the imagination. Not intelligent by any means—only in his own mind."

And Bob Thompson, the Bellevue detective who led his first murder investigation into the Rafay murders, agreed. After the verdict, he called Atif Rafay's uncle in Toronto; the man had always believed his nephew was guilty.

"When the jurors came back, and they said he was guilty, there was a sense of relief that finally, I could get on the telephone, call the victims up in Canada, and say, 'Justice is served.' 'Cause they'd waited a long time. Ten years is a long time to wait," Thompson said. "I don't feel vindicated. I just feel relieved that justice was served."

Thompson then paused and contemplated his successful investigation, the first and most memorable murder investigation of his career. He looked across at Van Sant and smiled.

"Yeah, the dumb cop outsmarted a couple of boy geniuses, I guess, huh?" He laughed with a sense of satisfaction.

Sebastian wrote letters to Jenna Jackson about how he was coping in prison. He contemplated shaving his head so he would look tougher. He felt that the prosecutors would like nothing more than for him to be killed in prison—and he was determined not to let this happen. He mostly wrote, in detail, about what went wrong during his trial—and about how he planned to get his conviction overturned.

His family and friends continued to speak out on his behalf, refusing to give up the fight.

"I think we've done some things wrong," Carol Burns told a reporter after her son was sentenced.

"We didn't talk to the press before, when all of this was going on. In hindsight, I think we should have screamed out loud."

And Sebastian's father gave a warning: "It could happen to any of your kids.

"Quite simply, it was about solving a murder case. And they've decided that my son and his friend are the guilty parties. And they have no evidence, but they've decided that. So, they still haven't solved the murders."

Epilogue

The appeals for Sebastian Burns and Atif Rafay are pending and their convictions could actually be overturned: They eventually will be heard by one of the most liberal appellate courts in the country, the Ninth Circuit Court of Appeals. But first, they must make their way through the Washington State appellate system, which could take several years. The courts will look at several issues, including whether it was legal to allow the confessions into a U.S. court, since the tactics used to get them were illegal in this country. They will also look at whether an expert should have been allowed to discuss the phenomenon of false confessions, and whether more information should have been admitted on other suspects that may have been ignored by the Bellevue police.

Sebastian Burns has been severely beaten twice by his fellow inmates. He has been moved to another prison for his own protection.

Atif is serving his life sentence at a different prison in Washington State.

Both men remain steadfast in their friendship and in their claims that they are innocent.